Baseball

Second Edition

ILLINOIS HISTORY OF SPORTS

Series Editors
Benjamin G. Rader
Randy Roberts

*A list of books in the series
appears at the end of this book.*

Baseball

A HISTORY OF AMERICA'S GAME

Benjamin G. Rader

UNIVERSITY OF ILLINOIS PRESS
Urbana and Chicago

© 2002 by the Board of Trustees of the University of Illinois
Manufactured in the United States of America
1 2 3 4 5 C P 5 4 3 2 1

∞ This book is printed on acid-free paper.

Library of Congress Cataloging-in-Publication Data
Rader, Benjamin G.
Baseball : a history of America's game / Benjamin G. Rader.—
2nd ed.
p.   cm. — (Illinois history of sports)
Includes bibliographical references and index.
ISBN 0-252-02703-5 (cloth : alk. paper)
ISBN 0-252-07013-5 (paper : alk. paper)
1. Baseball—United States—History. I. Title. II. Series.
GV863.A1R33   2002
796.357'0973—dc21   2001002477

To
    Anne Elizabeth Rader
    Stephen Lowell Rader

Contents

Preface   ix

Acknowledgments   xi

Introduction   1

1. The Fraternity and Its Game   5
2. A Commercial Spectacle   20
3. The First Professional Teams   31
4. The First Professional Leagues   43
5. The Players' Revolt   61
6. The Great Baseball War   79
7. Baseball's Coming of Age   92
8. The Big Fix   110
9. The Age of Ruth   124
10. An Age of Dynasties   137
11. Baseball's Great Experiment   155
12. The Last Days of the Old Game   170
13. Baseball in Trouble   186
14. The Empowerment of the Players   201
15. The Demise of Dynasties   218
16. A New Era   235

Bibliographical Essay   257

Index   265

Illustrations follow page 136

Preface

The aim of the second edition of *Baseball* remains the same as that of the first edition. I have sought to offer an entertaining and insightful account of the history of the game from both inside and outside the foul lines. Readers will continue to find substantial discussions of the history of the game on the playing field, its organizational and business side, and its relationship to the larger social and cultural forces in American history.

This edition also gave me the opportunity to make corrections and add new material. Although the first edition received a gratifyingly warm welcome from reviewers and the public alike, I quickly discovered that baseball aficionados are especially conscientious when it comes to getting the facts right. And this is as it should be. So in this revision I have not only endeavored to correct factual errors but have also in a few instances given ground on my views of important issues in baseball history. Even more important is the addition of new material. In particular, I have rewritten substantial parts of chapter 14, "The Empowerment of the Players," and chapter 15, "The Demise of Dynasties." Finally, readers of this edition will find an entirely new chapter on baseball in the 1990s. In chapter 16, "A New Era," I try to tell the stories of the new hitting barrage, the "Latino invasion," the building of retroparks, and the return of team dynasties.

Acknowledgments

Let me acknowledge first and foremost those who introduced me to ball playing. They were my schoolmates on the red-clay playgrounds of one-room schools in the southern Missouri Ozarks. During recess, girls and boys ranging in age from six or seven to fourteen or so gathered for a brisk game of "work-up." In work-up, players start in the outfield, working their way up with each out, from the outfield to third base, from third base to shortstop, and so on until finally getting an opportunity to hit. Players remain at bat as long as they do not make an out, but because in our game only two or three people were at bat, even a good hitter could become the victim of a "force out." A batter who has been retired must return to the outfield. Depending on the size and age of the players, we sometimes permitted "crossouts" as well. In a crossout, a player can put the runner out by throwing the ball between the runner and the next base. At the time, I had no idea that our schoolyard game was similar to a game from which modern baseball evolved or that I would one day write a history of the sport.

During this era of my life as well as in high school, two people in particular stimulated and sustained my interest in baseball. First was my brother Mike, who is a year younger than I am. On our isolated farm, my brother and I talked endlessly about the game, played catch at every spare moment, played on an assortment of teams together, and, whenever we could, co-erced our four younger siblings into practicing baseball or softball. The other was Harry Caray, the voice of the St. Louis Cardinals. I spent many hours listening to Caray's vivid accounts of the Cardinals on radio station KWPM in West Plains, Missouri. In the meantime, I became an avid reader of the daily sports page of the Springfield, Missouri *News-Leader.* An occasional delight (when I could afford it) was reading *The Sporting News,* where I learned about the intricate world of minor league baseball as well as about the big leagues.

In later years, attending college, teaching, doing "serious" research, and perhaps simply growing up, among other considerations, tempered my enthusiasm for "America's game." I returned to the subject only some twenty years ago, when I first began to encounter the books of Harold Seymour, David Voigt, Robert Peterson, Lawrence Ritter, Leverett Smith Jr., Robert Creamer, Steven Riess, Richard Crepeau, Melvin Adelman, Peter Levine, Larry Gerlach, and Jules Tygiel. This book owes something to each of these pioneers in what may be described as a new baseball history as well as to dozens of books and articles published more recently, including those by George Kirsch, Warren Goldstein, Charles Alexander, Eugene Murdoch, Bill James, Debra Shattuck, Rob Ruck, George Will, and James Miller. Even this list does not exhaust the extent of my obligations to the research and thoughts of others. I trust that the bibliographical essay at the end of the book more fully reflects that debt.

Several people contributed more directly to *Baseball: A History of America's Game.* They include the members of the Research Council of the University of Nebraska at Lincoln, who voted to give me financial assistance, the University of Nebraska for a faculty development leave, and John Peters, Peter Maslowski, and Richard L. Wentworth, each of whom offered advice and sustained my interest in this project. Ruth and Ted Gatter of Rye, New York, provided me with lodging, food, drink, and marvelous conversation while I did research in the New York Public Library. A trip from New York City, the historical birthplace of the modern game of baseball, to Cooperstown, New York, its mythical birthplace, brought me face to face with the big city and small town character of the game. In Cooperstown, Tom Hetiz and Bill Dean introduced me to the National Baseball Library; I was able to sample its rich holdings all too briefly. Equally helpful was Steven Gietscher, librarian of *The Sporting News* in St. Louis, who on several occasions located things for me and proffered suggestions. Back in Lincoln, Gretchen Holten of the University of Nebraska's Love Library routinely and generously used her remarkable skills in aiding and abetting my research. Joan Curtis did her usual superb work in reproducing the manuscript in several stages, and work-study students Michelle Diedrichsen and Reynolds Towns spent several tedious hours entering raw statistical data used in this book. For running the computer programs and analyzing the statistics, I am deeply indebted to my colleague Kenneth Winkle. Kenneth Winkle, Ken Gatter, Larry Gerlach, Christopher Kimball, Steven A. Riess, Jules Tygiel, and Bruce Bethell read and offered invaluable suggestions on the entire manuscript.

For assistance in doing this edition, I would also like to acknowledge especially Robert Adair, Thomas Altherr, Peter Bjarkman, Russell Crawford, Richard Crepeau, John Dreifort, Dane Kennedy, Kent Krause, Richard Larson, David Ogden, Jeff Powers-Beck, Anne Rader, Akim Rhinehart, and Ofer Rind. Furthermore, I am grateful to the Clay Thomas Fund of the University of Nebraska at Lincoln's Department of History for the financial aid that expedited the completion of this revision.

Finally, Barbara Koch Rader, my closest collaborator in this enterprise as in many others, not only listened to countless monologues but aided me in refining the ideas that eventually found their way into this book.

Baseball

Introduction

"It's our game," exclaimed poet Walt Whitman more than a century ago, "that's the chief fact in connection with it: America's game." He went on to explain that baseball "has the snap, go, fling of the American atmosphere—belongs as much to our institutions, fits into them as significantly, as our constitutions, laws: is just as important in the sum total of our historic life." Perhaps Whitman exaggerated baseball's importance and congruency with American life, but few would contend that the sport has been merely a simple or occasional diversion. Indeed, if forced to make a choice, most would side with Whitman. They would insist that baseball achieved a special prominence and permanence in the United States that in some respects makes its significance equivalent to that of business, politics, religion, ethnicity, or race.

Until recently, those attempting to tell the story of how baseball became so "important in the sum total of our historic life" focused almost exclusively on the history of the game between the foul lines. That is, they vividly—sometimes with nostalgia and often with more than a bit of hyperbole—recounted the feats of the great players and the great teams. In doing so they were not completely amiss. It would be foolish to ignore the drama and the significance of what took place on the playing field, of Harry Wright's Cincinnati Red Stockings, King Kelly, the Baltimore Orioles of the 1890s, Ty Cobb, Babe Ruth and the New York Yankees, Satchel Paige and Jackie Robinson, or Sammy Sosa and Mark McGwire.

But while recounting the exciting story of legendary players and teams, I try to do more. I attempt to tell a broader story, one that identifies the critical continuities and changes in the way the game was played and examines the creation and demise of team dynasties, the organization of baseball, the ethos of the game, and baseball's relationship to American society. This book might also be described as a history of baseball's culture, meaning the story of continuity and change in the game's rules, organizations, habits, customs, skills, and interactions with the larger society.

The larger story of America's game begins in the 1840s with an examination of a ball game anchored in the lives of young artisans and clerks. They formed voluntary associations or clubs and described themselves as members of a "base ball fraternity." This variety of baseball has never completely vanished; countless amateur and semiprofessional teams continued to play a version of it until the 1960s, and some of the rules and customs of the fraternity remain to this day. Even in the heyday of the fraternal era, however, a new baseball culture emerged, one that was tied to the commercial opportunities presented by the sport. With commercial baseball in the 1860s and 1870s came professional players whose roles resembled more the actors and actresses of the day than boys playing ball on empty lots or a group of young shipbuilders gathering to play at their clubhouses.

The growth of the professional game was inextricably linked with urban identities. Representative professional baseball teams exhibited a remarkable capacity for giving towns and cities deeper emotional identities; teams helped to define the particular character of an urban community, giving citizens a sometimes glorious sense of place and sharply drawn collective memories. Baseball sometimes furnished a respite, albeit a short one, from grinding and unfulfilling work and from the social stresses and dislocations of urban life. At its best, baseball could even reduce antagonisms arising from class, religious, ethnic, and racial divisions. In a nation comprising a multiplicity of ethnic, racial, and religious groups, one without a monarchy, an aristocracy, or a long, mystic past, the experience of playing, watching, and talking about baseball games became one of the nation's great common denominators. In the perceptive words of British novelist Virginia Woolf, it provided "a centre, a meeting place for the divers activities of a people whom a vast continent isolates [and] whom no tradition controls." No matter where you were, you pulled off the hit-and-run play, the double play, and the sacrifice bunt the same way in one town as in another.

In the first half of the twentieth century, baseball was, as Bill Veeck once put it, "the only game in town." Never before did the game occupy such a central place in American life. The entrepreneurs in charge of the representative nines in the larger cities established an entity that became known as organized baseball, which consisted of an elaborate hierarchy of major and minor professional leagues. They concocted an elaborate myth of the game's origins, erected great civic monuments in the form of ballparks made of steel and concrete, and instituted an annual fall rite known as the World Series. Led by Babe Ruth, the game propagated epic heroes whose dimensions of public involvement were equaled by few other figures in American history, and Ruth's team, the New York Yankees, became synonymous with success. In the front office, Branch Rickey, first of the St. Louis Cardinals and then of the Brooklyn Dodgers, not only brought to baseball business a new rationality but also, with his role in breaking the "color ban" in 1946, contributed directly to a new era of American race relations.

By midcentury, there were other games in town. After 1950 America's game confronted potent competition, not only from other professional sports (especially football) but more importantly from a shift by Americans from public to private, at-home diversions. Attendance at all levels of baseball fell, minor league baseball became a shell of its former self, and hundreds of semiprofessional and amateur teams folded. Professional baseball responded to the crisis by planting additional major league teams in new population centers, building new stadiums, and trying to harness the new technological marvel of television. Finally, the empowerment of the professional players in the last quarter of the twentieth century not only ended their serflike relationship to the owners but subtly altered the public's perceptions of the athletes and the game.

An analysis of baseball's recent troubles, however, should not obscure the game's continuing vitality and importance. Despite its limitations for conveying the nuances of baseball, television has allowed many more people to see the game played at the highest levels of excellence than ever before. In the 1980s and early 1990s both big league and minor league attendance increased appreciably. Perhaps no signs of the game's durability have been more important than the soaring interest in an alternative baseball culture represented in novels, poetry, nostalgic movies, rotisserie baseball, "sabermetrics," dozens of Web sites devoted exclusively to the game, and the collection of baseball souvenirs. Now college students can even take courses in baseball history and literature.

In the opening decade of the twenty-first century, as in the past, baseball's grip on the American people rests to a large extent on its power to evoke continuity. In the 1850s, just as today, three strikes retired a hitter and ninety feet separated the bases. Unique among American team games, baseball presents itself to the fan in startling clarity; each player stands alone on vast expanses of green, and the game's pace is slow enough to permit the mind to collect sharply etched memories, each of which can be analyzed repeatedly. Regardless of wars, economic catastrophes, natural disasters, or personal tragedies, the memories remain. In a world of seething change and uncertainty, baseball continues to offer comfort and reassurance; in this sense, it remains America's game.

1

The Fraternity and Its Game

In 1858, three years before the first shots were fired in the nation's terrible civil war, baseball excitement in the New York City area mounted to a fever pitch. The occasion was a best-of-three-game series between an all-star nine from Brooklyn and a team of New York City all-stars. After lengthy, sometimes acrimonious negotiations, the teams selected as the site for their series the Fashion Race Course, a popular Long Island horse racing track that featured a magnificent new stone grandstand. To get to the games, the fans crowded into carriages, omnibuses, and the special trains of the Flushing Railroad. Admission cost fifty cents, a price in those days equivalent to half a day's earnings for a common laborer. Proceeds from the games went not to the players but to a fireman's fund for widows and orphans. According to a press report, the spectators included "a galaxy of youth and beauty in female form, who . . . nerved the players to their task." Perhaps feminine comeliness steeled the resolve of the New Yorkers the most, for they won the first game, 22 to 18. In the second game the Brooklynites evened the series, winning 29 to 8, but then the New Yorkers rebounded to win the decisive third contest, and the championship, 29 to 18.

The all-star series of 1858 was only one among many sporting spectacles that suddenly burst on the nation in the middle decades of the nineteenth century. In the 1840s and 1850s, thousands of spectators gathered at tracks in virtually every state in the Union to watch horse and foot races; equal numbers thronged along the nation's harbor, lake, and river banks to observe boat races. Although a bare-knuckle prize fight rarely attracted more than a few hundred fans (being illegal everywhere and often scheduled in remote places), literally tens of thousands heard oral accounts or read about them in the newspapers. Prior to 1845, only a few scattered references exist of baseball games, but within fifteen years several hundred clubs had been formed, and more than ten thousand boys and young men played in club matches.

Two groups, each described by contemporaries as "fraternities," were of critical importance to the rise of organized sports in the 1840s and 1850s. One was known simply as the sporting fraternity, or "the fancy." The fancy shared a love of sports, especially those games that provided opportunities for drinking, wagering, and hearty male fellowship. Remaining mostly outside the mainstream of Victorian America, the sporting fraternity offered antebellum men, in particular the younger, unmarried, ethnic, working-class population, a sense of belonging and excitement, as well as a refuge from femininity, domesticity, and the demanding routines of the new industrial economy.

The other group, known as the ball-playing fraternity, came closer to meeting Victorian standards of propriety, though the behavior of the ball players and their followers frequently made them also suspect to the guardians of mid-nineteenth-century morality. The ball players organized voluntary associations, or clubs, for the playing of baseball. Representatives of the clubs wrote and revised the rules of play, appointed officials, scheduled matches, and in 1858 formed a national association. The ball-playing fraternity provided its informal membership with the direct excitement of playing ball games and with the indirect benefits arising from male camaraderie and exhibitions of manly physical skills.

⊞ ⊟ ⊞

The baseball fraternity had its origins in the widespread popularity of various sorts of bat-and-ball games and the special American penchant for forming voluntary associations. As Thomas Altherr has carefully documented, long before Abner Doubleday's alleged invention of baseball at Cooperstown, New York, in 1839, men and boys were playing a large variety of baseball-like games. During the Revolutionary War, for example, the soldiers frequently relieved boredom by resorting to "playing ball" or "base." Early bat-and-ball games might also be called "ball," "old cat," "barn ball," "town ball," "rounders," or even "base ball." Most of these games probably originated in England, though we know that Native Americans played a variety of bat-and-ball games as well. While no written rules existed (or at least have survived) for the earliest of these games, as early as 1767 an English children's book, *A Little Pretty Pocket-Book,* printed in London, contained engravings of scenes of boys playing games labeled as "stool-ball," "base-ball," and "trap-ball."

These early games required a ball, a stick with which to hit the ball, and one or more bases. The bases might be of stones, articles of clothing, trees or shrubs, or stakes driven into the ground. The ball might be fabricated on the spot. One of the players might offer a woolen stocking to be unraveled and wound around a bullet or a cork. The cover might consist of stitched leather. No one probably worried about the distances between bases nor the number of players on each side. There was no umpire. The object of the game was to throw a ball so that it could be hit easily by the batsman.

A decisive turning point in the emergence of the baseball fraternity came in 1842 and 1843 when a group of young clerks, storekeepers, professional men, brokers, and assorted "gentlemen" in New York City began playing a bat-and-ball game at the corner of 27th Street and Fourth Avenue in Manhattan. According to unverifiable baseball folklore, it was Alexander Joy Cartwright, a bank clerk and later a partner in a stationery shop, who in 1845 convinced the young men to form a club. They called their fledgling organization the New York Knickerbocker Base Ball club, thereby identifying themselves with the hoary mystique of the area's original Dutch settlers. For a playing site, they rented a portion of the Elysian Fields in Hoboken, New Jersey, a "most picturesque and delightful" place surrounded by woods and with easy access to New York City via the Barclay Street ferry. After a hard afternoon at play, the members regularly retreated to nearby McCarty's Hotel bar, where they could regale one another with manly talk and quench their thirst with spirituous drink. For a time, McCarty's may have also served as an informal clubhouse; at least it was there that the Knickerbockers held their second annual meeting.

The Knickerbocker Base Ball club bore only a faint resemblance to a modern professional or sandlot baseball club. In contemporary sports, the words *club* and *team* are used interchangeably. The main, if not the exclusive, purpose of such organizations is to play games against other teams and sometimes to make money. To the Knickerbockers, however, the term *club* meant far more than simply a team of baseball players bent on victory or monetary remuneration. The Knickerbocker club, like many of the other pioneering baseball clubs, was both an athletic and a social association. While providing opportunities for playing baseball, it also scheduled suppers, formal balls, and other festive occasions in the off-season. Individuals could acquire membership only by election; the club conscientiously tried to keep out those who had a "quarrelsome disposition" or who did not fit well into the group for other reasons. The Knickerbockers drew up bylaws, elected officers, and even fined members who breached the organization's code of dress and behavior. Club members had to purchase uniforms of blue woolen pantaloons, white flannel shirts, and straw hats and attend "Play Days" on Mondays and Thursdays. The Knickerbockers at one time had more than 200 members, many of whom played little if any baseball.

In 1845, the club set down in writing the rules for its game. As with the English game of rounders, the Knickerbocker game stipulated that the infield be diamond shaped, with a base at each corner. The umpire called no strikes or balls, but three pitches that had been swung at and missed retired the batsman. Tagging a runner between bases replaced "soaking" or "plugging," a painful feature of rounders in which base runners could be retired by striking them with a thrown ball. In another departure from rounders, the Knickerbockers limited the team at bat to only three outs. Fielders could obtain outs by catching the batted ball on the first bounce, in the air, throwing to first base ahead of the runner, or tagging the runner between bases. A game ended as soon as a team scored twenty-one "aces," or runs, provided that both teams had played an equal number of "innings." (Innings apparently was a term borrowed from cricket).

Other features of the Knickerbockers' game would be even less familiar to the modern fan. Instead of placing himself behind the catcher or in the field, the "umpire" (another term probably borrowed from cricket) sat at a table along the third base line, sometimes dressed in tails and a tall black top hat. Unless a play was so close that it was disputed by one of the team captains, the umpire never interfered with the course of the game. When a controversy did arise, it was the umpire's duty to weigh the merits of the opposing arguments carefully before rendering a decision. If uncertain of a proper ruling on a fair or foul ball, for instance, he could even request the opinions of nearby spectators. All of them being "gentlemen," it was presumed that the spectators would offer unbiased judgments.

Intraclub games began with the captains choosing sides, much in the manner of children on empty lots today. The captains called a tossed coin to see which team batted first. When the losing side took the field, all the infielders except the "short" fielder (the shortstop) usually stood atop their respective bases. The fielders wore no gloves, and the catcher used no protective gear. Hoping to catch pitches on the first bounce, the catcher stood several feet behind the "striker," or batter. Taking a running start, the "feeder," or pitcher, literally pitched (rather than threw) the ball underhanded with a straight arm from a distance of forty-five feet. Because the umpire called no strikes, the striker could wait patiently for a pitch to his liking. Except for fellow club members and occasional invited friends, few spectators witnessed the earliest contests.

The Knickerbockers were not the first baseball club in the country, nor did their formation immediately result in a flurry of interest by other young men in organizing such clubs. Newspaper reports indicate that one or more teams existed long before the Knickerbockers; in 1991, Tom Heitz, librarian of the Baseball Hall of Fame, reported finding an account from 12 July 1825 in which a group of nine men challenged any team in Delaware County, New York, to a game. Nonetheless, these early teams appear not to have survived for long. The Knickerbockers themselves suffered a crushing defeat (23-1) at the hands of a "New York Club" in 1846, but the winning club, if it ever existed as a separate entity, apparently met an early demise, and for a time the Knickerbockers themselves nearly collapsed from a lack of sufficient interest. They did not play another recorded game with an external foe until 1851.

Then suddenly, in the mid-1850s, a baseball mania swept through the metropolitan New York area. In 1854 and 1855 at least three new clubs appeared in Manhattan, while Brooklynites formed seven additional clubs. According to *Porter's Spirit of the Times* (1855), Brooklyn, which had once been known as the "City of Churches," was "fast earning the title of the 'City of Base Ball Clubs.'" The next year, the same sporting sheet reported that every empty lot within ten miles of New York City was being used as a ball field. According to "The Baseball Fever," a song that first appeared in 1857,

> Our merchants have to close their stores
> Their clerks away are staying,
> Contractors too, can do no work,
> Their hands are all out playing.

Men got up in the wee hours of the morning to practice before going to work; they spent their lunch hours playing catch; and after work, they rushed to the ball fields for yet more play. "The streets in the vicinity of our factories are now full at noon and evening of apprentices and others engaged in the simpler games of ball," reported the *Newark Daily Advertiser* in 1860. Doubtless some young men sacrificed their future careers in business or lost their jobs, all for the sake of the new game. Nothing, not even the biting cold of winter or expressions of displeasure by employers, seemed to chill their enthusiasm for baseball.

By the summer of 1861 at least 200 junior and senior teams were playing in Brooklyn, Queens, Manhattan, Westchester, and northern New Jersey. These teams were of two sorts. One set of teams, usually composed of petty merchants and clerks, organized social clubs such as the Knickerbockers. Although they frequently had enough resources to rent a club room or a clubhouse, they were nonetheless clearly less wealthy than the yachtsmen of the era or the members of the athletic clubs that grew in popularity in the 1870s and 1880s. The second kind of team arose from neighborhoods and workplaces. Young men from a particular neighborhood or those employed in a particular craft—shipwrights, butchers, firemen, post office employees, printing trade workers, and harness makers, for example—formed teams, some of which had no formal existence apart from the playing field. Because the activities of the latter teams, unless they were especially powerful, rarely appeared in the sporting sheets or the newspapers of the day, and because they generated few if any surviving records, we know far less about them than we do about the social clubs.

Even less information has survived about early African-American baseball. Antebellum slavery in the South and low incomes among free blacks in the North no doubt severely constricted the possibilities of forming clubs. Nonetheless, after the Civil War, there is scattered evidence of blacks organizing clubs in most of the larger cities. Apparently, the Pythians of Philadelphia were the first all-black team. As early as 1867, the Excelsiors of Philadelphia and the Uniques of Brooklyn played a game hailed by the press as the "colored championship of the United States." On their arrival in Brooklyn, the Excelsiors, dressed in full uniform and headed by their colorful fife and drum corps, marched through the city's streets to the ballpark. A large crowd gathered for the contest. With the Excelsiors ahead 42 to 37 after seven innings of play, the umpire called the game on account of darkness. Led again by their fife and drum corps, the Excelsiors and their supporters marched back to the East River, which they crossed by ferry to New York City for their return trip by train to Philadelphia.

In the first recorded intercollegiate baseball contest, one played by the rules of New England town ball rather than by those of New York, Amherst subdued Williams in 1859 by a lopsided score of 73-32. Unlike Williams, Amherst had trained carefully for the contest. According to a Williams professor, Amherst took "the game from the region of sport and carried it into the region of exact and laborious discipline." When the Amherst students learned of the win, they rang the chapel bell, lit a huge bonfire, and set off fireworks. The Monday following the game brought equally exciting news to the Amherst students; they had also defeated Williams at chess. Once more, "there was a universal ringing of bells, and firing of cannons; and throats already hoarse shouted again amid the general rejoicing." The Civil War temporarily set back the game on college campuses, but in the war's wake college clubs formed in all parts of the nation. It soon became the most widely played of all college sports.

⊡ ⊡ ⊡

Despite the widespread enthusiasm for baseball, not all men were equally devoted to the new game. In the early days of its history, established or would-be bankers, merchants, and industrialists had little use for baseball. A few of them played within their own inner social circle or lent their approval to the sport if it did not interfere with the work of their employees, but for the most part they saw it as a waste of valuable time. "The invariable question put to a young man applying for situations in New York," reported the secretary of the Irvington, New Jersey, baseball club in 1867, "is, whether they are members of ball clubs. If they answer in the affirmative, they are told that their services will not be needed." When the wealthy engaged in or patronized sports, it was usually restricted to such socially exclusive activities as yachting, horse racing, and (after the Civil

War) formal athletic clubs, polo, tennis, and golf. Because baseball entailed modest costs to play, it was poorly suited for those who turned to sports as a means of distinguishing themselves from the masses.

At the other end of the social spectrum, the casually employed, unskilled workers, who did the backbreaking chores of moving dirt at construction sites or loading and unloading wagons and ships, lacked the financial means or perhaps the inclination to join baseball clubs. Such men usually satisfied their needs for leisure in the patronage of saloons or in such "blood" sports as cockfights or rattings. In New York City, for example, they might visit Kit Bums's Sportsman Hall, where they could watch and wager on how long it would take a dog to kill a pit full of rats, or go to Tommy Norris's livery stable, where they could witness rattings, cockfights, goat fights, and even a boxing match between two women who were stripped nude above the waist. Finally, though baseball is steeped in the pastoral images of the American countryside, and rural people did play various ball games, the early fraternity was exclusively an urban phenomenon. In the antebellum era, no farmers are known to have formed clubs.

Instead of coming from the rich, the poor, or the farmers, the early fraternity's main support came from the clerks, those who occupied the bottom rung of the white-collar occupational ladder, and the artisans, those who occupied the top rung of the blue-collar occupational ladder. Although the clerks and artisans had adequate financial resources to permit them to form voluntary associations, and they had some control over their conditions and hours of work, both groups were experiencing profound changes in their ways of life.

At the beginning of the nineteenth century, skilled artisans took a fierce pride in their work and held esteemed positions in their communities. Working out of small shops and using the skills that had been passed down to them from earlier generations, they fashioned from start to finish most of the goods used by Americans: household utensils, furniture, carriages, harnesses, tools, and dozens of other items. Although the fast-growing factory system did not suddenly or completely annihilate the skilled handicraft mode of production, it required artisans with fewer skills, as well as a large unskilled or semiskilled work force. Factories more sharply segregated the roles of employer and employee, and they substituted a rigid discipline for the more casual work patterns of the past.

The socioeconomic role of clerks likewise underwent important changes. In the first quarter of the nineteenth century, working as a clerk was in effect an apprenticeship for many of the sons of the wealthy who aspired to become business or professional men. Employed in thousands of small offices, these young men learned the fundamentals of the business while serving as copyists of correspondence and business documents, bookkeepers, and collectors of invoices and in dozens of other capacities. But as the business and manufacturing concerns hired thousands of additional clerks to handle the expanded volume of transactions in the middle decades of the century, the older system of clerks as jacks-of-all-trades gave way to one wherein office workers performed specific tasks, such as copying documents or bookkeeping. With less opportunity for advancement, clerking for many became a dead-end occupation.

The ball-playing fraternity offered younger clerks and artisans satisfactions missing in their work as well as in other parts of their lives. Frank Pidgeon, captain of the "first nine" of the Brooklyn Eckfords, a club composed of shipbuilding artisans, offered two reasons for playing ball. First, "such sport as this brightens a man up, and improves him, both in mind and body," commented Pidgeon. Second, Pidgeon stressed the sheer pleasures of the experience itself: "We had some merry times among ourselves; we would forget business and everything else on Tuesday afternoons, go out in the green fields, don our ball suits, and go at it with a perfect rush. At such times, we were boys again."

Pidgeon's phrase, "we had some merry times among ourselves," suggests a larger function of the early games. Often unmarried and living away from home in impersonal boardinghouses, the young men sought excitement, opportunities to display their individual physical skills, companionship, and a sense of belonging. It was no accident that the early players described themselves as members of a ball-playing fraternity. The term *fraternity* implied a special closeness among the ball players, a literal brotherhood. In playing baseball and in such associated activities as eating, drinking, wagering, and talking together, the players consummated intensely shared experiences and friendships. As in a family, the ball players developed their own set of special understandings, argot, and expected behaviors.

Within many of the clubs, as Warren Goldstein has perceptively observed, pageantry and off-season social activities strengthened the bonds of male fellowship. While on the playing fields, the players donned colorful uniforms similar to those of the volunteer fire departments and the volunteer militia units of the day. Uniforms clearly distinguished the ball-playing fraternity from the general urban masses. In the more highly organized clubs, members met throughout the year to share food, drink, and good cheer. Some of the clubs scheduled an annual ball. For its second annual ball (1861) the shipbuilding artisans of Brooklyn's Eckford club decorated the dance hall "elegantly and profusely." A special treat was captain Frank Pidgeon, who exhibited his skill in the "Parisian style" of dancing. That same winter the Atlantics, another club of skilled workingmen from Brooklyn, were almost as active on the dance floor as they had been on the playing field during the previous summer. They scheduled eight "invitation hops" along with an annual ball.

Among the clubs, highly formal, even ritualized relationships helped preserve the integrity of the early fraternity. The clubs carefully distinguished between "friendly games" or "social games," on the one hand, and "matches" or "match games," on the other. Arrangement of a match game with another club's nine entailed a written challenge. If the challenge was accepted, then the captains of the respective nines would agree on an umpire and the press might be notified of the upcoming match. At the end of the game, the losing captain would make a short speech congratulating the winners and then present them with the game ball. The captain of the winning team responded with a speech praising the losers. The game ball was then inscribed with the date and score of the contest, wrapped in gold foil, and usually retired to the winner's trophy case.

Throughout the 1850s and into the 1860s, the host club provided visitors with an elaborate evening meal. In 1858, for example, "the Excelsior Club [of Brooklyn] was escorted to the Odd Fellows' Hall, Hoboken, by the Knickerbocker Club, and entertained in a splendid style. . . . Dodworth's Band was in attendance to enliven the scene." In the postgame gatherings, celebrations could become quite boisterous. A marked feature of the festivities, according to a press report in 1858, was "the indulgence of a prurient taste for indecent anecdotes and songs—a taste only to be gratified at the expense of true dignity and self-respect." "Evidence of dawn's appearance" occurred in Baltimore before the players finally called a halt to a postgame eating and drinking binge in 1860. Although the players were advised to abstain from "spirituous liquors," they were told that "to allay thirst and relieve exhaustion, lager-beer answers every reasonable purpose." An extreme example of the effectiveness of postgame rituals in promoting amity within the fraternity occurred in 1860. According to a New York *Clipper* report, after having shared a keg of lager, the players were unable to recall the score of a game that they had played earlier in the day. Little wonder that the early baseball fraternity experienced difficulties in winning support among suspicious Victorians!

Nonetheless, the fraternity persisted in trying. As *Porter's Spirit of the Times,* a weekly that was planted firmly in the fraternity's camp, put it in 1857, the ball player "must be sober and temperate. Patience, fortitude, self-denial, order, obedience, and good-humor, with an unruffled temper, are indispensable. . . . Such a game . . . teaches a love of order, discipline, and fair play." No one could have coined a more satisfactory list of Victorian virtues, all of which the game allegedly nurtured. Furthermore, the defenders of the game insisted that, unlike other sports, only baseball encouraged "manliness," or self-control, the opposite of boyishness or uninhibited behavior. For the sedentary clerks who had few opportunities to express their physicality in the workplace, the robustness of baseball may have been particularly appealing. Consistent with the argument that baseball was a manly game, widespread agitation arose within the fraternity in the 1860s for requiring that the fielders catch the ball "on the fly" rather than on the first bounce for a putout.

Play by boys, according to the *Brooklyn Eagle,* kept the youngsters "out of a great deal of mischief. . . . [Baseball] keeps them from hanging around [fire] engine houses, stables, and taverns." The game merited "the endorsement of every clergyman in the country," concluded Henry Chadwick, because it was a "remedy for the many evils resulting from the immoral associations [that] boys and young men of our cities are apt to become connected with." Perhaps such arguments relieved the anxieties of some, but they certainly failed to still completely public suspicions of the fraternity and its game.

⬜ ⬜ ⬜

In the 1850s and 1860s the "New York game," as the Knickerbockers' version of the sport came to be known, completely displaced competing forms of baseball. Part of the success of the New York game stemmed from its rules. Both spectators and players preferred the use of foul lines, a unique feature of the New York game that contained the play and allowed the fans to get closer to the field. The "three outs to end an inning" rule of the New York game permitted more offensive action than the "Massachusetts game" of "one out, all out." Finally, by restricting the length of a game to nine full innings (in 1857), the New York game usually ended within three hours, whereas a contest played by Massachusetts rules (which required the winning team to score a hundred runs) frequently failed to reach a conclusion before nightfall. Cricket, for a time an effective competitor of the New York game for popularity, was even slower; it sometimes took two full days to finish a match.

New York's pivotal position in the nation's commercial and communications network aided the city in achieving the triumph of its game. Visitors to Gotham on business or pleasure observed the new game and sometimes became infatuated with it; some of them, on returning home, introduced it to their friends. And, like the zealous missionaries of a new religious faith, New York baseball enthusiasts took their game everywhere they went: among other documented places, to Baltimore, St. Louis, New Orleans, Chicago, Washington, D.C., San Francisco, and Honolulu (to the latter by none other than Alexander Cartwright himself). The nation's leading sporting weeklies, *Porter's Spirit of the Times* (founded in 1831) and the New York *Clipper* (founded in 1853), both published in New York, took up the cause. They extolled the New York game in editorials, recounted the game's early history, printed the results of matches, and even instructed readers on how to form clubs.

No single journalist gave the New York game greater assistance than an English-born Brooklynite, Henry Chadwick. For many years, he wrote voluminously on baseball for the *Brooklyn Eagle* (1856–94) and the New York *Clipper* (1857–88). He also edited many of the annual guidebooks of the sport. Allegedly selling 50,000 copies, the first of these, *Beadle's Dime Base Ball Player* (1860), set the pattern for the rest. It contained some of Chadwick's newspaper articles, rules of the game, statistics for the previous year, and a summary of the physical and moral benefits of the sport. Chadwick also adapted from cricket the box score and batting averages, quantitative devices that enhanced baseball's appeal. Recognizing the importance of his contributions to the early game, contemporaries hailed Chadwick as the "Father of Baseball."

Nothing encouraged the diffusion of baseball outside the New York area more than the 1860 tours of the famed Brooklyn Excelsiors (meaning in this context a group that excels). News of the "crack club's" lopsided triumphs over teams in Albany, Troy, Buffalo, Rochester, and Newburgh flashed across the nation's telegraph wires. Albert Spalding, who in 1860 was just beginning his career as a ball player in the far-off Illinois prairies, later recalled that these matches inspired thousands of young men to hope "that they might win for their cities a glory akin to that which had been achieved for [Brooklyn]." That same summer, the Excelsiors proceeded on to Philadelphia and Baltimore. Their visit to Baltimore, according to the *Clipper,* advanced the cause of baseball in that city by at least three years. Partly because of the play of the Excelsiors in Philadelphia, George Kirsch has concluded that baseball in the City of Brotherly Love "exploded in popularity, leaving townball as a quaint relic of the past." The Excelsiors' skill, however, was not the only element helping to further the game; according to Henry Chadwick, the fact that the Excelsiors ranked "second to none . . . in social standing did more to establish baseball on a permanent and reputable footing than had been attempted by any other club."

As early as the mid-1850s New York's baseball fraternity began to promote the sport as "the national game." Such a strategy fitted perfectly the mood of the tense 1850s. In a decade that spawned the nativist, anti-Catholic Know Nothing political movement and the bitter sectional rivalries that were to culminate in the Civil War, yearnings for national unity spilled over into the sports arena. Few events captured the public imagination more than American challenges to English supremacy in horse racing, yachting, and prize fighting. Many of the first baseball clubs avowed their patriotism by taking on such names as American, Columbia, Eagle, Young America, Washington, Union, Liberty, and National. As the English had their cricket and the Germans had their *Turnvereins* (gymnastics clubs), *Porter's Spirit* declared in 1857, so should the Americans have "a game that could be termed a 'Native American Sport.'"

New Yorkers took the initiative in forming the first national association of baseball enthusiasts. Although the Knickerbockers were unable, or perhaps unwilling, to dictate the structure and rules of baseball for the entire nation, as the pioneering Marylebone Club of London had done for cricket in Britain, the Knickerbockers did establish an influential model for the organization of the early clubs, drew up the first rules, and issued the first call for a meeting of New York club delegates. Meeting in 1857, the clubs decided to form a larger organization that would make rules, regulate interclub competition, and preserve the fraternal character of the game. The next year the group called itself the National Association of Base Ball Players (NABBP), a misnomer inasmuch as only clubs in New York City and nearby areas initially belonged to the association. By 1861, however, clubs located in New Haven, Detroit, Philadelphia, Baltimore, and Washington, D.C., as well as in the New York area, sent delegates to the annual NABBP convention.

Finally, the Civil War (1861–65) helped ensure the dominance of the New York version of baseball. Many clubs folded as their members made their

way off to war, but at the same time, by bringing together massive numbers of young men in military units, the war replicated conditions similar
to those that existed among them in the cities. Seeking to escape boredom
and establish an identity in an all-male milieu, soldiers and sailors frequently turned to boxing, running, wrestling, shooting-at-the-mark, and baseball matches. The troops played both previously arranged and pick-up
games; they played both inside and outside the camp grounds. According
to baseball lore, a game between two teams of New York volunteer infan-
trymen at Hilton Head, South Carolina, attracted more than 40,000 soldiers. The attendance was probably exaggerated; without a grandstand
only a few thousand spectators could have seen much of the action. At any
rate, this exhibition of the New York game was said "to have lighted the
spark that caused" the postwar "baseball explosion." In the midst of another game in Texas, the Confederates launched a surprise assault on Union
troops. Although the Northern soldiers repulsed the charge and lost only
their center fielder to the enemy, they also had the misfortune of losing "the
only baseball in Alexandria."

Veterans of both armies returned home after the war, bringing with them
the game that many had encountered for the first time in the camps. Doubtless few Southerners saw the sport as an antidote for their traditional "list-
lessness and love of indolent pleasures," as Northerner Henry Chadwick
did, but they did take to the game's excitement. In the West, antebellum
Chicago had only four clubs, but by the second summer after the conflict
had ended at least thirty-two clubs were playing in the Windy City. Interest was sufficient in 1865 for the Chicago enthusiasts to form the North
Western Association of Base Ball Players, which included clubs from as far
away as St. Louis. By 1865 representation at the annual convention of the
NABBP had grown to include delegates from ninety-one clubs located in
ten states. Two years later the association elected its first non–New York-
er, Arthur Pue Gorman from Washington, D.C., as president and in 1868
held its first convention outside New York City (in Philadelphia).

⊡ ⊡ ⊡

Although baseball in organized forms had existed only for two decades
or so, the baseball fraternity was able to make a convincing case by the
end of the Civil War that its game should be labeled as *the* national game.
The fraternity had a substantial affiliation in all the major cities of the
Northeast, with some representation in the cities of the Midwest and the

Far West, and was spreading rapidly into the smaller towns and cities throughout the nation. No other organized American sport included so many participants or attracted so many persons who avidly followed the game as spectators. But at the very height of its apparent success, the fraternity confronted forces that would soon threaten its very existence.

2

A Commercial
Spectacle

In 1862, the same year that Alexander T. Stewart opened the nation's first
department store on Broadway and 10th Street in Manhattan, an enter-
prising Brooklynite, William H. Cammeyer, had a different idea for improving his financial fortunes. Why not seize on the opportunities offered
by the city's baseball mania? By converting his ice-skating pond at the
corner of Lee Avenue and Rutledge Street into an enclosed field, he could
charge fans a fee to watch the games played there. Acting on this thought,
Cammeyer proceeded to drain his pond, fill it with dirt, level the surface,
and build a fence around the plot. To provide seating for some 1,500 spectators, Cammeyer nailed together long wooden benches. In one corner of
the field he built a "commodious" clubhouse for the teams, and in another he erected a saloon to quench the thirst of fans. On opening day, 15 May
1862, flags, including the American flag and the pennants of local teams,
hung loosely in the breeze, and a band played "The Star Spangled Ban-

ner." Reflecting the high patriotic sentiments of the day, Cammeyer named his new field the "Union Grounds."

After the Civil War, dozens of entrepreneurs across the country followed a procedure similar to Cammeyer's. They enclosed grounds, sponsored special games, and offered money to participating teams while meeting their costs from gate receipts. Less frequently, the clubs themselves purchased a field, enclosed it, and charged admission. Typically, watching a routine game cost a fan ten cents, a major contest might be twenty-five cents, and even fifty cents was not an unusual charge for a championship game. Rather than relying exclusively on club membership dues to finance their teams, the clubs increasingly turned to the money that could be obtained from gate fees.

The "enclosure movement," as the drive to build fences around the grounds and charge admissions was called, had far-reaching implications for the baseball fraternity. To seize the full advantages offered by gate fees, teams had to play more games with external foes; by the late 1860s, several "first nines" were playing fifty or more games per season, and some of them were embarking on long summer tours as well. In policy matters, enclosure meant that ordinary club members increasingly deferred to the interests of the "first nine" and that clubs began to recruit members more on the basis of their playing skills rather than their general sociability. In short, the enclosure movement tended to subordinate fraternal concerns to commercial considerations. It was, as Henry Chadwick later wrote, "really the beginning of professional base ball playing."

⊞   ⊞   ⊞

Once a club scheduled its first match with another club, it set in motion the process by which that club moved away from its fraternal origins. External matches, on the whole, generated far greater excitement than intraclub games. "It is well known that where a lively, well contested and exciting game is in progress," concluded the New York *Clipper* in 1860, "there will ever be found crowds of interested spectators." The fans invariably chose sides; their own identities then became emotionally linked to the successes and failures of the teams for which they rooted. By providing urban dwellers with richer identities, the teams helped satisfy deep yearnings for belonging and rootedness in an exceptionally mobile society. Teams could also give neighborhoods, ethnic and occupational groups, and cities new and deeper emotional existences.

The growing popularity of championships added to the intensity of the interclub games. As early as 1859, Massachusetts held a statewide baseball championship at the Boston Agricultural Grounds, and seven years later the New England association awarded a silver ball for its championship. New York area teams first contended for a self-proclaimed national championship in 1860. According to the practice of the day, a club retained the championship until it lost a two-of-three series. A self-proclaimed 1866 World Championship Tournament in Rockford, Illinois, brought in teams from Detroit, Milwaukee, Dubuque, and Chicago. Two years later, Frank Queen, the publisher of the *Clipper*, offered a national championship trophy of a gold ball to the team with the best won-lost season record among the powerful New York nines.

Potential publicity, glory, gate receipts, and championships invariably encouraged a greater emphasis on the fortunes of the "first nine" at the expense of the other ball-playing club members. "All of those who would like to play an occasional game merely for recreation are precluded from doing so," lamented the Philadelphia *Sunday Dispatch* in 1866. "All the base ball clubs of any prominence give up their grounds entirely to [their] first nine, and out of several hundred members they are the only ones who derive any benefit whatever from the game." Such clubs then became in effect merely booster organizations for the first nines. Play became far more serious. When not playing, many of the first nines practiced nearly every day. Players began to specialize according to positions. The New York *Clipper* noted as early as 1861 that players could achieve "special excellence" only if they "permanently" occupied one position. "A first base player only, for instance, should be known as a first base player only, and the same as regards other bases, the pitcher, catcher, and the short field [shortstop]."

Interclub games could easily degenerate into ill will and a loss of self-control, both of which could seriously damage the larger interests of the fraternity. Spectators more frequently became boisterous participants in the games. As early as 1857, *Porter's Spirit of the Times* reported that, in a game in which the Excelsiors defeated the Niagaras, "some of the Niagaras' friends did not behave as gentlemen should." Whenever a pitch approached an Excelsior batter, some of the fans yelled "'shanks,' 'Shanghai,' and other words not quite as decent as the above." Large crowds sometimes interfered with the course of the game itself. When fans congregated in the outfield, fielders might have to retrieve balls from among a forest of legs. In a game in Philadelphia in 1860, so many fans crowded around third base that the other fielders "were at a loss to know whether the third base [was] occupied or not." Gangs of boys were particularly aggravating. "The noisy and ill-bred urchins . . . intrude themselves among the spectators and annoy and disturb everyone in the vicinity with bad language and rough conduct," reported a newspaper in a frequently repeated complaint of the day.

Baseball matches sometimes reflected fundamental ethnic and class rivalries. A manifest instance occurred in 1860 when the Excelsiors, a team that ranked "second to none in social standing" and was composed of Protestant, old-stock American clerks and petty merchants, met the Atlantics, a team composed mainly of Irish Catholic workingmen, in a three-game series for the New York championship. The teams split the first two games without incident, though more than 10,000 spectators attended each contest. In the final game, before a crowd estimated between 15,000 and 20,000, several close calls by the umpire triggered an outburst by the Atlantics rooters. They hooted and jeered. No one could restrain them, not even the efforts of the Atlantics players themselves or the 100 policemen stationed at the game to keep order. Accompanied by a shrill chorus of insults from the Atlantic fans, captain Joseph Leggett of the Excelsiors pulled his players off the field. As the Excelsiors' team omnibus departed, Atlantic rooters pelted it with stones.

More was at stake in the game than simply winning or losing. Albert Spalding, in a second-hand report, described the Atlantic fans as "utterly uncontrollable . . . thugs, gamblers, thieves, plug-uglies and rioters." The cause of the disorder, according to the *Clipper,* was "*the spirit of faction* . . . in which the foreign element [i.e., the Irish Americans] of our immense metropolitan population, and their . . . offspring, especially, delights to indulge." To both the Protestant old-stock and the Irish Catholic ethnic fans, the game had become a symbolic test of honor and supremacy. From that day to the time when both clubs disbanded in 1871, the Atlantics and Excelsiors never again met on the field of play.

Capitulation to the excitement of a hard-fought game was not limited to the spectators, or "kranks," as the more rabid of the fans came to be known. As the game's popularity spread among the workingmen and ethnics, groups not so encumbered by Victorian fears of unregulated passion, the players more frequently succumbed to their tempers, disputed umpires' decisions, and argued with their opponents or even their own teammates. In another game featuring the Atlantics—this time against Tammany Hall's New York Mutuals in 1863—the press reported that in the ninth inning "considerable 'chaffing' [took place] among the members of the two clubs." Both teams became "excited to an unusual degree" when William Mc-Keever of the Mutuals stepped up to bat with the tying run on first base. Trying to tempt McKeever into swinging at a bad pitch, the Atlantics pitch-er proceeded to throw more than fifty "bad" balls. In the words of a re-porter, McKeever then "allowed his temper to get the better of him."

As in this instance, amiable relationships among the players depended on their mutual willingness to adhere to the sport's conventions. No ex-plicit penalty prevented the Atlantics pitcher from deliberately throwing pitch after pitch outside the spot favored by the hitter, but it was under-stood that such behavior violated the spirit of the game. With a growing premium placed on winning, and without the restraints of an upper-class circle of "gentleman" sportsmen or a compelling tradition of "fair play" (as existed among the upper classes in England), the American baseball players tended to exploit every area within the game for which there was no explicit rule or no penalties levied for violations.

Because some batsmen had been too selective about the pitches that they were willing to swing at, the NABBP in 1858 authorized the umpire to call strikes on those hitters who repeatedly refused to swing at "good balls." This rule change encouraged the pitchers to throw harder but wilder, in-asmuch as they suffered no penalties for throwing "bad balls." In response to this new violation of the game's spirit, the NABBP in 1863 permitted the umpire to award first base to hitters who had been the recipients of three bad pitches. Although both these rules left the issue of whether to call balls and strikes to the umpire, it was only a matter of time before the official would have to make a judgment on every pitch thrown.

Acutely conscious that the loss of self-control potentially weakened fra-ternal bonds, the early clubs tried to deal with spectator and player misbe-havior in a variety of other ways. They fined club members for using pro-fane language, disputing umpire decisions, disobeying the captains, and other forms of disorderly conduct. In interclub matches, the umpire had the unenviable task of upholding the ideal of "gentlemanly behavior." "The position of the umpire," explained Henry Chadwick, "is an honorable one, but its duties are anything but agreeable, as it is next to impossible to give entire satisfaction to all parties concerned in a match." In recognition of the inadequacy of these restraints, and consistent with the Victorian notion that women possess special powers to domesticate men, the ball-playing fraternity frequently sought the patronage and influence of women. Men required feminine "confidence and approval," commented the *Clipper*, "as a kind of social regulator in the joyousness of our fun, to prevent it from becoming too boisterous." Ultimately, none of these measures ensured that early baseball would be freed from disorderly conduct.

☐ ☐ ☐

Earning money from gate receipts was only one source of profit arising from interclub baseball matches. Soon, gamblers were also exploiting the pecuniary opportunities presented by the games. Although roundly condemned by proper Victorians, gambling had been closely tied to such antebellum spectacles as horse races, billiard matches, prize fights, and pedestrian races. As early as 1840 almost any coffee house, billiard parlor, or saloon might harbor a gambling establishment. Many of the nineteenth-century sporting spectacles arose from spirited arguments over the merits of a horse, a prize fighter, or a runner. A wager and the scheduling of a contest then ensued. Few experiences equaled the intensity of wagering; for spectator, promoter, and athlete alike, winning a bet could be more important than the thrill of winning the contest itself. In wagering, one risked not only money but one's self-esteem as well. By choosing to bet on a particular team, the bettor might be making a statement of ethnic or occupational pride. Furthermore, wagering provided an opportunity to display skills for men who increasingly found such opportunities denied to them in their workplaces.

By the late 1860s, baseball offered the Victorian underworld rich opportunities to satisfy the widespread hunger for gambling. At some parks, gamblers openly touted their odds. In California, just as a fielder was about to catch a fly ball, the gamblers who had placed a bet on the side at bat would fire their six-shooters. On a few occasions, bettors even mobbed playing fields to prevent the completion of games in which they stood to lose money. "So common has betting become at baseball matches," complained a *Harper's Weekly* editor in 1867, "that the most respectable clubs in the country indulge in it to a highly culpable degree, and so common . . . the tricks by which games have been 'sold' for the benefit of the gamblers that the most respectable participants have been suspected of baseness."

Although newspapers frequently hinted at fixes throughout the late 1860s, they probably exaggerated the extent of the practice. Every time a favored team lost, fans were likely to suspect that the game was fixed. Nonetheless, the common practice of scheduling three-game championship series tempted teams to split the first two games so they could profit from a third contest.

There was one publicly disclosed admission of such a fixed game. In 1865, Thomas B. Devyr, a player for Tammany Hall's New York Mutuals, testified that William Wansley, a teammate, had approached him and another teammate, Edward Duffy, with a proposal to split $100 among them to throw a game against the Brooklyn Excelsiors. By winning the last two games of the three-game series, Wansley allegedly assured Devyr, "we can lose this game without doing the Club any harm." After disclosure of the fix at a hearing, the Mutuals promptly expelled all three offenders, but later, hoping to strengthen their team, they forgave their past transgressions, reinstating first Devyr in 1867, then Duffy in 1868, and finally Wansley in 1870.

By the mid-1860s, widespread charges of fixes, gambling, drinking, and general disorder seriously jeopardized the baseball fraternity's efforts to maintain Victorian respectability. Led by the evangelical Protestant clergy, proper Victorians frequently identified the game with the nineteenth-century underworld of commercial entertainment that included saloons, vaudeville, variety shows, billiard halls, gambling emporiums, and brothels. Like other commercial pastimes, baseball became a focal point of controversy in several cities. The city political machines and their bosses, who depended mainly on the support of the Catholic, ethnic, working-class vote, usually sided with commercial baseball, whereas the well-to-do, old-stock Protestants sided with the reformers who wanted to restrict or abolish commercial amusements.

Indeed, the "politicians are commencing to curry favor with the fraternity of ballplayers, as a class of our 'fellow citizens' worthy of the attention of 'our influential men,'" reported the *Clipper* as early as 1865. Politicians helped organize and fund teams. The New York Mutuals, for example, had been founded in 1857 by William Marcy Tweed, who was to become the infamous boss of Tammany Hall. The club's 1871 board of directors included city aldermen, state legislators, and local judges.

Recruiting club members exclusively for their playing talents represented yet another threat to the survival of the early baseball fraternity. Just as the 1860 tours of the powerful Excelsiors of Brooklyn had been instrumental in popularizing the New York game, the same club led the departure from exclusive reliance on regular membership as a pool of talent. Between 1857 and 1860 the Excelsiors strengthened their first nine by recruiting new members from the New York Cricket Club and the Star Club, a leading junior nine from Brooklyn. None of their new recruits was a more important symbol of baseball's future than James Creighton, "the sport's first superstar." Creighton was not only the game's premier pitcher (he threw what contemporaries called a "speed ball" and is alleged to have invented the curve ball), but he was also baseball's first known compensated player.

Although the National Association of Base Ball Players (NABBP) explicitly prohibited the employment of professional players, soon teams were extending sub rosa subsidies to players. As early as 1863, the *Brooklyn Eagle* reported that "ball matches have of late years got to be quite serious affairs, and some have even intimated that ballplaying has become quite a money making business, many finding it to pay well to play well." In the immediate postwar years professionalism became even more common; the majority of the players on the Atlantics, Eckfords, and Mutuals, the three most powerful nines in the metropolitan New York area, apparently were being paid to play.

Subsidies often took the form of a paying job that required little or no actual work. Many of the Mutuals, for example, held patronage positions with New York City's government. "The real birthplace of professional baseball" in Washington, D.C., was said to be among clerks employed in the United States Treasury Department. Comprising some of the best recruits in the East, nearly all of the 1867 Washington Nationals, the first eastern club to tour west of the Alleghenies, held jobs with the federal government. Adrian "Cap" Anson recalled that when he was a youth in Iowa in the late 1860s, "it was generally the custom to import from abroad some player who had made a name for himself . . . and furnish him with a business situation." An example was young Albert Spalding, who in 1867 accepted a position paying forty dollars a week with a Chicago wholesale grocery "with the understanding that my store duties would be nominal, a chance given to play ball frequently, without affecting my salary to reduce it."

As the game became more commercialized, its ambience changed. "Instead of legitimate trials of skill between clubs," lamented the Philadelphia *Sunday Mercury* in 1867, "we had conflicts in which animosities were engendered, gambling was fostered, and from which arose the effort to make ball-playing a regular business occupation." By the mid-1860s the postgame rituals of awarding the game ball to the winning team and of the home club hosting the visitors to an evening feast had all but vanished. The more skilled players increasingly cut their ties with their home clubs and offered their services to the team that offered them the most generous subsidies. This practice was known as "revolving." Perhaps the most extreme case was a player who, according to a newspaper report in 1866, had played with six different clubs during the previous three seasons.

❑ ❑ ❑

The history of the NABBP and its locally affiliated associations provides additional illumination on baseball's transition from a fraternal game into a commercial spectacle. Throughout its existence, the NABBP wrestled with several issues that threatened the fraternity's existence. One of the first of these was whether the association should have an open admissions policy. Should it, for example, welcome the membership of junior clubs, those composed of boys under the age of twenty-one? Exclusion of the juniors was necessary, the opponents successfully argued, to preserve the "manly" quality of the sport. Consistent with their effort to dissociate their game from youngsters, the association in 1863 also adopted a rule requiring that the ball be caught on the fly rather than on the first bounce for a putout.

Likewise, the association excluded black clubs. Although white and black clubs sometimes shared playing fields and on occasion played games against one another, both the NABBP in its 1867 convention and the New York state baseball association in 1870 flatly refused to admit black clubs. "If colored clubs were admitted," concluded the NABBP's nominating committee, resorting to the logic of a racist society, "there would be in all probability some division of feeling, whereas, by excluding them no injury could result to anyone."

To protect the fraternity from internal divisions—that is, in the words of the NABBP, to cultivate "kindly feelings among the different members of Base-Ball clubs"—the association tried to regulate player eligibility. Permitting players to revolve from one club to another during the season generated much ill-will within the fraternity and completely violated the belief that the players ought to have emotional ties to their clubs. In a vain effort to prevent revolving, the association in 1865 required that a player be a member of a club for at least thirty days prior to playing in an interclub game.

The use of professional players posed an equally serious problem for the fraternity. Unlike the wealthier sportsmen of the era, the baseball clubs rarely employed amateurism as a means of promoting social exclusivity. One of the few exceptions may have been the Knickerbockers, who, despite their pioneering role in baseball, had never been competitive in extramural competition. "The same standard still exists [21 years after the club's founding], no person can obtain admission in the club merely for his capacity as a player," reported Charles A. Peverelly in 1866. "He must also have the reputation of a gentleman." But neither the artisan nor the ethnic communities developed a tradition of amateurism, let alone using it to promote social exclusion. They had no objections in principle to play for pay. Instead, their opposition to paying players sprang mainly from the fact that it created two sharply different levels of skills within the fraternity. Such a division tended to erode the equality that was essential to the fraternity's existence.

In the end, the association was ineffective in forestalling the ascendancy of commercial baseball. To begin with, the great majority of clubs belonged to neither the NABBP nor a regional association. Secondly, the NABBP itself had no real power; ultimately, it had to rely entirely on the voluntary compliance of the member clubs. Finally, the association was rent by internal divisions. Even when paid players were first officially barred in 1859, some members of the NABBP protested that the ban discriminated against ordinary workingmen and was likely to retard improvements in the quality of play. By the late 1860s, critics of the rule pointed out that in practice it had become a "dead letter"; frank recognition of professionalism, they said, would eliminate the widespread hypocrisy of under-the-table payments to players. In 1868, the association voted to recognize two classes of players, one as professional and one as amateur, only to reverse itself the following year.

The issue of professionalism finally brought about the demise of the association in 1870. After a "spicy debate," two-thirds of the delegates to the NABBP convention voted against a resolution that condemned "the custom of publicly hiring men to play the game of base ball [as] reprehensible and injurious to the best interests of the game." "Under the pressure of the control of the professional managers," reported the *Clipper,* "the National Association gave up the ghost, and after a reputable existence of ten years and a decline in health during the last three, it adjourned sine die." In the following year, the professionals formed their own National Association of Professional Base Ball Players. In the same year, 1871, the opponents of professionalism, led by the New York Knickerbockers, responded by forming a new association that expressly tried to restore "the old status of base-ball playing," extending an invitation of membership to all clubs "which engage in the game for recreative exercise only, and not for gate money, receipts, or for pecuniary benefit only." By the 1870s, however, it was far too late to restore the original character of the game. In 1874 the new amateur association folded.

⊡ ⊡ ⊡

By the late 1860s, baseball was fully launched as a commercial enterprise. Enclosing the grounds and charging gate fees had become a common practice. Many clubs paid their most valued players in some fashion, and for the 1869 season the Cincinnati Red Stockings boldly announced that they would field an all-salaried nine. Although baseball continued to fulfill fraternal needs for thousands of young men and boys, the commercialization of the sport weakened fraternal bonds. Paid players became in effect employees, much like the professional actors and actresses of the day, and many of the clubs became joint-stock companies, organized in part for the express purpose of profiting from the sport. Yet commercialization by no means dampened public enthusiasm for the game. Professional players raised the quality of play to new heights, and the professional teams soon demonstrated that they could fan the fierce fires of local tribalism even more effectively than had their fraternal predecessors.

3

The First Professional Teams

Nothing surprised baseball enthusiasts more in 1869 than the performance of Cincinnati's Red Stockings. The nation's first publicly proclaimed all-salaried team swept through the 1869 season without a loss and with but one tie. The tie occurred when the Haymakers of Troy, New York, angered—or perhaps feigning anger—by an umpire's decision, left the field after five minutes of arguing. Some said that the Haymakers walked off to protect the bets of those who had wagered on a Troy victory. Be that as it may, more than 23,000 fans watched the Red Stockings invade baseball's citadel, metropolitan New York, where they handily defeated six foes considered up to that time the best in the game. The team then traveled by train on to the nation's capital in Washington, D.C., where President Ulysses S. Grant welcomed the western "Cinderella" team and complimented the members on their high standard of play.

On returning home, Cincinnatians gave the team a rousing welcome.

They organized a parade featuring carriages decorated with flags, plumes, and bright ribbons, and the Zouave band played the team song:

> We are a band of Ball Players
>   From Cincinnati City
> We go to toss the ball around,
>   and sing you our ditty.
> Hurrah! Hurrah!
> For the noble game, hurrah!
>   Red Stockings all
> We'll toss the ball.

The band escorted the team to the Gibson House hotel, where that evening at a lavish banquet a local lumber company presented the players with an icon of their success, a huge, specially turned bat that was eighteen inches thick in the fattest part and sixteen feet long. "Glory, they've advertised the city—advertised us, sir, and helped our business," exulted a delighted Cincinnati businessman. In September, the Red Stockings crossed the country on the newly completed transcontinental railroad and played a series of games in California. Altogether, according to one estimate, they traveled by rail, stage, and ship 11,877 miles, and more than 200,000 fans watched their games.

The national attention bestowed on the Red Stockings in 1869 provoked the envy of cities elsewhere. They soon formed their own representative professional nines, thereby signaling the end of one era and the beginning of another. Although hundreds of teams continued to play as amateur or semiprofessional outfits, it was the joint-stock clubs fielding paid players in the rapidly growing cities of the Midwest—or "the West," as the region was called in those days—that determined the main directions of baseball's history in the 1870s and 1880s.

▣ ▣ ▣

Nothing contributed more to the enthusiasm for the creation of representative nines than the intense rivalry among nineteenth-century cities. Older eastern cities could to some degree take their eminence for granted; they already had familiar physical edifices, hallowed civic monuments, and long-established institutions that gave them a sense of continuity, permanence, and achievement. Even in the East, however, a smaller city might see in its baseball team an opportunity to embarrass a larger neighbor. "If we are ahead of the big city in nothing else," crowed the *Brooklyn Eagle* in 1862, "we can beat her in baseball." Nonetheless, until the formation of the Giants in 1883, local baseball enthusiasts regarded such a powerful team as the Mutuals as only one among several strong New York teams, none of which individually they considered to be *the* New York team.

Interurban rivalry among the upstart cities of the West, rather than among the older eastern cities, first stimulated the enthusiasm for the formation of representative pro teams. In the West, only a few decades separated small, sleepy trading posts from large, bustling cities. Uncertain about their city's status but hopeful for its future, local newspapermen, merchants, and manufacturers frequently resorted to strident boosterism. They tried to bolster their extravagant claims in behalf of their cities by conjuring up suitable institutions, including churches, parks, hospitals, opera houses, libraries, colleges, and representative baseball nines.

Chicago, a longtime Cincinnati rival for midwestern supremacy, was a classic instance. Prior to 1870, Chicago, like other larger cities, had been the home of several dozen baseball clubs, none of which could be said to have represented the city as a whole. Cincinnati's success with a representative pro team in 1869 changed all that. Chicago "could not see her commercial rival on the Ohio bearing off the honors of the national game," declared the Windy City's *Lakeside Monthly.* "So Chicago went to work." Among others, Joseph Medill of the *Chicago Tribune* and Potter Palmer, owner of the famed Palmer House hotel, rose to the occasion by organizing the White Stockings baseball club as a joint-stock company. They "raised $20,000 with which to employ a nine that should," in the words of an envious Boston newspaper, "'sweep the board.'"

As it had in Chicago, the decision by a group of small-time entrepreneurs, politicians, and civic boosters to field a representative pro team in Cincinnati arose more from dreams of promoting the city's reputation, advancing personal political careers, and taking revenge against a local rival than from the lure of potential profits. In 1868 the Buckeye Base Ball Club of Cincinnati had, according to the *Spirit of the Times,* ignored all the fraternity's principles; it had "shipped players in from Washington to take part in this game, and even went so far . . . as to drug some of the players of the Cincinnati [Red Stockings Club] and to bribe others." But neither were the Red Stockings innocents. A year earlier, Aaron B. Champion, a twenty-six-year-old attorney with soaring political ambitions, had reorganized the club as a joint-stock company. Over the next two years, by vigorously pushing stock sales and subscriptions among local businessmen and politicians, Champion recruited more than 350 club members and raised enough money to employ star players from the East. In fact, only one local man, Charles Gould, the first baseman, graced the roster of the powerful ten-man 1869 Red Stockings squad. "Had the Cincinnati Base Ball Club depended upon home talent it would never have been heard from outside its own locality," observed the *National Chronicle.*

No outsider was more important to the Red Stockings' success than Harry Wright. Born in England to a father who played professional cricket, Wright gained his first organized ball-playing experience at the St. George's Cricket Club in Staten Island, New York. He served as the club's bowler and assisted his father, who was the club's pro, in teaching the nuances of the sport to the other club members. Like many cricketers of the day, Wright soon took up baseball; he played for a time in the outfield for the legendary New York Knickerbockers. In 1865 he moved on to Cincinnati, where he received a salary of $1,200 as an instructor and player for the Union Cricket Club. The following summer he switched to playing baseball exclusively. The Cincinnati Base Ball Club paid him $1,200 to serve as a player, captain, chief recruiter, and publicist for their baseball team. Other players on the 1869 team received salaries ranging from $1,400 for George Wright, Harry's brother, to $600 for Richard Hurley, the team's lone substitute. Altogether, Wright disbursed $9,300 in salaries.

Despite the 1869 team's fantastic success on the playing field, Wright experienced headaches in managing the first publicly all-salaried team. Sometimes gate receipts did not equal team expenses. For example, in Mansfield, Ohio, the club grossed only $50, and in Cleveland $81. No opponent showed up for a game scheduled in Syracuse, New York. At times the players cut practices, missed trains, imbibed too much strong drink, and stayed up into the wee hours of the morning. Wright's eccentric pitcher, Asa Brainard, was a special problem. During one game, a wild rabbit ran across the infield in front of Brainard. He impulsively turned and hurled the ball at the frightened bunny. Brainard's throw not only missed the elusive rabbit but sent the ball rolling into the crowd, allowing two rival runners to score. Fortunately, not all was lost, for the powerful Red Stockings won the game anyway. After deducting all expenses, Champion reported a profit of only $1.25 for the season.

The Cincinnati club remained undefeated until a year later. On 14 June 1870, after having won twenty-six consecutive games during the spring, the Atlantics upset them 8-7 in eleven innings before a crowd of 20,000 at the Capitoline Grounds in Brooklyn. During the 1870 campaign they lost five more games. The exact reasons for the team's demise in September are unknown. In November, amidst much grumbling about the team's management, the club stockholders ousted Champion. It may have been that the players were demanding too much in salaries. At any rate, the team's financial prospects were too dim to attract additional investments. With the dissolution of the famed team, Harry Wright took four of his players with him to form the nucleus of a team that would represent Boston. The others went to Washington, where they played for the Olympics club.

□ □ □

Although fielding a baseball team could on occasion attract more attention to a city than building hospitals, opera houses, or libraries, it could also backfire, as the Cincinnati experience suggested. After all, by necessity, for every team that wins there is another team that loses. A losing team then (as now) could evoke negative publicity, feelings of inferiority, and even depression among the city's residents. After the St. Louis Brown Stockings defeated the Chicago White Stockings in 1875, a Chicago newspaper reported that "a deep gloom settled over the city. Friends refused to recognize friends, lovers became estranged, and business was suspended. All Chicago went to a funeral, and the time, since then, has dragged wearily along, as though it were no object to live longer in this world." From a more practical standpoint, a losing team usually meant declining attendance and frequently financial losses to those who had invested in it.

As a business proposition, baseball faced other difficulties. The ricocheting business cycle could play havoc with the best-laid plans. During the periods of unemployment or falling incomes, families were more likely to forgo tickets to baseball games than food or shelter. As with farming, day after day of adverse weather could also quickly destroy the fortunes of an otherwise promising ball club. Finally, despite its claims to being the national game, until at least the first decades of the twentieth century, pro baseball enjoyed at best only lukewarm acceptance among proper Victorians. Without the patronage of a vast range of old-stock middle-class Protestants, the game depended for its support mainly on ethnics and workingmen (both of whom enjoyed less than average amounts of discretionary income) and on the middle- and upper-income ranks unrestrained by Victorian attitudes.

Given these handicaps, pro baseball teams, like most small businesses then and since, experienced staggering rates of failure. Ted Vincent, a modern student of the pro teams in the postbellum era, has found that three-fourths of them failed to survive for more than two years. Leagues of representative teams were equally fragile. Far more typical than the National Association of Professional Base Ball Players (1871–75), the National League (1876–present), and the American Association (1881–91) was the Southern League. Prior to 1900, the Southern League collapsed before the end of the season no fewer than seven times (1886, 1888, 1889, 1893, 1894, 1898, and 1899) and did not play at all during three seasons (1890, 1891, and 1897). By 1900 no fewer then eighteen different cities had fielded teams in the loop.

Contrary to press reports of the day, those who formed or invested in the nineteenth-century joint-stock company pro clubs were rarely either "leading citizens" in their communities or "magnates," to use a term popularized in the 1890s by big league club owners themselves and by Albert Spalding in his early history of the game. Families of old wealth, in particular, looked on pro baseball with profound suspicion. "Our professional baseball, with its paid players and its thousands of smoking, and sometimes umpire-baiting spectators, is doing more harm than good," concluded *Outing*, a sports magazine that catered to the wealthy elite. "The spectators are wasting two or three hours of fresh air and sunshine looking at what they ought to be doing." Neither were the newly created captains of industry, commerce, and finance likely to invest in pro baseball clubs. They were too clever for that; they recognized that greater financial rewards with fewer risks could be had by placing their money in other enterprises.

In his study of 1,263 nineteenth-century investors in both major and minor league professional baseball, Vincent found that they came predominantly from the ranks of small merchants, billiard parlor operators, saloon keepers, theater owners and managers, clerks, salesmen, and professional politicians. Many such men were less concerned about direct financial returns from the game than in using baseball's high visibility as a means of advancing their political or commercial interests. In addition, players themselves sometimes purchased stocks; Albert Spalding, Charles Comiskey, Connie Mack, and Clark Griffith eventually became baseball entrepreneurs in their own right. In the 1880s and 1890s, as the opportunities for profit increased, brewers, realtors, and traction (streetcar) company owners also became important investors. Such men benefitted in direct ways from concession sales or from the location of ballparks. Frequently excluded from opportunities in more respectable business arenas, German and German-Jewish ethnics became increasingly conspicuous in the late nineteenth century by their disproportionate presence in the pro game (as they were in the theater and other forms of commercial amusement of the day).

Although then as today the press talked of pro baseball as though it were one of the nation's major business enterprises, such descriptions wildly exaggerated the size of club operations. The gross receipts of a typical nineteenth-century pro baseball team were closer to those of a corner saloon than to those of Andrew Carnegie's steel works or John D. Rockefeller's oil empire. The 1875 Bostons, the most financially successful team of the 1870s, generated gross receipts of $38,000; from these the club netted $3,261. The 1881 Chicago White Stockings received $32,000 from the gate, whereas the New York Giants of 1887 broke all attendance records and may have received as much as $70,000 in gross revenues. All these figures were well above average for the baseball clubs of their respective eras, and, although they were not mean sums for that day, they paled beside Andrew Carnegie's income. The steel magnate earned more than that weekly!

In addition to the joint-stock representative pro teams in the larger cities, boosters or the players themselves organized hundreds of semiprofessional, or "cooperative," nines. These teams might pay only the pitcher on a per game basis; all other players might either receive no pay at all or split whatever was left from gate receipts after expenses had been deducted. Because of their baseball skills, such players often obtained sinecures in local businesses or industry. In order to enhance their prospects of winning symbolic contests against rival towns, clubs frequently scoured the surrounding region for talent. Although the clubs rarely survived for more than a season or two, a new team frequently arose out of the ashes of an expired club. As for the players, with opportunities for exhibitions of physical manliness limited by the radical changes in nineteenth-century workplaces and the prevailing Victorian restraints on self-expression, semipro baseball provided them with an exciting arena for the display of their physical prowess and aggressiveness in a controlled setting.

The representative team was only one way, albeit ultimately the most important, of organizing a pro team. Beginning in the 1880s, a dozen or more pro barnstorming teams also regularly toured the nation. Some were temporary aggregates composed of nationally known players who sought to increase their earnings by embarking on off-season tours. Others were more permanent outfits. Even the best of the representative nines feared the barnstorming Hop Bitters, based in Rochester, New York. The Hop Bitters bore the name of (and thereby advertised) a popular patent medicine of the day, one that claimed to be "the Invalid's Friend & Hope." Asa

T. Soule, the concoctor of the drug and owner of the team, claimed that he gave each of his players a teaspoonful of the nostrum before every game. When the team lost, which it rarely did, he doubled the dosage.

Barnstorming black nines could be equally effective on the playing field. Although the itinerant black teams did not reach the heyday of their popularity until the twentieth century, in the late 1880s the powerful Cuban Giants, formed in 1885 by a group of ball-playing hotel waiters at the Argyle, a famed resort on Long Island's South Shore, took on all comers. The Giants eventually booked some 150 games a season, mostly against white clubs. In 1887 they took a long western tour on which they played major league clubs in Cincinnati and Indianapolis, as well as several minor league teams. "The Cuban Giants . . . have defeated the New Yorks, 4 games out of 5, and are now virtually champions of the world," reported the *Indianapolis Freedman* in 1888. But "the St. Louis Browns, Detroit and Chicagos, afflicted by Negro-phobia and unable to bear the odium of being beaten by colored men, refused to accept their challenge."

Probably nothing about baseball shocked Victorian sensibilities more than the barnstorming women's teams. There are scattered reports of amateur women's nines in the fraternal era; for example, as early as 1866, Vassar college students organized two clubs. In the 1880s a few entertainment entrepreneurs exploited the public fascination with the bizarre by forming women's pro teams. One of the most notorious of these was Harry H. Freeman's "buxom beauties," who "paraded the streets [of New Orleans] in full uniform, and created an impression that base ball, played by shapely . . . girls, must be attractive." "The short-skirted ball tossers" played poorly, continued a newspaper report in 1885, but they "try and play hard even if they do not succeed better than girls are expected to with the national game." Given prevailing notions of Victorian womanhood, Freeman had difficulties recruiting players. In 1886, New Orleans officials arraigned Freeman "on the charge of being a dangerous and suspicious character." He was accused of "inducing young girls to leave their homes and parents to join his troupe of base ball players." In order to heist Florence Harris, one of his recruits, out of the Crescent City undetected, Freeman cut off her dark hair and had her don a blonde wig.

⊞ ⊞ ⊞

Ballparks also indicated the early pro game's modest business dimensions. Unlike the great railway terminals or the massive banks of the day, only a

few of the nineteenth-century baseball parks could be considered significant civic monuments. Nearly all of them, even in the larger cities, were
inexpensive, jerry-built, wooden structures that were doomed to become
early victims of decay, termites, fire, or even collapse from the excessive
weight of fans. Indeed, fans sometimes lost their lives from falling stands.
The worst disaster in baseball history occurred at Philadelphia in 1903
when a collapsed railing sent twelve persons reeling to their deaths. On
five separate occasions during the 1890s fires ravaged Sportsman's Park
in St. Louis, and in 1894 alone fire leveled the stands in four National
League cities. Because of the stands' temporary nature, the cheapness with
which they could be built, and improvements or changes in mass transit,
teams rarely occupied the same park for more than a few seasons. The
Chicago White Stockings, for example, played at six different sites between
1870 and 1894.

Wooden fences kept out nonpaying spectators, though some fans avoided
paying an admission by watching games through cracks or knotholes in
the boards (hence the terms *knothole clubs* and *knothole gangs*). Larger
parks had roofs to protect some of the spectators from the sun. Less expensive, unprotected seats consisted of unpainted, sun-bleached boards
(hence the term *bleachers*). To provide additional seats for major games,
park owners frequently nailed together temporary stands of raw pine. At
several parks, the tradition of permitting fans to congregate along the foul
lines remained intact until well into the twentieth century; at big games,
fans also watched from in front of the outfield fences. As the game pro-
gressed, such fans tended to inch closer to the action, sometimes interfer-
ing with play. Even as late as the first decade of the twentieth century, richer
patrons could also view the games from the comfort of their carriages
parked in the outfield.

Lake Front Stadium in Chicago was one of the more lavish facilities of
the 1880s. Reportedly costing the White Stockings the princely sum of
$10,000 to remodel in 1883, the park accommodated 10,000 patrons; it
had a band pagoda near the main entrance and, for wealthier fans, eighteen boxes featuring arm chairs and curtains to keep out the sun or the
gaze of unwelcome viewers. The box seat of Albert Spalding, the club's
president, even came equipped with a telephone connected to the clubhouse
"to enable [Spalding] to conduct the details of the game without leaving
his seat." To handle the crowds and maintain the grounds, the "palatial"
park required forty-one uniformed attendants.

Lake Front Stadium was better suited to meet the needs of spectators than it was for playing baseball. The distances between home plate and the outfield fences were the shortest in major league history. A fly ball of only 196 feet in right field, 300 feet in center field, and a mere 180 feet in left field could reach the outfield fence. Even against a baseball that was quite soft by modern standards, these bandbox dimensions enabled Ed Williams of the White Stockings to hit twenty-seven home runs in 1884, a major league record that stood until Babe Ruth broke it in 1919. In 1884, although no other club totaled more than fourteen homers, Chicago boasted four players who hit more than twenty.

As with the theater, circuses, and other forms of commercial entertainment, colorful pageantry was a conspicuous part of the early pro game. Flags and pennants flew from outfield fences, and patriotic buntings of red, white, and blue frequently festooned the grandstands. During lulls between innings, brass bands sometimes entertained fans. Vendors hawked concessions and scorecards at all parks, but the lack of a public address system or numbers on players' uniforms challenged the fan's ingenuity in following the action. Because the playing facilities had no showers or changing rooms for visitors, the players—in full uniform—usually rode out to the parks from their hotels in open omnibuses drawn by horses, sometimes bursting into the team's song on the way. Such a spectacle helped lure customers to the game. This practice was not officially abandoned until 1912, when the American League finally required all its teams to provide dressing rooms. Apparently, however, cleanliness and the reduction of pungent odors were not major concerns of the day. A physician warned managers against having their players take "dangerous and useless showers," but he did advise them to require a weekly supervised bath.

Early professional ball games attracted motley crowds. The *St. Louis Post-Dispatch* reported in 1883 that "a glance at the audience on any fine day at the ball park will reveal . . . telegraph operators, printers who work at night, travelling men [salesmen] . . . men of leisure . . . men of capital, bank clerks who get away at 3 P.M., real estate men . . . barkeepers . . . hotel clerks, actors and employees of the theater, policemen and firemen on their day off . . . clerks and salesmen temporarily out of work . . . butchers [and] bakers." Clubs in several cities specifically arranged their games for the convenience of white-collar workers. So that stockbrokers and their associates could easily get to the park after the close of Chicago's Board of Trade, the White Stockings set their starting time at 2:30 in the afternoon; likewise, the 3:30 starting time of the New York Giants allowed the Wall Street crowd ample time to get across town to the ball field. For the convenience of government clerks, Washington's teams scheduled their games at 4:30 in the afternoon.

Although young, white-collar workers were conspicuous at games, it is far less certain how many blue-collar, ethnic workingmen attended games. Steep ticket prices (a minimum of fifty cents to National League games during the last quarter of the century), the cost of horse car or electric trolley fare to the ballpark, the necessity of play during the daylight hours, and the ban on Sunday games in most cities all restricted potential attendance by unskilled workingmen. A *New York Times* report of an 1888 Memorial Day game at the Polo Grounds noted the unusual enthusiasm of the men and boys who normally were confined to "shops and factories during the week days, and who [had] to content themselves for months with reading accounts of games."

Nonetheless, newspapers frequently commented on the presence of the Irish in Boston and New York and the Germans in Cincinnati and St. Louis. Although the original Polo Grounds obtained its name from the polo played there by publisher James Gordon Bennett and his wealthy friends, that association faded when the area was converted into a ball field; by the 1880s, the bleachers had become known as "Burkeville," named after the predominantly Irish fans who sat there. Several other fields had "Kerry Patches," which also referred to sections occupied regularly by the Irish kranks. Rather than coming from the factories or large-scale shops, these ethnic fans probably came from the ranks of petty shopkeepers, skilled workingmen, public officialdom, and other occupations less encumbered by income constraints and with schedules sufficiently flexible to allow attendance at weekday games.

Compared to men, women rarely patronized pro baseball. Despite the fact that special ladies' days were scheduled and special sections of the stands were reserved for women as early as the 1880s, their attendance apparently varied greatly according to time and place. For example, in 1875 the press reported that large numbers of women were attending games in Hartford and Boston, but in that same year the presence of a single "lady who seemed to take a great interest in the proceedings" of a game at the Union Grounds in Brooklyn occasioned comment in a local newspaper. A decade later, however, a report of a game between the top contenders for the National League pennant at the Polo Grounds contained these words: "The ladies are regular and numerous attendants at the grounds. The hundreds of them who stood on the seats and screamed and waved their handkerchiefs and brandished their fans in ecstasies of applause yesterday knew enough to come early and avoid the crush." Yet this account should not be considered representative or typical; it leaves an exaggerated impression of the number of women spectators and their involvement in the game. Early photographs reveal an overwhelming preponderance of males at most games.

◻ ◻ ◻

During the 1870s and 1880s the professional teams fully established their ascendancy over all of baseball. The Cincinnati Red Stockings and dozens of other clubs soon proved that full-time salaried players could nearly always outperform those who held down other jobs during the playing season. Seizing mainly on urban rivalries, an assortment of civic boosters, small-time entrepreneurs, and politicians organized hundreds of professional and semiprofessional teams. Although adverse weather, poor play, mismanagement, and the peculiar nature of the enterprise, among other reasons, caused nearly all the teams to fail financially within only a year or two of their founding, new nines soon filled their places. The next important stage in the history of the professional game was the formation of leagues of the representative teams.

4

The First
Professional Leagues

Armed with endorsements of four western clubs, William Ambrose Hulbert, president of the Chicago Base Ball Club, met on 2 February 1876 with representatives of six eastern clubs at the Central Hotel in Manhattan. Nothing could deter Hulbert, not even the rain and the gale-force winds that whipped through Manhattan's streets at seventy miles per hour. According to baseball lore, after all the delegates had entered his room, he locked the door behind them and then, with a dramatic flourish, dropped the key into his pocket. Hulbert thereby symbolically held the eastern men captive until they agreed to his plan for the creation of a radically new professional baseball league. They discussed and refined Hulbert's proposal into the evening hours before finally signing a pact creating the National League of Professional Base Ball Clubs (NL). Appropriately, given baseball's claim as the national pastime, the fateful meeting took place during the nation's centennial year of 1876. Perhaps it should also be remembered that the league began play in the same spring that chiefs Rain-in-the-Face,

Sitting Bull, and Crazy Horse annihilated General George A. Custer and his troops near the Little Big Horn River in southern Montana.

The creation of the NL, along with more than a dozen other leagues during the 1870s and 1880s, was an important step in the evolution of professional baseball. Although professional baseball leagues only gradually evolved into the economic cartels familiar to fans today, baseball men early on recognized that the formation of leagues could promote their mutual interests. The first pro baseball league, the National Association of Professional Base Ball Players (1871–75), had no grand plan for winning public favor or maximizing the income of its member clubs. It was merely a loose confederation designed to provide a system for naming a national championship team. But its successor, Hulbert's National League, aspired to become a circuit composed of only the premier clubs. It sharply restricted the number of clubs that could join the league, took steps to curb player freedom, and sought, not altogether successfully, to present itself as a fortress of Victorian propriety.

◫ ◫ ◫

On 17 March 1871, St. Patrick's Day, ten delegates representing clubs fielding professional baseball teams met in New York City, where they founded the first organized league, the National Association of Professional Base Ball Players, usually known simply as the National Association (NA). Although the inclusion of "Base Ball Players" in the title of the new association suggested that it was a player-controlled organization, the players did not entirely dominate either the NA or most of its member clubs. True, of the eleven teams that enlisted for the first season, five were described as "cooperative" nines. Organized by the players themselves and thus without the patronage of a joint-stock company, the cooperative teams paid expenses from gate receipts; if there was any money left over, they divided it among the players. Nonetheless, Harry Wright, who was as concerned with club management as with the fate of the players, was the only active player at the 1871 NA founding meeting. Apart from Wright, only two (or possibly three) active players ever attended the annual conventions of the NA. The NA did elect player-captain Robert Ferguson, who was associated at different times with the New York Mutuals, Brooklyn Atlantics, and the Hartfords, as president for two terms, but Ferguson himself acknowledged that the league presidency was a ceremonial position. The club directors bestowed it on him as a token recognition of the "playing class's" contribution to the game.

Although the National Association exhibited few characteristics of a modern sports league cartel, it was important to the history of professional baseball. With the demise of the fraternal-oriented National Association of Base Ball Players in 1870, the new association became by default the rule-making body for all of baseball. Never again would the fraternal-centered version of baseball significantly affect the game's rules. More importantly, the NA also established a procedure for naming a pro team as the national champion. Each club was to play a best-of-five-game series with all other members. Such a system was awkward, inasmuch as teams did not play the same number of championship games during the season and each club had to schedule its own games. To maximize revenues, the clubs scheduled many games against non-NA foes.

In 1871, the association's first season of play, Chicago's White Stockings, the Athletics of Philadelphia, and the Bostons embarked on an exciting three-way race for the championship pennant. Unfortunately, Chicago's Great Fire burned down the White Stockings' new field, which seated 7,000 spectators. Although the White Stockings lost their park, uniforms, and equipment in the fire, they decided to carry on anyway. Wearing suits of "various hues and makes, ludicrous in the extreme" that had been loaned to them by other nines, the ill-dressed and ill-fated Chicagoans lost the flag by a single game on the last day of the season to the Philadelphians. Because of the Great Fire, Chicago did not field an association team in either the 1872 or 1873 season.

For the next four seasons (1872–75), no club successfully contested the hegemony of the Bostons, as Harry Wright's team was known. Led by their gaunt, full-bearded, clerical-looking manager, the team won four consecutive pennants and compiled a staggering 227-60 cumulative won-lost record. In 1875, the final season of the association, Boston ran away with the league flag, winning seventy-one games and losing only eight. In terms of the NA's total welfare, the Bostons may have been too good; other teams paled in comparison. It must have been difficult for Brooklynites, for example, to grow excited about their Atlantics. During the 1875 campaign, the abysmal Atlantics won only two of forty-six league games.

Boston's phenomenal success stemmed in large part from the recruitment of superior players. Wright had at his disposal his brother George, a superb fielding, hard-hitting shortstop. At second base, he employed Roscoe

Barnes, the league's perennial batting champion, and behind the plate was the league's most admired superstar, Jim "Deacon" White. White picked up his nickname because, unlike most of his fellow players, he regularly attended church services, toted a Bible with him wherever he went, and always behaved as "a gentleman in his professional and private life." In the pitcher's box, Wright had big Albert Spalding, who at six feet and two inches in height towered over his contemporaries and was the league's most successful hurler. Spalding compiled a 207-56 won-lost record and a .320 batting average while at Boston. "On receiving the ball," read a contemporary account of Spalding's pitching style, ". . . he gazes at it two or three minutes in a contemplative way, and then turns it around once or twice to be sure that it is not an orange or coconut. Assured that he has the genuine article . . . and after a scowl at the short stop, and a glance at homeplate, [he] finally delivers the ball with the precision of a cannon shot."

Although notions of the earlier fraternal era lingered on in Wright's thinking, he approached the game in a far more businesslike manner than did most of the other men associated with the pro game. Whereas stockholders frequently placed more value on potential psychic and political rewards than on profits, Wright depended on baseball for his livelihood. "Base ball is now a business," he flatly explained in a letter to Nicholas Young of the Washington Olympics. The pro clubs, he maintained, should drop freewheeling practices that, while admittedly enhancing a sense of equality and fraternity among the players, might impair a team's prospects for success. Wright not only carefully managed such details as club scheduling and finances but, above all, firmly established his authority over the players. Acting as a paternalistic patriarch, he even dictated their living arrangements. In Boston, "George [Wright], Harry [Wright], and [Charles] Gould live together," reported the *Spirit of the Times* in 1871, "and the other seven 'boys' live next door in a private house, so they are all under Harry's wing." No longer did the players rule their own destinies. At least for the Bostons, a clear-cut employer-employee relationship existed between the manager and his "boys."

⊡ ⊡ ⊡

Although no fewer than fifteen new clubs were clamoring to get into the National Association for the 1876 campaign and more than 3,000 fans frequently attended the games of major foes, not all was well with the loop. Not only did it suffer from Boston's lopsided superiority on the playing field, but for those who believed that pro baseball could achieve greater success by mirroring Victorian America, the NA was little short of a disaster. Rather than serving as models of order and propriety, association games too frequently erupted into incivility and anarchy. Ugly confrontations and long delays in play regularly arose over the choice of umpires and their decisions. As in the past, the NA, which required that the home teams pay umpires $5 per game, followed the practice of having the home team pick an umpire from a list of names submitted by the visitors. But with money now at stake and fraternal ties largely eroded, nothing kept home teams from objecting to all the proposed arbiters. Accompanied by growing crowd unrest, arguments over the choice of an umpire sometimes held up starting the contests for an hour or more.

Agreement on an official for the game by no means terminated the possibility of controversy. Umpires held unenviable positions. They needed to master a complex set of rapidly changing rules, they had to make countless decisions during the course of a game, and given the size of the playing field, a single umpire was sometimes in a poor position to make good calls. Until the practice was prohibited in 1880, umpires still occasionally consulted with nearby players or bystanders before rendering a final decision on fly ball or base calls. Frequently confronted with vociferous complaints about their rulings from players, managers, and fans (who as likely as not had wagered on the contest), it was little wonder that umpires sometimes lost their tempers or simply quit in the middle of games. Few umpires, however, responded as forcefully as Robert Ferguson. Angered by the "growling" of Mutuals' catcher Robert Hicks, Ferguson, while serving as umpire of a game between the Lord Baltimores and the Mutuals in 1873, grabbed a bat and broke the offender's arm in two places. He thereby disabled Hicks "for the remainder of the game." At the game's conclusion, a constable stepped forward to arrest Ferguson, but the injured catcher refused to press charges.

Game fixing and gambling also plainly mocked Victorian values. Wagering on games was common everywhere; both Brooklyn and Philadelphia even allowed pool selling in their parks. The frequency of game fixing cannot be precisely determined, but players on some teams, such as the Mutuals of New York City, acquired a notorious reputation for their willingness to take money from gamblers in exchange for playing poorly enough to lose games. In the 1874 and 1875 seasons, newspapers repeatedly reported instances of suspected game fixing by the Mutuals. Referring to an 1874 win by the White Stockings over the Mutuals, the *Chicago Tribune* declared that "for the first time in the history of baseball in Chicago, the national game has been disgraced by a palpable and unbelievable fraud." According to the *Tribune*, there was "ample reason to believe that at least four [Mutuals] players were hired to throw the game and had no intention of winning at any stage." This and more than a dozen similar incidents, none of which led to punitive action by the NA's judiciary committee, cast a dark shadow of suspicion over the "squareness" of association games.

Nevertheless, neither Boston's dominance on the playing field, the behavior of ball players, nor the common practice of players revolving from one club to another is sufficient in itself to explain the association's demise. The National League coup of 1876 was mostly the work of a single individual, William Ambrose Hulbert. The burly Hulbert had no nostalgia for the earlier fraternal game. As a successful Chicago coal merchant, an active Republican, and a member of the city's prestigious Board of Trade, he approached baseball solely from the perspective of a businessman, politician, and civic booster. Hulbert loved Chicago. "I would rather be a lamp-post in Chicago than a millionaire in any other city," he allegedly said repeatedly. In the wake of Chicago's Great Fire of 1871, Hulbert saw in professional baseball an opportunity to promote the revival of his beloved city.

For baseball to contribute to the Windy City's civic renewal, the team had to perform well enough to engender pride in its accomplishments. Therefore, Hulbert, as president of the White Stockings, set about recruiting the best players he could find. He secretly and boldly defied the NA rule against signing players from other clubs while the season was in progress. In the midst of the 1875 campaign he persuaded Albert Spalding to join the White Stockings as a pitcher, captain, and manager for the upcoming 1876 season in exchange for a salary of $2,000 plus 25 percent of the team's gate receipts. On receiving the news that Spalding and three other Boston players had defected to Chicago, the Worcester *Spy* reported that "Boston is in mourning. Like Rachel weeping for her children, she refuses to be comforted because [her] famous baseball nine . . . the city's most cherished possession, has been captured by Chicago."

Hulbert's employment of Spalding was especially fortuitous. The charismatic Spalding not only was a superb pitcher, but he also aided Hulbert in convincing Boston stars Jim White, Cal McVey, and Roscoe Barnes, along with Philadelphia's hero Adrian "Cap" Anson, to sign contracts with Chicago. Fear that the eastern clubs might retaliate for these audacious player raids by expelling the Chicago recruits and perhaps the club itself from the NA was, according to Spalding, the inspiration for Hulbert's conception of an entirely new league. "Spalding," Hulbert exclaimed, "I have a new scheme. Let us anticipate the Eastern cusses and organize a new association . . . and then we'll see who will do the expelling."

Hulbert and his cohort concluded that pro baseball could be stabilized by forming a league restricted to the most powerful representative nines of the larger cities. The National Association had allowed any club fielding a pro team, regardless of whether it was located in a small town or the nation's largest city, to join and compete for the championship pennant. The only requirement was that the aspiring club pay a $10 entry fee. Thus, dozens of clubs from both the smaller towns and the big cities had regularly joined and shortly dropped out; several did not even complete a single season of play. Under such unstable conditions, fans in the large cities had special difficulties identifying a particular team as the city's representative nine. That fifteen additional clubs were seeking admission to the association for the 1876 season created a special sense of urgency among those seeking to form a new circuit. If the "whole gang be let in," predicted the *Chicago Tribune,* half the clubs would fail to meet expenses. The only solution, the *Tribune* concluded, was either to reform the NA or form a new league organized as a "closed corporation." Hulbert adopted essentially the latter idea.

Composed initially of teams located in Boston, Chicago, Cincinnati, Hartford, Louisville, New York, Philadelphia, and St. Louis, the National League departed sharply from the practices of the NA. To offset some of the disparities in the markets arising from differences in population among the NL cities, the league provided that visiting teams would receive 50 percent of the base admission price to each game. (As higher-priced seats were added to league ballparks, the share of total receipts going to visiting teams fell.) A club wishing to join the new league had to obtain the approval of the existing clubs, only one club could represent each city, and no club could be located in a city with a population of less than 75,000. Each club enjoyed a territorial monopoly in another sense. When a team from one league city, such as the Chicago White Stockings or the Bostons, came to another league town, they could play no other pro club except the NL team representing that city. The founders hoped that these strictures would enable them to establish a premier circuit, one that would establish a clearly separate identity and a superior quality of play compared to competing baseball clubs or leagues.

The NL abandoned all pretenses of being a player-centered enterprise.

Although player delegates were not specifically prohibited from attending annual league meetings until 1878, by confining the game to "regular [joint-] stock companies," the NL got rid of the cooperative nines that had played in the NA. It also quickly implemented labor policies similar to those of the industrial corporations of the day. Although the NL founders did not initially have enough gall or foresight to bind players to one club for their entire playing careers—or perhaps they doubted the legality of such a move—they did forbid negotiations with players affiliated with other clubs while the season was in progress and granted the clubs the power to expel players from the league for violating team rules.

Led by Albert Spalding, the league founders nourished the legend that the NL saved professional baseball from utter ruin. Had it not been for the timely creation of the NL and the sagacious decisions of its leaders, so the fable went, the national pastime would have continued its downward slide into complete degradation. The league introduced a new player discipline; it avowed to end rowdy behavior and make "Base Ball playing respectable and honorable." In a further bid to dissociate itself from the NA, portray itself as a civic rather than a profit-driven enterprise, and appease suspicious Victorians, the league organizers banned Sunday games (officially in 1878) as well as liquor sales and gambling in their parks. They also hoped that a minimum admission price of fifty cents would prevent attendance by ruffians while encouraging "the better classes [to] patronize the game a great deal more." No doubt at a cost of some support among the working class, especially working-class ethnics, the NL ostentatiously presented itself as the national pastime's main moral guardian.

These measures by no means ensured the fledgling league's survival. Custodians of Victorian propriety remained suspicious. "You should never go to a ball game," lectured Pittsburgh Judge J. W. F. White in 1887 to a defendant in a larceny case. "Baseball is one of the evils of the day." Although on paper few other business cartels bound their membership in so many particulars, like other gentlemen's agreements, the baseball cartel had no legal standing; its restrictive agreements could not be enforced in the courts. Therefore, each club was ultimately free to place its interests ahead of the league's welfare. "The [baseball] magnate must be a strong man among strong men," concluded Spalding years later, "else other club owners in the league will combine in their own interests against him and his interests." With its effectiveness entirely dependent on the voluntary compliance of the member clubs, the NL faced awesome challenges to its very existence.

⊡ ⊡ ⊡

Both on and off the field of play, Chicago's baseball men orchestrated the NL's early history. Off the diamond, there was the formidable duo of William Hulbert and Albert Spalding, who had founded the NL and put together the 1876 "all-star" White Stockings team. Spalding pitched and managed the White Stockings to the 1876 NL championship, but thereafter until his retirement in 1878 he played sparingly. In the meantime, he charted the beginning of another important career. In February of 1876 the *Chicago Tribune* announced that Spalding was opening a "large emporium in Chicago, where he will sell all kinds of baseball goods and turn his place into the headquarters for the Western Ball Clubs." He obtained the exclusive right to furnish the official NL baseball and to publish *Spalding's Official Baseball Guide,* an annual that included the league rules, records, articles, and Spalding's views on the main issues confronting the game. Spalding later expanded his business into both the manufacturing and retailing of sporting goods, and it soon became the largest such organization in the world.

While Spalding was launching himself as a sporting goods entrepreneur, Hulbert guided the NL through its perilous early years. An industrial depression in the late 1870s furnished the league with its first great challenge. With widespread unemployment and reduced incomes for many, the amount of money available for leisure expenditures dropped drastically. For the 1876 season probably none of the clubs save Chicago earned a profit. Hoping to avoid further financial losses, both the Athletics of Philadelphia and the Mutuals of New York decided to forgo their final western road tours. Hulbert, who had been installed as the league president after Morgan G. Bulkeley of Hartford had been chosen by lot as president the first year, responded sternly. He obtained the expulsion of both clubs, thus denying the NL access to the nation's two largest cities. Even the tears of the Athletics' contrite president failed to reverse Hulbert's decision.

In 1881, when the Cincinnati club persisted in selling beer at its park and playing Sunday games, Hulbert hounded them out of the league as well. "We respectfully suggest, that while the league is in the missionary field," responded Oliver P. Caylor of the Cincinnati *Enquirer,* ". . . they [also] turn their attention to Chicago and prohibit the admission to the Lake Street grounds of the great number of prostitutes who patronize the game up there." Caylor's red herring apparently availed nothing but perhaps chuckles. Hulbert was determined that no club would successfully challenge the league's authority.

Hulbert likewise cracked down on loose player behavior. Charges surfaced at the conclusion of the 1877 season that four Louisville Grays' players had fixed games. The powerful Grays needed to win only eight games to clinch the championship pennant, but during the stretch drive the talented four played like a team of local sandlotters. They made costly errors and carelessly got picked off bases. Even worse, one of the four, James Devlin, the Grays' star pitcher, suddenly lost his stuff. A subsequent league investigation found the players guilty of taking money for throwing the games. Hulbert again acted without mercy; he promptly banned the four culprits from the NL for life. Pleading abject poverty, Devlin regularly begged the NL for reinstatement. "I am living from hand to mouth all winter [and] I have not got a Stitch of Clothing [n]or has my wife and Child," Devlin lamented in a letter to Harry Wright. But the league did not bend. On one occasion, according to Spalding's recollection, Hulbert gave the offender $50 from his own pocket while exclaiming, "Damn you, you have sold a game, you are dishonest, and [the] National League will not stand for it." At the tender age of thirty-three, the pathetic Devlin died (cause unknown) while serving as a Philadelphia policeman.

Although Hulbert's stern measures against clubs and players strengthened the National League's authority and its image of integrity, such actions failed to ensure the prosperity of league franchises. Indeed, during its first fifteen years of existence, twenty-two different cities had teams in the NL; only Boston and Chicago fielded clubs for the entire 1876–90 era. Until the mid-1880s, the NL could be accurately described as "Chicago's league," for not only did Chicago men manage the league, but the other teams in the NL depended to a large extent on the revenues they received from playing the White Stockings.

Neither did the NL establish its ascendancy over all of professional baseball. Indeed, dozens of strong pro clubs continued to operate independently of the NL. In 1877 delegates from eighteen of these clubs founded the International Association of Professional Base Ball Players, which, since it allowed any club to join, resembled the old National Association. Nor did Hulbert's loop establish its clear-cut ascendancy on the playing field. Several nonleague pro teams were fully as good as the NL teams. In 1877 alone, according to a careful count by Harold Seymour, NL teams lost seventy-two games to outside foes, and even at that the league teams were frequently accused of avoiding the strong independent clubs.

Acting in the monopolistic manner of the industrial corporations of the day, the NL tried to control or eliminate competition from other teams and leagues. In 1877 it organized the League Alliance. All pro clubs that joined the alliance would have their territorial rights and player contracts protected from one another as well as from the NL clubs. Conversely, clubs that refused to join the alliance could have their rosters preyed upon freely by other clubs. The NL also welcomed into its fold the stronger International Association clubs. Conveniently overlooking its requirement that franchises could be located only in cities with 75,000 or more residents, the NL took in clubs from three smaller cities: Syracuse and Troy, New York, and Worcester, Massachusetts. Finally, the league ordered a halt to all games with nonleague foes on league grounds, thereby cutting off lucrative earnings by outsiders in NL ballparks.

The high-handed methods by which the National League was undertaking "to control the baseball fraternity" was "unreasonably absurd," declared A. B. Rankin, a leader of the International Association. "Are we to submit to the caprice of a clique, or ring?" he asked rhetorically. Yet the dream of resurrecting a loosely formed association to which all pro baseball teams could freely join and through which they could compete with one another for a championship pennant was rapidly fading. By the time the International Association collapsed in 1880, the NL's more binding kind of cartel had demonstrated a capacity to withstand conflicts among its members and challenges from both the players and teams outside the league's fold.

In 1882 Hulbert died, and Spalding assumed his mantle. At the age of thirty-two, Spalding became president of the White Stockings, a position he held until 1891, and though he did not serve as league president (an office of nominal authority after Hulbert's death), he was the most dominant voice in league counsels. Ostensibly to convert foreigners to baseball but no doubt to expand sales of his sporting goods as well, in 1888–89 Spalding arranged a highly publicized worldwide tour that matched his Chicago team against a team of NL all-stars. Although the foreigners were singularly unimpressed with the exhibitions of America's national game, and although Spalding lost money on the venture, the exotic nature of baseball games in far-off Australia, in the shadows of Egyptian pyramids, in Rome's Colosseum, and on the leading cricket grounds of England intrigued Americans at home.

As Hulbert and Spalding directed the destinies of the NL off the field, on the diamond no players were more important than Chicagoans Adrian "Cap" (so named because of his captaincy of the team) Anson and

Michael "King" Kelly. They formed the nucleus of one of the most powerful teams in big league history; in the 1880s the White Stockings won
five pennants in seven years. In that decade only Anson was left from the
championship squad of 1876, but the six-foot, two-inch, 200-pound-plus
first baseman, "a veritable giant," as he was described by contemporaries, continued to be one of the best players in the game, even until his retirement in 1897. He won four league batting crowns and in twenty-two
seasons failed to hit .300 only twice. Anson became the playing manager
of the White Stockings in 1879, a position he retained until his retirement.
The fans loved to hear Anson, who had a booming voice, bellow out directions to the players or epithets aimed at the umpire. One of Anson's
recruits, lightning-fast but weak-hitting William "Billy" Sunday, later
achieved renown as one of the nation's leading evangelists.

    King Kelly competed with Anson for the adoration of Chicago kranks.
A colorful player both on and off the field, Kelly excelled at hitting and
base running. "Slide, Kelly, Slide!" later became a hit song. Apart from
baseball, Kelly loved horses and drinking. Tall, dark, and handsome, "as
Celtic as Mrs. Murphy's pig," he was one of the first of many players who
trod the boards of vaudeville; he starred in a skit titled "He Would be an
Actor, or The Ball Player's Revenge." Kelly inspired many legends, most
of which revolved around his opportunism and trickery. During one game,
as the sun began to set toward the end of the twelfth inning, Kelly pulled
one of his most startling stunts. With two out and the bases full, Kelly, as
the right fielder, leapt into the twilight trying to catch a mighty drive that
would win the game. As he came down, he held his glove high in the air
and jauntily jogged to the dugout. The umpire bellowed: "Out number
three! Game called on account of darkness!" "Nice catch, Kell," exclaimed
his teammates. "Not at all, at all," Kelly responded. "'Twent a mile above
my head." In the days before players wore gloves, however, Kelly was no
iron man. While catching in a game for Cincinnati in 1879, a Cal McVey
pitch bruised his hand. Kelly refused to intercept any more of McVey's
"cannonball" pitches, so the Cincinnati manager brought in a slower-
throwing "change pitcher" who, according to a press report, proceeded
to "take his lumps" from the Providence club.

    In 1887 Spalding shocked the baseball world by selling Kelly to the
Boston team for the then-astronomical sum of $10,000. The Boston fans
promptly labeled him "the $10,000 Beauty," after a local actress who used
that title as a promotional gimmick. If anything, the Boston Irish loved
Kelly more than his followers in Chicago did. The fans even chipped in

their hard-won earnings to buy the King a pair of handsome gray horses and a fancy gig so that he could ride out to the ballpark on Washington Street in proper style. Kelly added to the grandeur of the occasion by wearing needle-pointed shoes and a tall top hat.

⊡ ⊟ ⊡

"Beer Ball League," hooted the *Chicago Tribune,* a mouthpiece of the National League, in 1881. The *Tribune* referred to the newly created American Association of Base Ball Clubs (AA). And it was true that brewery owners sat on the boards of directors of six of the clubs in the new association. In addition, the AA brazenly authorized the sale of beer at its games, permitted play on Sundays (in cities where it was legal), and set a base admission price of a mere twenty-five cents a game. By such measures, the AA sought to tap into a large pool of potential baseball fans who had been abandoned by the NL's ostentatious capitulation to Victorian standards of propriety. Few ethnics or workingmen cared a whit for either temperance or a strict Sabbath. Indeed, few occasions pleased them more than the opportunity to drink beer on a hot Sunday afternoon while watching a ball game.

The stage for the creation of the AA had been set by the return of prosperity in the 1880s. Industrial production again leapt forward, real incomes rose, and from both the European and American countrysides millions flocked into the nation's cities. Cut off from their traditional rural and village pastimes, the urban dwellers sought excitement and communal experiences in commercial recreation. They increasingly patronized theaters, circuses, dance halls, saloons, and commercial sports. Responding to the growing spectator demand for baseball, the number of pro teams and pro leagues proliferated. Not only did two new leagues—the American Association (1882–91) and the Union Association (1884)—challenge the NL directly for major league status, but by the end of the decade seventeen other pro leagues existed, scattered from Maine to California.

The initiative for the American Association came mainly from Alfred H. Spink of St. Louis and Oliver P. Caylor of Cincinnati, two sportswriters whose cities had been squeezed out of the NL. Both cities had large German ethnic constituencies that enjoyed beer drinking and Continental Sundays. In St. Louis, Spink found an invaluable ally in Christopher Von der Ahe, a thick-accented German immigrant. In the summer of 1881 the two men added Sunday baseball games and beer to the other attractions of Von der Ahe's amusement park. Such a formula worked wonders, attracting unusually large crowds. Among the teams that cashed in on the opportunity offered by the St. Louisians were Caylor's newly organized Cincinnati Reds and the Dubuque, Iowa, Rabbits, who featured a young ex-newsboy, Charles Comiskey, at first base. Witnessing the success of Spink and Von der Ahe, entrepreneurs in Cincinnati, Baltimore, Louisville, Philadelphia, and Pittsburgh joined the St. Louisians to form the AA in 1882.

The NL recognized in the AA a serious challenge to its claim as the nation's only major league. The NL quickly reversed its long-standing ban on baseball in New York and Philadelphia. It gently pushed aside the existing clubs in the smaller cities of Troy and Worcester and in 1883 welcomed John Day's Gothams (soon to be known as the Giants) from New York and the Philadelphias (later to be known as the Phillies) of Alfred J. Reach. To prevent all-out guerrilla warfare for players, after the 1882 season NL president Abraham G. Mills, who was yet another leader from the Chicago club, engineered a tripartite truce with the AA and the Northwestern League, a minor league operating in Michigan, Ohio, and Illinois. At the heart of the 1882 agreement was the mutual recognition of reserved players and the establishment of exclusive territorial rights.

National League Cities, 1876–1902
(pennant-winning years in parentheses)

Baltimore, 1891–99 (1894–96)
Boston, 1876–1902 (1877–78, 1883, 1891–93, 1897–98)
Brooklyn, 1890–1902 (1890, 1899–1900)
Buffalo, 1879–85
Chicago, 1876–1902 (1876, 1880–82, 1885–86)
Cincinnati, 1876–80, 1890–1902
Cleveland, 1879–84, 1889–99
Detroit, 1881–88 (1887)
Hartford, 1876–77
Indianapolis, 1878, 1887–89
Kansas City, 1886
Louisville, 1876–77, 1892–99
Milwaukee, 1878
New York, 1876, 1883–1902 (1888–89)
Philadelphia, 1876, 1883–1902
Pittsburgh, 1887–1902 (1901–2)
Providence, 1878–85 (1879, 1884)

St. Louis, 1876–77, 1885–86, 1892–1902
Syracuse, 1879
Troy, 1879–82
Washington, 1886–89, 1892–99
Worcester, 1880–82

American Association Cities, 1882–91
(pennant-winning years in parentheses)

Baltimore, 1882–91
Boston, 1891 (1891)
Brooklyn, 1884–90 (1889)
Cincinnati, 1882–89, 1891 (1882)
Cleveland, 1887–88
Columbus, 1883–84, 1889–91
Indianapolis, 1884
Kansas City, 1888–89
Louisville, 1882–91 (1890)
Milwaukee, 1891
New York, 1883–87 (1884)
Philadelphia, 1882–91 (1883)
Pittsburgh, 1882–86
Richmond, 1884
Rochester, 1890
St. Louis, 1882–91 (1885–88)
Syracuse, 1890
Toledo, 1884, 1890
Washington, 1884, 1891

The guns of warfare had hardly been silenced when a third contender for big league status, the Union Association, entered the fray. Unlike many of the men behind the AA, the Union Association's founder and financial angel, Henry V. Lucas, a young St. Louis millionaire, was not motivated by the financial opportunities to be derived from beer or Sunday games. An ardent fan and apparently sympathetic to players' resentments arising from their inabilities to offer their services to the highest bidder, Lucas (or "Saint Lucas," as he was dubbed by an irreverent press) determined to build a circuit without strictures on player freedom. Although Lucas's eight-team loop attracted a few first-rate players from the NL and the AA, there were simply not enough fans to support thirty-four big league teams. After Lu-

cas's fortune had been dissipated and "his combativeness destroyed," the
NL extended mercy to him and the players who had jumped to his Union
Association. At the close of the 1884 season, the NL allowed the disloyal
players to return and provided Lucas with a franchise in St. Louis.

In the meantime, the predecessor of baseball's modern World Series began to take shape. In the fall of 1883 clubs from the two leagues played
fifty-eight exhibition games against one another, but the AA's Philadelphia
Athletics, after having lost seven of eight exhibition games to lesser NL
foes, prudently decided to cancel a postseason series with the NL champion Bostons. The next year the NL pennant-winning Providence team won
all three postseason games from the AA's flag-bearing New York Metropolitans, but these games attracted negligible public attention. A turning
point came in 1885, when Von der Ahe's St. Louis Browns and Spalding's
Chicago White Stockings played a controversial postseason series. The
Browns won the three games completed, but one game ended in a tie because of darkness, and the umpire forfeited another game to Chicago after St. Louis manager Charles Comiskey angrily protested an umpire's call
by taking his team off the field.

In 1886 the teams confronted each other again in the first contest to be
billed as "the world's championship." A wager between Spalding and Von
der Ahe calling for the winner to receive all the gate receipts added to the
public excitement. The series started in Chicago, where the White Stockings "Chicagoed" (shutouts in those days were called "Chicago" games)
the Browns 6-0, but the next day the St. Louisians reciprocated the em-
barrassment by Chicagoing the Chicagoans 12-0. Chicago took the final
game in the Windy City, but then disaster befell the proud White Stockings. In St. Louis the Browns swept the remaining three games and took
the championship.

A jubilant Chris Von der Ahe ordered up champagne for his players.
Spalding, on the other hand, was furious. He refused even to pay the White
Stockings' train fare back home. He, along with his manager Cap Anson,
privately blamed the club's humiliating losses on the nightly drinking sprees
of the players. He sold the main offenders (including King Kelly) to other
clubs and the next spring shipped the team off to Hot Springs, Arkansas,
with instructions for Anson to work the liquor out of the players' systems.
The strategy apparently misfired, for Chicago failed even to win the NL
flag in 1887.

No rules or formulas governed the conduct of these early series. One
league champion challenged, the other accepted, and then they agreed on

such details as the number of games, where they would be played, and how the gate receipts would be divided. For instance, the series of 1887 between the Browns and the Detroits called for fifteen games to be played in St. Louis, Detroit, Pittsburgh, Brooklyn, New York, Philadelphia, Washington, Boston, Baltimore, and Chicago. The series netted about $12,000 for each team. Although by 1886 the series had become a more or less established fixture, it came to an end in 1890 because soon thereafter the AA and NL commenced another trade war. If the series proved nothing else, it demonstrated the equality of AA teams on the playing field. The powerful St. Louis Browns, managed by young Charles Comiskey, won four consecutive pennants (1885–88) and a postseason championship from the NL pennant winner in 1886.

The AA departed from the NL not only by aggressively and openly seeking the patronage of ethnics and workingmen but by fielding black players on one of its teams. Unofficial bans had prevented blacks from playing in either the National Association or the National League, but as early as 1872 a black player, John "Bud" Fowler, played on a white pro team located in New Castle, Pennsylvania. For a dozen years he performed in obscurity before surfacing again in 1884 on the roster of a club in Stillwater, Minnesota, in the Northwestern League. "The poor fellow's skin is against him," reported *Sporting Life* at the end of the 1885 season. "With his splendid abilities he would long ago have been on some good club had his color been white instead of black. Those who know say there is no better second baseman in the country." In the mid-1880s the color line briefly relaxed. Along with Fowler, at least fifty-four other blacks played on racially integrated professional teams between 1883 and 1898. Among them were a pair of brothers, Moses and Welday Walker, who played in 1884 with Toledo of the AA. But the Walkers lasted only one campaign.

The season of 1887 was a turning point for race relations in baseball. During that summer, several events signaled a retreat from integration that would end by the turn of the century in the total exclusion of blacks from professional white baseball. The biggest blow came in the International League, a top-flight minor league in which six of its ten teams fielded black players. "How far will the mania for engaging colored players go?" queried *Sporting Life*. In July, in the face of protests from some of the white players, the league banned the admission of any more blacks into the circuit. Only a few days later Cap Anson refused to allow his White Stockings to take the field against Newark, an International League team, in an exhibition contest unless George Stovey, Newark's star black hurler, was kept out of the game. Although Stovey won a record-shattering thirty-three games, he was dropped by Newark at the end of the season. After 1887 conditions rapidly worsened, climaxing in the complete exclusion of blacks from white professional teams. The banning of blacks in white professional baseball corresponded in time with a more general implementation of segregation in the United States.

⊟   ⊟   ⊟

In the meantime, as the 1880s closed, both the NL and AA faced new challenges. Internecine warfare threatened the AA's very existence. Although Von der Ahe on several occasions lent financial aid to his less fortunate fellow AA owners, he also embarked on a personal vendetta against the Brooklyn Bridegrooms (so named because several of the players got married, an unusual occurrence in an age when the overwhelming majority of the players were bachelors). When the association chose a puppet of Von der Ahe as president in 1890, Brooklyn and Cincinnati angrily pulled out of the AA and joined the NL. To accommodate the two new clubs, the NL conveniently ignored the Tripartite Agreement that it had signed in 1882. But from the standpoint of the owners in both leagues, an even more ominous shadow fell across baseball. In 1890, the players launched a formidable uprising of their own.

5

The
Players' Revolt

John Montgomery "Monte" Ward was an exceptional ball player whose talents extended far beyond the diamond. As a pitcher with the 1879 Providence Grays, he compiled a 44-18 record and topped the NL in strikeouts, victories, and winning percentage. When a sore arm cut short his pitching career, he switched to shortstop, where he led the New York Giants to the World Championship over the St. Louis Browns in 1888. He also earned both a bachelor's and a law degree from Columbia University while playing ball during the summer. He allegedly learned five foreign languages, tried unsuccessfully to get the Giants to sign a black pitcher (George Stovey), wrote baseball articles regularly for national periodicals as well as a popular book on the game, and married a beautiful New York showgirl (Helen Dauvray). Although he was of Scots-English descent, his lucid blue eyes, high cheek bones, and personal charisma led New York fans to the mistaken inference that he was of Irish origins. Ward did nothing to disabuse them of that conclusion. In the wake of the 1888 championship season, no one in Gotham exceeded Ward's popularity.

In the late 1880s Ward brought his multiple skills to the players' cause. In a series of articles published between 1886 and 1888, he called attention to baseball's peculiar labor-management relationship. The reserve clause in player contracts and the buying and selling of players, wrote Ward, was "a conspiracy, pure and simple, on the part of the clubs by which they are making money rightfully belonging to the players." To whip up support among the players for a collective response, Ward turned to the Brotherhood of Professional Base Ball Players. The players' brotherhood had been initially founded in 1885 as a secret lodge to provide financial aid to their sick and indigent "brothers," but it gradually took on the character of a regular labor union. In 1890 the players' brotherhood led the players into a full-scale revolt against the club owners.

⊟   ⊟   ⊟

While leagues locked in fierce combat with one another for profits and ultimately for survival itself, an equally serious conflict raged between club management and the players. Notions and practices lingering from the fraternal era, the similarities between the experience of "playing" for pay and "working" for pay, and the high salaries received by ball players to some degree mitigated potential antagonism. These distinctive characteristics also made baseball's labor-management conflicts somewhat different from those that existed between employees and employers in other sectors of the economy. Nonetheless, in the 1880s, a decade racked by a spectacular series of industrial strikes, both the players and the owners became increasingly conscious of what Albert Spalding later termed "the irrepressible conflict between Labor and Capital."

Nothing was more critical to a club's financial success than obtaining high-quality players while containing salaries. Salaries constituted the largest single item in franchise expenses. For example, between 1876 and 1879 the Boston club paid out 64.4 percent of its costs to the players. Superior players resulted in winning teams, which in turn usually increased attendance and produced more gate receipts. But in a free labor market—that is, when players were free to transfer to the club making them the best offer—escalating salary costs could offset the additional revenues generated by fielding a better team.

At the outset of the professional game, club management sought ways to reduce the impact of a free market for player services. The first professional league, the National Association, had prohibited players from revolving from one club to another while the season was in progress. The National League retained this provision, but in 1879 it took an additional step that would revolutionize the history of the player-management relationship. Apparently responding to the immediate threat of the richer Chicago club cornering the best players, the NL clubs secretly agreed that each could "reserve," or hold off the market, five players; all other clubs agreed not to negotiate with these five players. Such a stricture rested on gentlemen's agreements rather than the law. The NL quickly learned that the player reservation system could also be used to contain salaries. "All the delegates believe that this rule will solve the problem of how to reduce wages," reported Oliver P. Caylor in the Cincinnati *Enquirer* in 1879. According to economist Gerald Scully, Boston's salaries fell by 20 percent following the adoption of the 1879 agreement. Little wonder, then, that by 1883 both the National League and American Association clubs reserved eleven men, virtually their entire teams in that day.

For nearly a century, until the mid-1970s, the reserve clause in player contracts remained the backbone of management's control of the players. Containing a provision that bound a player to his team for a year after his initial contract had expired, the clause in effect allowed the club that first signed an athlete a lifetime option on that player's services. Negotiating individually and without the freedom to sign with a competing club, a player had only two weapons with which to respond: either refuse to play until offered a salary to his liking or quit baseball. Neither alternative was attractive. "Holding out" could mean a loss of income for the playing time that a player had cost the club, and most players could not find jobs outside baseball that paid equally well. The reserve clause also made it possible for clubs to buy and sell player contracts, or, in non-legalistic parlance, to buy and sell players.

Although in theory the reserve clause permitted the clubs to drive salaries down to near the rate of other skilled occupations, baseball players in fact consistently earned twice and sometimes even three times as much as an experienced craftsman. In other words, clubs did not fully employ the reserve clause's potential for curbing salaries. Personal likings of players by club management and the belief that men content with their salaries would perform better, among other considerations, restrained impulses to offer minimal salaries.

Well before club directors had stumbled onto the advantages of the reserve clause, they had collided with the players on another front. Like the industrial magnates of the day, club management sought a sober, well-rested, disciplined work force. Serious-minded, orderly ball players would perform better on the field, management reasoned, and they would attract more public support, especially among those concerned with the maintenance of Victorian propriety.

Ball players, however, rarely behaved as management thought they should. Even the players of the earlier fraternal era, who had been mainly artisans and clerks of Protestant, old-stock (English) origins, had by no means been exemplary Victorians. Whereas the old stock by and large frowned on professional baseball as a career choice, growing numbers of the players (perhaps even a majority by the 1890s) came from the ranks of the Irish and German working classes, in which (at least for the Irish) drinking, brawling, and display were a conspicuous part of their male homosocial worlds. Henry Chadwick estimated that at least a fifth of all big-leaguers worked in saloons in the off season, and of those who operated a business after retirement, 80 percent were saloonkeepers. In addition, the ball players were young, usually unmarried, and with great quantities of free time unoccupied by team practices or games. Away from the diamond, they frequented billiard halls, loitered in saloons, and consorted with gamblers and showpeople. Finally, with the growing separation of management and labor in baseball, management could no longer depend on fraternal constraints to curb player misbehavior. Even the term *fraternity* increasingly fell into disuse.

Professional baseball publicists, management, and some of the players themselves found in the concept of professionalization a partial substitute for fraternity. As in such emerging white-collar professions as medicine, law, and engineering, pro baseball players were urged to consider themselves members of a highly exclusive, specially skilled work force. As a profession, the players should close ranks against those who damaged their reputations. "Now, as with the lawyer or physician whose professional status is degraded by the actions of the pettifogger and quack," observed Henry Chadwick, "so it is with the professional athlete whose reputation necessarily suffers from the conduct of the class who lower their occupations by degrading associations [and] dissipated habits." To the degree that the professionalization of ball playing succeeded, it drove a wedge between the current lives of the players and their tumultuous working-class origins.

From the standpoint of management, neither disciplinary measures nor internal restraints arising from professionalization were entirely successful. Player drinking especially proved intractable to management control. Although it is impossible to determine precisely the degree to which drinking directly affected player performance, press reports, legends, and the disciplinary measures of the clubs indicate that many players regularly made their way to the saloons in the evenings after the games, and more than a few imbibed before the games commenced in the afternoons. There are several press reports, perhaps exaggerated and no doubt in some cases even false, of players taking the field while drunk.

Throughout the 1880s the National League campaigned against player drinking. Before the 1880 season opened, every NL player received a stern but fatherly warning titled an "Address to Players," which noted that intemperance resulted "in the loss of money [that the player] spends in the gratification of his appetite for liquor; [and] cutting the other way in the loss of his standing in the profession." "Hereafter," the address warned, "it is not proposed to tolerate drunkenness or bummerism"; players guilty of such behavior would be "absolutely shelved." But such dire threats apparently contained more rhetorical flourish than substance. Owners were especially reluctant to dismiss star players for their peccadillos. Nonetheless, two years later, the NL took more drastic action: It officially dismissed ten players, all of whom possessed marginal skills, and blacklisted them for life. "A professional player who is skilled in his work . . . and who weakens his play by indulgence in liquor," declared *Spalding's Guide*, "is a fool unfit for a position on any first-class team."

No one fought harder in principle against player drinking than Albert Spalding. In May 1884, for example, he fined Frank Flint and George Gore $50 each on the grounds that "dissipation" had diminished "their skill." While warning them that a second offense would double the fine, Spalding also upbraided his manager, Cap Anson. You must "be more strict in your discipline," Spalding wrote to Anson. Anson should enforce the eleven o'clock curfew on the players, Spalding said, even if it required the employment of detectives "to keep them in their rooms."

The ring leader of the carousing Chicago ball players was none other than King Kelly. Spalding once hired a Pinkerton detective to follow Kelly and his mates. Seven of them, the detective reported, spent almost every night going "up and down Clark Street [in Chicago] all over the tenderloin districts, through the whole roster of saloons and 'speakeasy' resorts." After Spalding had the report read to the team, Kelly finally broke the long silence. "I have to offer only one amendment," said Kelly. "In that place where the detective reports me as taking a lemonade at 3 A.M. he's off. It was straight whiskey; I never drank a lemonade at that hour in my life." In 1887, the season after the White Stockings had lost the World Championship to the St. Louis Browns and failed to take the NL flag, Spalding was so infuriated with Kelly and his drinking companions that he told the press that "we shall no longer endure the criticism of the respectable people because of drunkenness in the Chicago nine." Whether driven by anger over player drinking or by lucrative deals offered by other clubs, Spalding proceeded to sell or trade away his entire outfield, which included Kelly, as well as his star pitchers, Jim McCormick and John Clarkson.

◫   ◫   ◫

The highly publicized sale of Kelly for $10,000 to Boston dramatized to the players their utter powerlessness in obtaining compensation for themselves from the sale of their contracts to other clubs. Along with clashes between players and management over drinking, rising salary expectations stemming from baseball's growing prosperity in the 1880s, and the leadership provided by Monte Ward, the sale triggered a full-scale revolt among the professional players. In 1887 a Brotherhood of Professional Base Ball Players committee headed by Ward succeeded in obtaining a meeting with the owners to discuss the players' grievances.

At that meeting, Spalding, who represented the owners, outfinessed the players on every count. First, he quickly acquiesced to the committee's request for a uniform player contract that spelled out more specifically the rights and duties of both the owners and the players. With this gesture having put the players in a conciliatory mood, Spalding then presented his arguments in favor of the reserve clause. He concluded by confessing that the reserve clause was a less than perfect instrument and that he would be happy to entertain any alternatives suggested by the committee. Caught unprepared, the players were completely stymied by Spalding's apparent willingness to revise or even abolish the reserve clause. "The reserve rule, on the whole, is a bad one," Ward told a reporter afterward, "but it cannot be rectified save by injuring the interests of the men who invest their money [in baseball], and that is not the object of the Brotherhood." Perhaps unwittingly, Ward had expressed the position of management as effectively as Spalding himself could have done.

But player-management harmony was short-lived. Without the benefit of sage advice from Spalding, who was away from the country on his world baseball tour, the owners in 1888 adopted a salary classification plan that inflamed the players. In order to cap escalating salaries, John T. Brush, the major owner of the Indianapolis club, proposed that the NL president classify all players on the basis of their skill and personal character. Class A players, the highest category, would receive salaries of $2,500; class B, $2,250; and so on down the line to class E, who were to be paid $1,500. Had the Brush classification plan been effectively enforced, it would have drastically reduced salaries across the board, but in fact many players surreptitiously received far more than the figure called for by the plan. For instance, in addition to paying King Kelly $2,500, Boston apparently proffered their star an additional $5,000 for his photograph. As abhorrent as the idea of salary caps was to the players, however, the humiliating spectacle of having themselves "graded like so many cattle" for the slaughter was even worse. To the players, classification vividly signified their abject and complete surrender to the authority of the owners.

Led by Ward, during the season of 1889 the NL players formed a plan to end their subordination to the owners. It entailed fashioning their own league, the Players League (PL). As they visited each city to play ball, they secretly recruited financial backers, the most important being Al Johnson, a Cleveland streetcar magnate, and lined up additional players for the new circuit. In November 1889, the players' brotherhood issued a public "manifesto." Like the documents of many other reform movements, the manifesto recalled a mythic golden age, an age of baseball when the owners allegedly were interested only in the welfare of the game. "There was a time," read the manifesto, "when the [National] League stood for integrity and fair dealing. . . . Once it looked to the elevation of the game and an honest exhibition of the sport; today its eyes are on the turnstile. Men have come into the business for no other motive than to exploit it for every dollar." Appealing to the growing public hostility toward monopolies, the manifesto charged that the NL was "a combination . . . stronger than the strongest trust." It was "able to enforce arbitrary measures, and the player had either to submit or get out of the profession in which he had spent years in attaining a proficiency."

The NL held its annual meeting shortly after the brotherhood's declaration of war. Apparently at the instigation of Spalding, it quickly dropped the Brush classification plan, a step that, had it been taken earlier, might have prevented the war in the first place. The league then responded with its own mythical interpretation of baseball's past. According to the NL manifesto, only the sagacious actions of the owners in 1876 had saved baseball from utter ruin brought on by the misbehavior of the players. In 1876, the league had "rescued from destruction" the national game that was "threatened by the dishonesty and dissipation of the players." Only the "stringent rules and ironclad contracts [that] it developed . . . elevated and perpetuated [baseball] into the most glorious and honorable sport on the green earth."

Undeterred by the NL manifesto, the PL commenced play in the summer of 1890. By planting seven franchises in NL cities and successfully luring away most of its veteran players, the players' circuit challenged the senior loop directly. The PL dropped the hated reserve clause and the blacklist. The PL also obtained enough financial backing from local politicians, streetcar owners, and other small-time entrepreneurs—they were, in fact, strikingly similar to those who invested in NL and AA franchises—to ensure initial success. In a novel departure from the traditions of private enterprise, an eight-man board composed of four players and four "contributors," as the financial investors were dubbed, managed each club. After all expenses had been paid, including player salaries, the contributors would receive the first $10,000 in profit; additional profits would be shared with the players.

Spalding headed the NL's war committee appointed to suppress the player uprising. Capitalizing on the popular fears of the day, he denounced the players as "hot headed anarchists" who were bent on a terrorism that was characteristic of "revolutionary movements." "Don't mistake [the players] for . . . poor, miserable, overworked, under-paid haggards, [or] starving slaves," warned one newspaper. Instead, the players were overpaid men of leisure. Unlike ordinary workingmen, according to critics, the typical ball player arose at around 10:00 A.M., ate breakfast, took a nap, ate lunch at 2:00 P.M., strolled out to the park at about 3:00 P.M., engaged in light exercise for about two hours, returned to his hotel for dinner, and then spent the evening with a woman at the theater or at an elegant saloon drinking with his companions. The players frequently wore fur-lined coats, silk hats, and expensive jewels in their scarfs. Like showpeople and other dandies about town, they smoked twenty-five cent Henry Clay, Reina Victoria, or Rosa Perfecto cigars rather than the nickel El Toros of the working class.

Although some, but by no means all, of the newspapers happily denounced the players, Spalding had far less success in prosecuting the players for violating the reserve clause. The courts held that the reserve clause lacked "mutuality"; in other words, it was one-sided in favor of the owners. With these decisions, the players could jump to the new circuit with legal impunity. Efforts to bribe star players to stay in the loop also fared poorly. Spalding offered King Kelly a "blank check" to remain in the league, but Kelly, after taking a long walk to think it over, refused, saying "I can't go back on the boys." Apart from Cap Anson and Harry Wright, nearly all the better known National Leaguers jumped to the new circuit.

None of the three big leagues—the NL, PL, or the American Association—profited from the 1890 season. At the outset, the players' brotherhood made questionable decisions. By refusing to permit Sunday games, barring beer at games, and charging a fifty-cent gate fee, the PL opted for Victorian respectability rather than trying to appeal directly to ethnic, working-class fans. Although the PL's superior quality of play attracted more fans than did the NL, frequent competition on the same day in the same city for the same customers and a long spell of wet weather in September cost both leagues heavily. The Boston Reds, which featured King Kelly, won the PL pennant, and enjoyed the warm support of the local Democratic machine, was apparently the only PL franchise to turn a profit. Unknown to the players' brotherhood, none of the NL clubs made money; John Day's New York Giants had to receive a large subsidy from the other NL club owners merely to finish the 1890 season.

In the end, fan support and high-quality baseball were not enough to ensure the PL's success. During the season, rumors circulated that some of the PL's financial angels had met secretly with Spalding; whether true or not, several of them were anxious to avoid further financial injury. When Spalding called for a peace meeting at his Fifth Avenue Hotel suite in New York in October 1890, he refused to negotiate with Ward or any of the other players. While the brotherhood men seethed, in the words of Spalding, "the monied men met with the monied men." By a combination of complex stratagems that included buying out PL backers and allowing them to invest in NL clubs, Spalding brought down the PL. As a sop to the rebel players, he allowed them to return to their original NL and AA teams without penalties. With a rhetorical flourish, Spalding announced what might be considered the players' valediction: "When the spring comes and the grass is green upon the last resting place of anarchy, the National [League] will rise again in all its weight and restore . . . to all its purity [our] national pastime the great game of base ball."

▣ ▣ ▣

Rather than ushering in an era of permanent peace and purity, however, the suppression of the player insurrection set the stage for yet another trade war between the National League and the American Association. The confused situation in the wake of the PL collapse provided new opportunities for clubs in both leagues to strengthen their player rosters. According to the terms by which the PL had been dissolved, each owner was to send to a national board (composed of representatives of both the AA and the NL) a list of players with whom they had contracts prior to the 1890 season. For unknown reasons—perhaps simply ignorance—the new owners of the AA's Philadelphia franchise neglected to register with the national board two of their star players, Louis Bierbauer and Harry Stovey. The NL's Pittsburgh club promptly signed Bierbauer to a contract. "Pirates!" responded the angry AA clubs, and the Pittsburgh team has been known as the Pirates ever since. Philadelphia asked that Bierbauer's contract be returned to them, but at a hearing the board "reluctantly" ruled in favor of Pittsburgh. In response to this decision, as well as to other steps by NL clubs to corner player talent, the AA voted to withdraw from the National Agreement. "It was bad enough to have Spalding's fingers on our throats for nine long years," declared AA vice-president Billy Barnie. "Spalding says he wants war and we will give it to him."

And they did. For the 1891 season the association recruited additional financial backers, pooled its resources, planted competing franchises in Cincinnati, Philadelphia, and Boston, and raided NL player rosters. Unfortunately for the AA, it placed much of its hopes on the shoulders of King Kelly, but even the King could not salvage the beleaguered Cincinnati franchise. When Cincinnati folded in August, Kelly moved on to the association's Boston club. More than 10,000 fans greeted the return of their hero, but Kelly played only a week for the league-leading Red Stockings before jumping to the rival Boston Beaneaters of the National League. With Kelly leading the way, the Beaneaters proceeded to win eighteen consecutive games, enough for them to win the NL title. In the meantime, while Kelly and his mates were capturing the attention of the entire city, the desperate Red Stockings were reduced to scheduling games over the noon hour.

Both sides suffered heavily from the "Second Association War." The entire structure of professional baseball was in jeopardy. Already weakened by the financial losses incurred during the player insurrection of 1890, the leagues had added to their woes in 1891 by contending with one another for players. Player salaries had shot up spectacularly. To avoid further expenses, leaders in both leagues sought to end the bitter struggle. The truce, the National Agreement of 1892, called for a new twelve-team NL composed of the original eight NL clubs plus four clubs from the AA. The new loop allegedly paid $130,000 (the cost to be assessed equally against each club) for the rights of five remaining AA franchises. "Many people seem to think that the National League bought peace dearly in paying $130,000 for it, but according to my way of figuring the price was cheap," NL president Nick Young informed the press. With competition for players eliminated, the NL "will save nearly all of that during the next five years in salaries."

National League Cities, 1892–99

Baltimore	Louisville
Boston	New York
Brooklyn	Philadelphia
Chicago	Pittsburgh
Cincinnati	St. Louis
Cleveland	Washington

Young may have been right. Although the absence of financial records makes it impossible to know how much the new circuit saved on salaries, the evidence is clear that it soon took on some of the trappings of an "undisguised monopoly," as one newspaper put it. In a decade that witnessed banker J. Pierpont Morgan's creation of giant holding companies in the railroad, electrical, and farm machinery industries, the absorption of the AA "enabled the [baseball] magnates to do about as they please without hindrance."

The players were the first to feel the weight of the new regime. To recover the losses suffered from the PL and AA wars, the owners were determined to hack down player salaries. Rather than engage in open bidding for the players left over from the reduction of big league clubs from seventeen to twelve, a two-man committee arbitrarily distributed the surplus players where they thought it would help equalize competition. The owners did not even await the conclusion of the 1892 season before they reduced club rosters from fifteen to twelve players and slashed player salaries 30 to 40 percent. When John Glasscock, a St. Louis player, was called into the office of St. Louis club president Christopher Von der Ahe, he cracked, "Excuse me, . . . I'm going into Von der Ahe's barber shop to get my salary shave." He got a closer shave than he expected: a $500 reduction at midseason. NL president Nick Young did not find Glasscock's remark funny. "We are through with the hurrah business," he grimly explained. "We [the owners] propose now to get a share of the money." The owners cut salaries again in 1893. For the remaining seasons of the 1890s the league imposed an unofficial $2,400 salary cap.

Without competing leagues and with a general economic depression in the mid-1890s, there was little that the players could do but take their cuts or, as James Hart, president of the Chicago club uncharitably put it, "retire from the business." The players no longer enjoyed a strong bargaining position. In a satiric letter to William Joyce, Monte Ward, who was now serving as Brooklyn's manager, vividly revealed the new status of the players. To a request by Joyce for a $200 advance on his salary, Ward responded, "Haven't you heard yet of the consolidation of the League and Association into one big league[?] And, if so; don't you understand that the days of advance money are past[?] Why, my innocent William, hereafter it is the players who are to pay advance money to the magnates. . . . Your inning is over, my boy."

▣ ▣ ▣

The fans cared little whether the players could command their "innings" at the salary table. They were far more attentive to the players' innings on the diamond. And there, in the game played between the foul lines, the turbulent 1890s may have been the single most important decade in baseball history. That decade established the broad pattern of play that would prevail for at least the next three decades.

A major rule change encouraged the new pattern. In 1893 the league required that the pitcher deliver the ball with his back foot anchored on a rubber slab (rather than allowing him to take a skip step within a five-and-a-half-by-four-foot box) and lengthened the distance between pitcher's mound and home plate to sixty feet, six inches, which was ten feet longer than it had been a dozen years earlier. Since the early days of the game, the delicate balance between offense and defense had been subject to several changes. In the 1870s and 1880s the rule governing how high the pitcher could raise his arm above his waist while delivering the ball had been gradually relaxed until overhand pitching was fully legalized in 1884. In 1887 batters lost the privilege of asking for a pitch above or below the waist, but it was not until 1901 that fouls first counted as strikes. The rule makers also repeatedly altered the number of pitches thrown outside the strike zone that entitled the runner to first base before settling on the present number of four in 1889.

Because underhand pitching places little stress on the arm, the hurlers of that era, like modern softball pitchers, threw day in and day out, in some instances completing more than eighty games during a single season. Unless injured, a pitcher was expected to work the entire nine innings. Prior to 1889 substitutes could be brought into a game only when a regular had suffered a serious injury (a determination made by the opposing captain); captains therefore usually had a backup or "change" pitcher who played in the outfield. If desired, the captain could simply have the two players exchange positions.

Although controversy and unverifiable legends abound about who deserves credit (and when) for the "firsts" in baseball's defensive tactics, it is clear that many tactics familiar to the modern fan had become commonplace by the 1880s. Even as late as 1886 a chart in *Beadle's Dime Base-Ball Player* shows the shortstop playing near the base line halfway between second and third base and the second basemen standing only slightly off the bag on the opposite side, but as early as the 1860s infielders had begun to inch away from their respective bases and managers had begun to place their quickest player at shortstop. According to baseball legend, 1875 was something of a major turning point in the use of baseball equipment; in that year catchers first donned masks and a fielder first wore gloves. Rather than being used to improve fielding, these skin-tight gloves (with the ends of the fingers cut off to improve throwing) were initially used solely to protect the hands from the sting of the ball. In 1887 Charley Cushman, manager of the International League champion Toronto club, introduced the practice of having his right-handed infielders wear gloves only on their left hands. Ridiculed for their lack of manliness in wearing gloves, a few players continued to play without them as late as the 1890s.

By modern standards, fielding was no doubt poor, a conclusion justified by the large numbers of errors recorded by the scorekeepers. When, during the first game of the National League's inaugural season of 1876, the Boston club made twenty-four miscues and their St. Louis opponents sixteen, the totals were unusual enough for a newspaper to comment that "never before was there a professional game played which was so full of disgusting muffs, disgraceful fumbles and loose and slovenly play." Even the 1886 National League pennant-winning Chicago nine committed 475 miscues in 124 games, whereas the league's worst fielding team, the Athletics of Philadelphia, mishandled the ball 637 times. These numbers are high by modern standards, but part of the reason must have been that playing surfaces were far rougher then than today and that the players were without the advantages of large, formed gloves.

The 1893 rule change that lengthened the pitching distance and required the pitcher to keep his back foot in place while delivering the ball immediately reversed a downward trend in hitting. Whereas only nine batters hit .300 or better in 1892, twenty-six accomplished the feat in 1893. Total runs per game rose 25 percent (to more than thirteen per game), and the number of strikeouts dropped by half. For the next season, the 1894 campaign, the league as a whole hit a stunning .309, with Philadelphia leading the pack at .349. Hugh Duffy took individual honors in 1894 with .438, which, except for James "Tip" O'Neil's inflated average of .492 in 1887 (a season in which bases on balls counted as hits), was an all-time major league record. During the 1890s seven men hit over .400, including Jesse Burkett, who scaled the barrier three times.

Although the 1890s were well known for lusty hitting, that decade also saw the burgeoning popularity of what eventually became known as "scientific" or "inside" baseball. The practitioners of the scientific game claimed to use brains as well as brawn to enhance their prospects of winning. As early as 1889, when star player Fred Pfeffer of the Chicago White Stockings wrote a little treatise titled *Scientific Baseball*, adherents of the new style spoke of "playing the percentages." Thus, on defense managers tried to place "every player in the right place at the right time." They assigned their "brainiest" players to the positions requiring the greatest mental effort; shortstops, for example, acquired reputations for being smarter and quicker than first basemen or outfielders. Playing the percentages also meant drilling the players in such fundamentals as throwing to the right base and backing each other up in the event of muffed balls. Because the slightest hesitation might make the difference between winning and losing, managers sought to nurture in players an ability to make correct split-second decisions in game situations. Because the effective practice of scientific baseball required careful attention to numerous details, the managers of such teams repeatedly drilled their players on fundamentals and frequently acquired reputations for being martinets.

Apart from the sacrifice bunt, which could be executed far more easily after the pitching distance had been increased, no part of inside baseball offensive strategy was more ingenious than the hit-and-run play. No one knows when the play was first consciously used. Many years after its alleged inception, both Cap Anson of the White Stockings and John J. McGraw of the Baltimore Orioles tried to claim credit for it. However, a modern student of the game, Bill James, has reported the contents of an essay written by Monte Ward that offers solid evidence that Boston's Tom McCarthy was the first manager to make wide use of the hit-and-run tactic. Writing in 1893, Ward disclosed,

The Bostons . . . work this scheme: The man on first makes a bluff attempt to steal second, but runs back to first. By this it becomes known whether the second baseman or the short stop is going to cover second for the throw from the catcher. Then the batsman gets a signal from the man on first that [he] is going to steal on a certain pitched ball. The moment he starts for second the batsman just pushes the ball for the place occupied only a moment before by the infielder who has gone to cover second base.

James speculates that Ward picked up this tactic from McCarthy, who then taught it to William "Wee Willie" Keeler. When Keeler was traded from Ward's New York Giants to Baltimore in 1894, he introduced it to his teammates there, including McGraw. No matter who deserves credit for its invention, in the 1890s both Boston and Baltimore developed the play into a fine art. In the twentieth century, it became a standard part of nearly every team's offensive repertoire.

The 1890s witnessed other offensive innovations. One was the "Baltimore chop." Seizing the advantage of sun-baked infields, the Orioles learned to swing down on the pitch, causing the ball to hit near home plate and to bounce high into the air, which allowed the batter to reach first base safely ahead of the throw. Both the Orioles and the Boston Beaneaters also exploited more fully the possibilities of daring baserunning. Rather than always "playing it safe," they frequently tried to take an extra base on hits to the outfield or to steal bases off pitched balls. The Orioles regularly had five or more players who stole thirty or more bases per season. The decade's most effective runner was Boston's William "Billy" Hamilton. An ideal leadoff hitter, Hamilton hit for a high average, walked often, struck out rarely, and took an extra base at every opportunity. With a total of 937 stolen bases (which in that decade included "stretching" hits into extra bases), he was the decade's premier base stealer.

Inside baseball could also include scrappiness, or what contemporaries called "rowdiness." From the outset of the professional game, play had become increasingly bellicose. In the 1880s both Cap Anson, as manager of the White Stockings, and Charles Comiskey, as pilot of the Brown Stockings, had earned reputations for their loud complaints about the decisions of umpires and their verbal harangues of opposing players. But in the 1890s the game moved far beyond verbal jousting. The most startling change was in the actual or threatened use of physical force. Nothing was more feared than being the victim of razor-sharp steel spikes (unless it was being hit in the head by a pitch). Players deliberately slid into bases with their spiked shoes flying high to intimidate or actually inflict deep flesh wounds to

defensive players. Violent acts also included infielders tripping and blocking base runners or grabbing players by the belt as they tried to tag up after
a fly ball to the outfield, catchers throwing their masks in front of runners
coming into home plate, and outright fist fighting. John Heydler, an umpire in the 1890s (and later NL president), described the leading offenders, the Baltimore Orioles, as "mean, vicious, ready at any time to maim
a rival player or an umpire, if it helped their cause. . . . The worst of it was
that they got by with much of their brow beating and hooliganism. Other
clubs patterned after them."

The game's increasing rowdiness arose from more than a recognition of
its usefulness in winning games. Part of it may have been a consequence
of players discharging frustrations against one another that had origins in
their declining status vis-à-vis management; in addition, however, by the
1890s large numbers of new ethnics, in particular the Irish, had achieved
a conspicuous place in the sport. "In fact, so many Irish were in the game,"
Harold Seymour has written, "that some thought they had a special talent for ball playing." In the face of this influx, ethno-religious conflicts
sometimes smoldered into open eruptions. John Warner of the Boston
Beaneaters, for example, was notorious for his efforts to make life miserable for Irish Catholic players.

Nonetheless, the Irish seemed to have held their own and more. Main-
stays of the brawling Baltimore Orioles included Irish Americans Edward
"Ned" Hanlon (their manager), John J. "Muggsy" McGraw at third base,
shortstop Hugh Jennings, first baseman Jack "Dirty Jack" Doyle, outfielders Joe Kelley and William Henry "Wee Willie" Keeler, and pitchers
Arlie Pond, John "Sadie" McMahon, Joe Corbett (younger brother of
heavyweight boxer James J. Corbett, who defeated John L. Sullivan for
the championship in 1892), and handsome Anthony Mullane. In the
1890s the uninhibited, clamorous, working-class and ethnic culture from
which these players (and growing numbers of others) originated spilled
over onto the diamond. Less self-restrained than the old-stock, Protestant
players, the Irish brought to the playing field far more physical and emotional expressiveness.

Nor did owners or managers do much to restrain rough play. "A milk and
water, goody-goody player can't wear a Cleveland uniform," their fiery
manager, Oliver "Pat" Tebeau, flatly declared. In the 1890s some if not most
of the owners believed that the fans enjoyed rowdy play. "Patrons like to
see a little scrappiness in the game," explained Baltimore manager Ned
Hanlon in 1897; "[they] would be very dissatisfied . . . to [see] players slink-

ing away like whipped schoolboys . . . afraid to turn their heads for fear of a heavy fine from some swelled umpire." Agreeing with Hanlon's opinion, the owners sometimes paid the fines of their players, refused to employ more than one umpire for each game, and denied umpires enough authority to check player behavior. "It is the fashion now for every player to froth at the mouth and emit shrieks of anguish whenever a decision is given which is adverse to the interest of [his] club," explained Tim Keefe, when he quit the league's umpiring staff in midseason of 1895. By modern standards, the league tolerated the shameless abuse of its arbiters.

Except for the players' league year of 1890, Boston, Baltimore, and Brooklyn, three teams known for their skills at playing inside baseball, won all the NL titles in the 1890s. Boston led the way with three consecutive flags in 1891–93 and two more in 1897 and 1898, all under one manager, Frank Selee, who was said to be the "brainiest, cleverest and best" field general in the game. Selee was apparently the first nonplayer to manage a team; he also sat on the bench in street clothes rather than in uniform. Apart from featuring a coordinated offensive attack, Boston had perhaps the decade's most effective pitcher in Charles "Kid" Nichols, who won more than twenty-five games in nine consecutive seasons.

In Baltimore, Ned Hanlon, the "Napoleon of base ball managers," got rid of "the old lushers" and replaced them with the remarkable group of young Irish players who made the Orioles famous for their brawling and effectiveness at executing scientific baseball. Perhaps even more critical to the Orioles' success was Hanlon's use of his pitchers. Lengthening the pitching distance in 1893 had placed far more stress on the hurler's arm. Although opposing clubs were slow to adjust to the change (most of them initially carried only four pitchers on their entire roster) Hanlon quickly responded by spreading the work among six different hurlers. The colorful Orioles won three straight pennants (1894–96) and finished second in 1897 and 1898. When the Baltimore franchise moved to Brooklyn in 1899, Hanlon proceeded to win flags the next two seasons there as well. Six of Hanlon's players eventually became big league managers themselves (and among them won twenty-two pennants), helping ensure the continuing popularity of his style of play in the twentieth century.

▣ ▣ ▣

The successful suppression of the great player uprising in 1890 and the collapse of the American Association at the end of the 1891 season left big league baseball in the unencumbered hands of the National League. Although rule changes introduced a hitting deluge and inside baseball excited fan interest, from a business standpoint the 1890s were a grim decade for the league. With the return of prosperity at the turn of the century, however, a new contender for big league status entered the fray: the American League, led by the indomitable Byron Bancroft "Ban" Johnson.

6

The Great Baseball War

On the evening of 11 December 1902, Ban Johnson, president of the American League, and Charles Somers, the new league's main financial angel, sat down to eat in the dining room of the Criterion Hotel in New York City. In the midst of their meal, Frank Robison, James Hart, and August "Garry" Herrmann, all of the National League, approached them. "I knew in an instant," Johnson later recalled, "the purpose of their visit and after greetings all around they informed me [that] they composed a committee of the old league to wait on me and see if peace terms could be arranged." Johnson assured them of his willingness to terminate hostilities. Nearly a month later, on 9 January 1903, committees from both leagues met in Cincinnati, where they hammered out the final wording of a peace settlement that officially ended the "Great Baseball War."

The origins of the Great Baseball War encompassed more than simply a clash between rival sets of entrepreneurs, though of course neither group was immune to the profit imperative. During the 1890s the NL never recovered the prosperity it had enjoyed in the 1880s; estimates by Bill James place average game attendance between 2,000 and 3,000, which was 500 to 1,000 less than it had been for the 1880s. Apart from the general economic depression that followed the Panic of 1893 and the growing competition from other forms of commercial amusements, the leaderless league failed to develop a competitive format that resulted in interesting pennant races, exciting postseason series, and championships won by clubs representing the nation's more populous cities. Nor did the NL owners, with their ostentatious posturing as great magnates, endear themselves or their game to baseball fans. In the meantime, the Western League (renamed the American League [AL] in 1900) not only audaciously invaded NL cities with its teams but also tried to seize the mantle of Victorian propriety from the senior loop. The AL augmented the power of its umpires, disciplined unruly players, and took steps to prevent wagering at ball games. Enjoying the firm direction of Ban Johnson, the financial resources of Charles Somers, and a more positive public image than the NL's, the upstart AL quickly established itself as a formidable foe of the older loop.

▣   ▣   ▣

"Where, oh where is the National League drifting to?" asked Tim Murnane in the Boston *Globe* in 1896. No one could say for certain in 1896, but it was already clear that the league was wandering into troubled times. For instance, the NL failed to develop an adequate substitute for the popular "World Championship series" of the 1880s. An 1892 experiment that involved splitting the season into halves and having the winners meet in a postseason playoff utterly failed to arouse fan interest. The next year, the champion Bostons had to be satisfied with the Dauvray Cup, which may have advanced the career of its donor, Monte Ward's stunningly beautiful wife, actress Helen Dauvray, but left the fans without the thrills of a postseason championship series. Nor was a satisfactory alternative to be found in the Temple Cup, offered by William C. Temple of Pittsburgh from 1894 through 1897 to the winner of a seven-game series between the first- and second-place teams. The cup seemed to render the regular season championship meaningless, the players did not take winning the series seriously, and the fans were treated each year to a public squabble among the players about how the series receipts ought to be divided.

The twelve-team loop likewise failed to maximize fan interest in regular season play. The dominance of three cities (Baltimore, Boston, and

Brooklyn won all the flags in the 1890s) and the absence of good teams in New York, Philadelphia, and Chicago, the nation's most populous cities, adversely affected the entire league's potential attendance and revenues. In particular, Chicago, once the mainstay of professional baseball, fell on hard times; after 1891, the team never finished better than fourth place. The low attendance that resulted from Chicago's poor performance, concluded a reporter in 1896, "cost the league thousands of dollars."

With twelve teams, too many cities fielded nines that were out of the pennant race early in the season and had abysmal won-lost records. At the end of each season, as many as eighty-four wins separated the last- and the first-place teams. Fans in St. Louis and Louisville had special difficulties getting excited about their clubs; they occupied last place for five of the eight years that the twelve-team circuit existed. But no team in major league history performed more miserably than the once-proud Cleveland Spiders. After their roster had been plundered by owner Frank Robison to furnish additional talent for his other NL team (the St. Louis Browns), the Spiders finished the 1899 campaign with only 20 wins in 154 games. When fewer than 200 fans began to show up regularly for Cleveland's home games, the disgusted Robison ordered them to play the final two months of their season on the road. Sportswriters then dubbed them the "Exiles."

Relaxation of the traditional bans on Sunday baseball, sales of beer and liquor on the grounds, and twenty-five cent admission charges reflected a fundamental change in the league's direction. During the 1880s the American Association had profited from Sunday play, but Albert Spalding, fearing that it offended "the better classes," had steadfastly opposed NL play on the Sabbath. However, as part of the peace settlement creating the twelve-team league in 1892, the four former AA clubs were allowed to continue playing Sunday ball. Soon big Sunday gates in St. Louis, Baltimore, Washington, and Louisville broke down the resistance of even the Chicago White Stockings, though laws continued to ban Sunday ball in New York, Philadelphia, and Pittsburgh.

The league also relaxed its longstanding vigilance against gambling and gamblers. In the 1890s open gambling returned to several big league parks; knots of bettors could even be seen congregating in and under the grandstands. Owners, players, and managers no longer made serious efforts to disguise their own betting. For example, Cap Anson regularly placed public bets on his White Stockings, and Monte Ward won twenty shares of Giants stock from a club director, Edward Talcott, as the result of a wager on where New York would finish in the 1892 standings.

Open gambling was only one symptom of the NL's growing unruliness. Fan uprisings erupted with startling frequency, especially when the fans, who were all too often inebriated, were denied access to the field because of their overflowing numbers, when they concluded that the umpire had rendered unfair decisions against the home team, or when they had lost bets or feared that their bets were in jeopardy. In particular, the greater rowdiness among the players and managers incited growing spectator rowdiness. Not only did witnessing brawls on the field stimulate fierce fan responses, but many players and managers deliberately played to the home crowd, hoping that the fans' outbursts might affect the outcome of the game. Apart from their stories about fans yelling insults and obscenities at umpires and opposing teams, newspapers reported a rising frequency of physical assaults by fans. On leaving the field at the completion of games, umpires and opposing players sometimes had to run a gauntlet of verbal and physical abuse. "It is impossible for a respectable woman to go to the games in the National League without running the risk of hearing language which is disgraceful," complained veteran George Wright in a *Sporting Life* interview. In particular, according to sportswriter Hugh Fullerton, the "Baltimore park reeked with obscenity and profanity." Whether such language actually kept female fans away from the ballparks is unclear. At any rate, reluctant to pay the costs for additional policing and fearful that aggressive countermeasures might reduce total attendance, the owners did little to control disorder.

Late in the decade, the NL finally took some steps to curb the more boisterous forms of player behavior. In 1897 it tightened the rules against using the body to block runners off the bases. The following year, the league adopted a document titled "A Measure for the Suppression of Obscene, Indecent and Vulgar Language upon the Ball Field," or the so-called Brush Purification Plan, which was apparently aimed mainly at the Baltimore Orioles. Henceforth, any player who addressed a fellow player or an umpire in a "filthy" manner could be subjected to a fine or even lifetime banishment from the game. Although manager Ned Hanlon said that his Orioles could "be counted on as one of the reformers," one of his star players, John McGraw, was not so certain. McGraw worried that enforcement of the plan might require him to "abandon my profession entirely." McGraw need not have had such a fear, for not a single player or manager was brought before the league for violating the plan. "I can only conclude," one writer observed, "that in the season past not one reference was made [by a player or a manager] to the maternal ancestry of any umpire; [and] not once was any umpire or opposing player asked to accomplish the physically impossible."

⊞ ⊟ ⊞

Responsibility for the drift in league affairs ultimately rested with the club owners. Nicholas Young, the affable NL president from 1885 to 1901, lacked the personality, vision, time, and owner support to exercise strong leadership. Throughout most of his tenure, Young continued to hold down a full-time clerk's position in the United States Treasury Department. In earlier times, league direction had come mainly from the Chicago club, both because of the special talents of William Hulbert and Albert Spalding and because the other owners had recognized that the league's overall prosperity depended so much on the success of the Chicago franchise. But the NL no longer had Hulbert or Spalding at the helm. Hulbert had long been dead, and Spalding, after having suppressed the player uprising of 1890, retired as president of the White Stockings in 1891 to devote more time to his sporting goods business and his private life.

The logical heir to Chicago was New York, but two circumstances in the 1890s militated against that franchise's leadership. One was the growing number of club owners who sought in baseball a means to gain public recognition for their achievements and their sagacity, something they sensed had been denied them in their other enterprises. Then, as today, an obscure brewer, stock broker, or shipbuilder could be transformed instantly into a public celebrity by purchasing a big league franchise. Using baseball as a vehicle for self-advertisement encouraged the owners to pose as great magnates. Imitating the Rockefellers, Carnegies, and Morgans of the day, they sometimes ruled their fiefdoms with an utter disregard for the public, their employees (the players), or their fellow owners.

Second, during the 1890s the New York Giants neither fielded a strong team nor had an owner who could unite his faction-prone fellows. Indeed, the New York franchise entered the decade in shambles. The great player insurrection of 1890 nearly destroyed the Giants, forcing the team's owner, John B. Day, to beg his colleagues for help. Believing that New York must be saved from collapse "at all hazards," the Spalding brothers (Albert and J. Walter) of Chicago, Arthur Soden of Boston, John T. Brush of Indianapolis, and Al Reach of Philadelphia, owners of competing clubs, purchased stock in the ailing franchise. Although their funds kept the Giants afloat, the club's fortunes did not improve. From 1890 through 1902, the team never won a pennant and finished the season in the bottom half of the standings ten times.

Rather than providing the league with direction, Andrew Freedman, the president of the Giants from 1895 to 1902, was himself a major source of controversy. Although bold, imaginative, and sometimes charming, Freedman, a realtor and a Tammany Hall henchman of German-Jewish ancestry, was utterly devoid of tact, highly sensitive to criticism, and inclined to act impulsively. From the outset of his ownership, he embarked on a running feud with the New York press. At various times he barred at least six reporters from the Polo Grounds for criticism of the team's management and once punched a *New York Times* reporter in the face for suggesting that the team would perform better with another owner. Nor did the tempestuous Freedman single out newspapers when making enemies. During his eight-year reign, he hired and fired no fewer than a dozen managers (including the legendary Cap Anson, who lasted only twenty-two games), successfully barred two umpires from working in the Polo Grounds, and antagonized nearly all the old-timers (including the venerable Henry Chadwick) who were associated with the professional game.

Two drawn-out, highly publicized disputes with players further damaged Freedman's reputation. Even though his popular fastball pitcher Amos Rusie had won twenty-four games and led the league in both strikeouts and shutouts for the ninth-place Giants in 1895, Freedman was not satisfied. He fined Rusie $200 for allegedly breaking training rules and an indifferent performance in the season's final game. Rusie interpreted the fine as simply a pretext for cutting his salary. Freedman then added to Rusie's anger by insisting that the pitcher take a salary cut of $600 for the following season. Rusie refused, sat out the 1896 season, and took the Giants to court. "Every independent fair-thinking man is with Rusie," reported *The Sporting News*. Wall Street brokers rallied behind Rusie by hanging a large sign in a Manhattan store window urging the fans to boycott Giants games; the police even had to break up a crowd that had gathered in front of the store to express its approval. Rather than face the prospect of having Rusie test the reserve clause in the courts and further alienate fans who sympathized with the holdout, Freedman's fellow owners contributed funds (reportedly $3,000) that permitted an out-of-court settlement with the Giants' star pitcher.

Deep-seated anti-Semitism added to Freedman's problems. During an 1898 game in New York, Orioles outfielder Howard "Ducky" Holmes responded to taunts from former teammates by shouting "Well I'm glad

I'm not working for a sheeny any more." Enraged, Freedman leapt out of his box and ran onto the field. He demanded that umpire Tom Lynch expel Holmes from the game. When Lynch, claiming that he had not heard the remark, refused, Freedman pulled his team off the field, forfeited the game, and refunded the fans' money. The league then fined Freedman $1,000 and suspended Holmes for the duration of the season. The players, the newspapers, and most of the owners sided with Holmes. *Sporting Life* reflected the casual anti-Semitism of the day when it declared that the suspension of Holmes for the "trifling offense" of "insulting the Hebrew race" was a "perversion of justice." Only ten days after the incident, the league reinstated Holmes.

Although an unequivocal failure in public relations, Freedman understood well the fundamentals of baseball as a business enterprise. He recognized that profits from baseball could be maximized only when franchises in the largest cities fielded good teams and when the league maintained at least a semblance of competitive balance. Practically, then, the NL needed to become more than an economic cartel based on gentlemen's agreements to preserve exclusive markets and rights to player contracts. According to Freedman, the league had to transform itself into a genuine trust, or holding company, in which each franchise would turn over control of its operations to a single body managed by a strong president. To ensure that the large cities fielded competitive teams and to reduce sharp disparities in performance in the league as a whole, Freedman would have had the trust redistribute players, perhaps even annually. This blatant violation of competitive principles not only came at the very time of a great public outcry against monopolies but also would have substantially reduced the power of the individual magnates; the latter ensured its rejection by Freedman's fellow owners.

Nevertheless, the growing practice of syndicate baseball—that is, the ownership by a person or persons of stock in more than one NL franchise—was hardly more acceptable to the public than Freedman's proposed trust. In the late 1890s three NL franchises became virtually the farm clubs of three other league franchises. When Cleveland Spiders owner Frank Robison obtained control of the St. Louis Browns in 1899, he transferred stars Jesse Burkett and Cy Young from the Spiders to the Browns, and when Barney Dreyfus, owner of Louisville, purchased control of Pittsburgh, he moved Honus Wagner and Fred Clarke to the Pirates. Perhaps no interlocking ownership reflected a more cynical disregard for hometown fans than the Baltimore-Brooklyn nexus. When Baltimore brewer Harry Von der

Hoorst and his field manager, Ned Hanlon, bought a controlling interest in the Brooklyn club, they immediately shifted Willie Keeler, Joe Kelley, and Hughie Jennings, among other Orioles, to the Superbas. Stocked with the Baltimore stars and with Ned Hanlon as its manager, the Superbas won NL pennants in both 1899 and 1900.

The resulting lopsided pennant races and hostile public reaction in cities victimized by syndicate baseball contributed to a growing demand for a reduction in the size of the league. Andrew Freedman led the fight. Still sulking over the Ducky Holmes affair and enraged by syndicate baseball, Freedman threatened "not to improve the New York Club until the circuit [was] reduced." In 1900, the league dropped the franchises for Cleveland, Baltimore, Louisville (all of which had been victims of syndicate baseball), and Washington. The buyout cost the eight surviving franchises $104,000, which was to be paid off by a levy on future gate receipts. This left a circuit consisting of Boston, Brooklyn, New York, Philadelphia, Pittsburgh, Cincinnati, Chicago, and St. Louis, one that remained intact until 1953, when Boston moved its franchise to Milwaukee.

▣ ▣ ▣

While the NL drifted through the 1890s, Byron Bancroft "Ban" Johnson, a flamboyant man who was large in both mind and body, laid the foundations for a successful challenge to the league's monopoly over big league baseball. According to legend, the American League's conception took place in 1893 at the Ten-Minute Club on Vine Street in Cincinnati. Both by day and night, German workingmen, ward heelers, con men, and sporting women, all of whom loved their bratwurst, beer, and beans, crowded into Vine Street drinking places. The Ten-Minute Club, one of the street's less raucous establishments, had the happy rule that a person at each table had to place an order every ten minutes or the patrons of that table would be asked to leave. It was there, according to Johnson's recollections, that he, a twenty-nine-year-old sportswriter for the Cincinnati *Commercial-Appeal*, and Charles Comiskey, the thirty-three-year-old manager of the local NL Reds, first explored the idea that would one day blossom into the American League.

The story may be apocryphal, but there is no doubt that as a Cincinnati sportswriter between 1887 and 1894 Johnson acquired an acute knowledge of both the internal and external workings of professional baseball. He concluded in the pages of the *Commercial-Appeal* that the game had two main problems: "a lack of harmony" among the owners and dissolute behavior among the players. In 1894, he got an opportunity to apply his ideas when, at the recommendation of Comiskey, a group of owners asked him to take the presidency of a minor league circuit, the revived Western League. Never before had a league president in the majors or the minors thrown himself so completely into the task. Johnson single-handedly set up the league's schedule of games, took steps to end the abuse of umpires, enforced tough standards of player behavior, and worked tirelessly at keeping ailing franchises afloat. The sporting press soon hailed "the hustling Western League chief" as the most successful baseball league president in the nation.

From the outset of his tenure, Johnson chaffed under the right of the NL to draft players from his league. In those days, players rarely began their professional careers by signing a contract with a big league franchise and then being assigned by that club to play on a minor league team. Instead, the typical professional player was first discovered, signed to a contract, and nurtured by an independently owned and operated minor league franchise. In accordance with the National Agreement of 1892, a compact to which nearly all the professional leagues were signatories, the minor league franchises held reserve rights in their players, but the major leagues could obtain such players by either drafting (paying a set price at the end of each season) or buying players from the minors before the annual draft.

Although the draft at least forced the NL to pay minor league franchises something for their players, Johnson objected that the draft price of $500 per WL player was frequently far less than the typical player's worth and that the draft regularly wreaked havoc with minor league stability. For example, the draft nearly destroyed the WL champion Minneapolis team of 1896; the next year Minneapolis barely managed to stay out of the cellar. Nonetheless, concerned mainly with the welfare of their own clubs, the NL owners rejected Johnson's proposals that the draft price be increased to $1,000 and that a player become eligible for the draft only after he had played two seasons in the WL.

Johnson's failure to obtain relief from the NL on the draft encouraged him to take the first steps that would lead to a complete severance of the WL's relationship with the senior loop. In order to give the WL more of a national character, he renamed it the "American League" in 1900 and formulated plans for invading Chicago. According to legend, during a long drinking session, Johnson convinced James Hart, president of Chicago's NL team (now called the Cubs rather than the White Stockings), to allow

Charles Comiskey to transfer his St. Paul team to the Windy City. As concessions to Hart, Comiskey's team was to be located on the South Side (far away from the Cubs), could not use the name "Chicago" on its uniforms, and (as a minor league club) would permit the Cubs to draft two of its players at the end of each season. Comiskey's team became the modern White Sox.

Chronology of the Great Baseball War

1894—Revived Western League forms with Johnson as president.
1900—Western League renamed the American League.
  —AL plants franchises in Chicago, Cleveland, Baltimore, and Washington.
1901—Johnson declares the AL a major league.
  —At least 74 NL players jump to the AL.
1902—Bitter internal struggle over the presidency divides NL owners.
  —AL draws 2.2 million fans; the NL, 1.7 million fans.
1903—AL plants a franchise in New York City, which would become the Yankees.
1903—National Agreement signed, creating the National Commission as professional baseball's governing body.

In the meantime, in his bid to establish the independence of the AL, a fortuitous set of external circumstances came to Johnson's aid. One was the decision of the National League to reduce the number of its franchises from twelve to eight. In 1900 Johnson planted franchises in Cleveland, Baltimore, and Washington, cities vacated by the NL. Another was the economy. At the turn of the century, the economy rebounded vigorously, releasing a flood of new money that consumers could use for commercial amusements. Even without players of big league caliber, the AL (as well as the NL) had a good season at the gate in 1900. A third was Charles A. Somers, a prosperous young Cleveland coal merchant. Somers helped bankroll franchises in Cleveland, Chicago, Philadelphia, and Boston. As Eugene Murdock, Johnson's biographer, has so succinctly put it, "Ban Johnson built the American League, but Charles Somers paid the bills." Finally, a new player uprising against the NL, led by the formation of the Players' Protective Association, suddenly improved the AL's prospects of successfully raiding the senior circuit for established stars.

Johnson was now prepared to make a complete break with the senior circuit. In 1901 he pulled out of the National Agreement of 1892, declared the AL a major league, and took measures to place his league on a wartime footing. To assure each member club "that it will be fully protected and in no danger of desertion by the other clubs in the event of a baseball crisis," Johnson required each franchise to assign to him 51 percent of its stock to be held in escrow. Thus, while a state of war existed, no AL franchise could make an important decision without first consulting Johnson. He urged AL owners to execute a massive player raid on NL teams. Offered higher salaries, the players left the senior loop in droves. Soon, former National Leaguers represented more than half of the players on AL rosters.

No player was more important in establishing the AL's credibility on the playing field than Napoleon "Nap" Lajoie, who was of French-Canadian ancestry. An established superstar with the NL's Philadelphia Phillies, Lajoie jumped to Connie Mack's Philadelphia Athletics in 1901, where he led the AL in batting (.422), home runs, doubles, runs scored, runs batted in, and slugging percentage. The NL Phillies obtained from the Pennsylvania Supreme Court an injunction (based on Lajoie's alleged violation of the reserve clause) that barred him from playing with the Athletics, but the legal victory soon proved hollow. The Athletics traded Lajoie to Cleveland, where the court order had no standing. Whenever Cleveland was to play in Philadelphia, Lajoie simply did not accompany the team; instead, he spent the time enjoying the beach at Atlantic City, New Jersey. Fortunately for the AL, within weeks of the Lajoie ruling, courts in St. Louis and New York rendered decisions favorable to players who had jumped to the new league.

Johnson soon regretted the decision of another NL star, John J. McGraw, to defect to the AL. A clash between the two men was inevitable. At first, Johnson enthusiastically encouraged McGraw's desertion, and McGraw welcomed the opportunity to become a player, manager, and part owner of the AL's Baltimore franchise. But McGraw had also been a member of the brawling Orioles of the 1890s, viewed umpires as natural enemies, and saw the game itself as a conflict little short of actual warfare. Led by McGraw, the ex-NL players brought to the AL their confrontational playing style. Throughout the season of 1901, Johnson, who had taken great pains to establish the AL as a model for player decorum, tried to contain rowdy play without permanently suspending the guilty players. Although Johnson and McGraw clashed on several occasions during 1901, McGraw somehow survived the season. In the spring of 1902 McGraw continued his abuse of umpires. Johnson finally ordered his indefinite suspension. McGraw then asked for his release from the Orioles and signed a contract to become player-manager of Andrew Freedman's New York Giants. McGraw and Johnson remained implacable enemies for the remainder of their lives.

The setbacks represented in the defection of McGraw and the virtual collapse of the Baltimore franchise were offset by soaring AL attendance and internal divisions within the NL. For the 1902 season the AL outdrew the senior circuit by 2.2 to 1.7 million fans. In the face of the AL challenge, the NL owners were more divided than ever before. Their wrangling reached a bitter climax in 1901 when news was leaked to the press that four owners had met at Andrew Freedman's estate in Red Bank, New Jersey, where they had put together a proposal to transform the NL into a trust or holding company. An opposing faction nominated Albert Spalding for the league presidency. The owners split evenly, four in favor and four against Spalding. When the Red Bank men walked out of the meeting, the Spalding bloc met in a rump session and elected their man president. An impasse continued until the spring of 1902, when Spalding finally resigned the office that may never have been his legally in the first place. The league management was then temporarily assumed by a three-man committee until Harry C. Pulliam, the secretary-treasurer of the Pittsburgh Pirates, was elected president later in the year.

The Great Baseball War's final battle revolved around Johnson's planting of a franchise in New York City. Initially, Freedman, with his Tammany Hall and real estate connections, blocked the AL's entry into New York. Freedman personally controlled the Polo Grounds, as well as several other potential park sites, and threatened to use his political influence to have streets cut through those that he did not control. By reaching a deal with an opposing Tammany faction, Johnson finally succeeded in bypassing Freedman. He awarded the AL's New York franchise, which was known at first as the Highlanders and later as the Yankees, to poolroom king Frank Farrell and former police chief William Devery, a protégé of Tammany bosses William Croker and Tim Sullivan. The New York franchise completed an AL circuit consisting of Boston, New York, Philadelphia, Washington, Detroit, Cleveland, Chicago, and St. Louis, one that remained fixed for a half century. In the meantime, Freedman, who was busily occupied building the New York subway system, sold most of his stock in the Giants for $125,000 to John T. Brush, the former owner of the Cincinnati Reds.

With the successful invasion of New York by the AL and the proven success of the junior loop at the gate in 1902, the war-weary senior circuit finally sued for peace. The result of the negotiations, the National Agreement of 1903, became the new centerpiece of professional baseball. The leagues agreed to recognize each other's reserve clauses and established a three-man commission to oversee all of what was becoming known as organized baseball. Composed of the presidents of the two leagues and a third member chosen by them, the commission served mainly as a judicial body to resolve disputes between the leagues and controversies involving the minor leagues.

The agreement also incorporated the existing minor league structure. In 1901, to protect their interests during the Great Baseball War, the minor leagues had created their own National Association of Professional Baseball Leagues and set up a hierarchy of minor leagues from A through D. The system set salary limits and permitted A leagues to draft players from B leagues, B from C, and so on, for a set price. The 1903 agreement recognized the territorial monopolies of the minor league clubs, granted them reserve rights in players, and set up a new system by which the major leagues could draft players from the minors. With the return of prosperity in the early twentieth century, minor league baseball enjoyed a rapid expansion.

▣ ▣ ▣

For big league baseball, the 1903 agreement ended a long era of league and franchise instability. With the acknowledgment of the American League as an equal partner, only one other circuit, the Federal League (1913–15), would ever again seriously contend for big league status. Until the Boston Braves moved to Milwaukee in 1953, not a single club relocated to another city. Ten cities—Boston, New York (including Brooklyn), Philadelphia, Washington, Pittsburgh, Cleveland, Cincinnati, Detroit, Chicago, and St. Louis—hosted all the teams in the two eight-team circuits. The 1903 agreement also established the possibility for an exciting climax to each season of play. The annual playoff between the flagbearers of the two leagues became known as the World Series.

7

Baseball's Coming of Age

No one at first expected the World Series to become a national rite that equaled or surpassed the excitement of Independence Day, Washington's Birthday, or tippling on New Year's Eve. At first, scheduling any kind of postseason championship series between the two leagues remained in serious doubt. The National Agreement of 1903 did not provide for a playoff, and although Boston and Pittsburgh agreed to a best-of-nine-game series in 1903 (won by Boston of the AL), the NL's New York Giants refused to play the AL champion Boston Red Sox in 1904. John T. Brush, the Giants owner, contemptuously dismissed the Red Sox as a "minor league" team. Perhaps it was the subsequent outcry against the Giants for cowardliness that led Brush himself to propose a mandatory seven-game postseason series between the champions of the two leagues. At any rate, within a decade after 1904, the outcome of the series absorbed the attention of millions. Fans congregated in the streets to watch the play-by-play as reported on boards posted in front of newspaper offices, and, reportedly, the series sometimes even delayed the proceedings of the United States Supreme Court.

The World Series, along with the thrills of regular season play, the construction of great ballparks of concrete and steel, the nurturing of a legend of baseball's uniquely American origins, and the game's continuing power to bind communities and neighborhoods together, all signified the coming of age of professional baseball. Indeed, amid the general economic prosperity of the first two decades of the twentieth century, baseball achieved a new institutional prominence and permanency in American life, in some respects equivalent to that of the state, the church, and the family. "Every city, town, and village in America has its team," observed the St. Louis *Globe and Commercial Advertiser* in 1905. Boys everywhere grew up reading baseball fiction, learning the rudiments of the game, and dreaming of one day becoming diamond heroes themselves.

Even the president of the United States extended his endorsement. In 1910, William Howard Taft, who was so broad-beamed that a row of seats had to be unscrewed and replaced with a sofa to provide him with adequate seating, established the precedent for the ritual of the president opening each season by throwing out the first ball. "Base-ball unites all classes and conditions of men," reported *Scribner's Magazine*, "from the White House through every person of our cosmopolite population." The song "Take Me Out to the Ball Game" (1908), with lyrics by Albert von Tilzer and music by Jack Norworth, emerged as the game's unofficial anthem. Sung by popular crooner Bill Murray, it was the number-one hit record in 1908 and, next to "Happy Birthday," quickly became the best-known song in the nation. No other sport, or so it seemed to contemporary observers, captured the essence of the nation's character quite as much as baseball. Such a contention was beyond debate, declared Albert Spalding in 1911; it was like saying "two plus two equal four."

❏ ❏ ❏

Contributing to the notion that the game embodied the nation's character was the invention of the myth that baseball was solely of American origins. The myth-creating process may have begun in 1889, when National League authorities threw a resplendent banquet at Delmonico's in New York City to welcome the return to American shores of Albert Spalding and his troupe of ball players from an around-the-world goodwill tour on behalf of the national game. Some 300 celebrities attended the event, including author

Mark Twain and future president Theodore Roosevelt. At the conclusion of the four-course meal, Abraham G. Mills, the fourth president of the NL, rose to speak. Perhaps carried away by the momentous nature of the occasion or by too many toasts of red wine, Mills exclaimed that both "patriotism and research" revealed baseball to be an original American game. The audience warmly responded: "No rounders! No rounders!" According to the New York *Clipper,* Mills's assertion "forever squelched" the insidious rumor that America's national game had foreign origins.

But the rumor could not be suppressed so easily. No less an authority than Henry Chadwick, the game's most knowledgeable historian, disagreed. He continued to insist that baseball had evolved from the English game of rounders. Finally, in 1905 Albert Spalding, responding to an essay by Chadwick, decided that a special commission of seven men (including two United States senators) of "high repute and undoubted knowledge of Base Ball" ought to be appointed to resolve the issue for all time. Chaired by the same Abraham G. Mills who had denounced the rounders theory of baseball's origins in 1889, the commission engaged in no firsthand research. Rather than employ someone to rummage through dusty old newspapers and other documents, Spalding invited anyone in the nation who had information on the origins of the game to send it in for the commission's evaluation.

Not surprisingly, given its composition, in 1907 the commission rejected Chadwick's thesis that baseball had evolved from rounders; nonetheless, it arrived at an unanticipated conclusion. The commission claimed to have unearthed a single progenitor of the national game. "According to the best evidence obtainable to date," read the commission's final report, the Civil War hero General Abner Doubleday conceived of baseball at Cooperstown, New York, in 1839. To support the Doubleday hypothesis, the commission relied on a single source, the recollections of Abner Graves, a former resident of Cooperstown. Sixty-eight years after the alleged event, Graves recalled that in the spring of 1839 Doubleday "designed the game to be played by definite teams or sides. Doubleday called the game Base Ball, for there were four bases in it." (In his two-volume memoir, written before his death in 1893, Doubleday did not once mention baseball, let alone seize the opportunity to stake his claim as the game's creator.) There the matter stood until 1939, when a librarian, Robert W. Henderson, convincingly demonstrated that the rules of rounders and baseball had at one time in their respective evolutions been nearly identical.

Despite the contrary evidence offered by Henderson and by several historians since, the myth has remained alive. In 1939 the major leagues com-
memorated the "centennial" of baseball with impressive ceremonies at
Cooperstown. That year they dedicated the Hall of Fame, presented a
pageant celebrating Doubleday's contribution, and staged an all-star game
between teams of former all-time great players. The United States government joined the festivities by issuing a commemorative stamp marking
1839 as the birth date of the national game. As Jews and Christians have
their Jerusalem and Moslems their Mecca, baseball fans now had their
special place, the pastoral village of Cooperstown. Each year thousands
of American "pilgrims" trek to the "shrine," Baseball's Hall of Fame and
Museum. There, as Harold Seymour has shrewdly observed, they can see
statues and pictures of their former heroes and observe their "relics": old
bats, balls, and uniforms. They can visit the "hallowed ground" of Doubleday Field, where young Doubleday was said to have first played the
game. And each year sports writers dutifully select great players of the past
for "enshrinement," after which they become "immortals."

▣ ▣ ▣

Just as the jerry-built wooden parks of the past suggested early professional
baseball's marginal, transitory character, the construction of fifteen massive ballparks of concrete and steel between 1909 and 1923 bore mute
testimony to the sport's coming of age. Awash with infusions of new money
that came from a twofold increase in attendance during the first decade
of the twentieth century (reaching an average of 6,133 per game by 1910)
and dreaming of even more fans, the major league owners set out on a
ballpark building binge.

It all began in 1909, when Benjamin Shibe erected Shibe Park in Philadelphia (later known as Connie Mack Stadium) and Barney Dreyfus built
Forbes Field in Pittsburgh. "For architectural beauty, imposing size, solid
construction and for public comfort and convenience," declared the *Reach
Guide* in 1910, "[Forbes Field] has not a superior in the world." On Sundays (Sunday baseball was still illegal in Pittsburgh) the local residents came
out in droves just to marvel at the new structure. The towering triple-
decked park seated 23,000 patrons and included electric elevators, tele-
phones, and inclined ramps to ease the movement of fans. Forbes Field "has
inaugurated a new era in base ball," concluded *Sporting Life*.

To invoke the past and inspire awe, the stadium architects frequently turned to classical motifs. Chicago's Comiskey Park emulated Rome's Colosseum, Cincinnati's Redland Field resembled a classical arena, and Philadelphia's Shibe Park included a massive three-story front with Ionic pilasters that flanked recessed arches. Only Boston's Fenway Park presented a traditional facade of red brick. Initially, several of the parks banned advertising on the outfield walls because, as Cincinnati's Garry Herrmann put it, they did not want to spoil "the artistic appearance of the yard[s]."

Unaided by public funding or the right of eminent domain, the owners were unable to clear out large spaces in the inner city (as modern stadium builders do). Instead, they built on cheaper land outside the central business district, though they kept in mind access to public transportation; for instance, a dozen streetcar and subway lines served Brooklyn's Ebbets Field. In addition, the new parks put an end to the flexibility of the wooden era; once situated, it was prohibitively expensive to relocate or to rebuild the huge, fireproof parks. When faced with the need to expand seating, the owners had to work within the constraints of the existing sites and structures.

Ebbets Field in Brooklyn was a classic example. In 1908, Charles Ebbets, the club's major stockholder, decided to put up a new park in Pigtown, a four-and-a-half-acre landfill where nearby farmers brought their pigs to feed on the fetid, steaming garbage deposited there by the local shantytown dwellers. To obtain the land from the fifteen separate owners at a reasonable cost, Ebbets formed a dummy corporation and kept his ultimate plans for the site a secret. Even then, the total costs of acquiring the plot soared to nearly $200,000, forcing Ebbets to seek additional capital by selling half the club's stock to a pair of local contractors with political connections. The final costs for erecting Ebbets Field exceeded a million dollars, no mean sum for that day. The new field initially had a seating capacity of 18,000, distributed in a two-tiered grandstand that extended from the foul pole in right field, around home base, and just past third base in left field.

In Ebbets Field, as was typical of the earlier wooden parks, great distances originally separated home plate from the outfield fences. Though the location of Bedford Avenue forced the construction of a wall in right field only 301 feet from home plate, the left-field fence stood at 419 feet, and the center-field wall at 477 feet from home base, both nearly unreachable for hitters. When faced with the need to expand seating capacity, Ebbets had too much invested to rebuild or relocate the field. The most economical solution for maximizing seating was to place grandstands along the foul lines beyond third and first base or in front of the existing out-field walls. By erecting new stands in front of the walls in left and center field, Ebbets Field eventually increased its seating capacity to 31,497; simultaneously, it became a favorite park of long-ball hitters. Although the left-field fence was 347 feet from home plate, the power alley in left was only a bit further, and the straightaway center-field wall stood only 397 feet from home plate.

The parks of steel and concrete served as more than giant arenas for commercial entertainment. They were akin to the great public buildings, skyscrapers, and railway terminals of the day; they were edifices that local residents proudly pointed to as evidence of their city's size and achievements. They also served as retreats from the noise, dirt, and squalor of the industrial city. On entering the grounds, the fans were transported into a nonurban universe of open vistas, green grass, and clean, white boundaries. As Steven Riess has observed, the owners gave their new parks pastoral names—Ebbets Field, Sportsman Park, the Polo Grounds. Such nomenclature remained popular until 1923, when Yankee Stadium was built. Parks since then have had more urban or futuristic names: Shea Stadium, the Astrodome, and the Skydome. Unlike the modern, symmetrical, multisport stadiums built in the 1960s and 1970s, each of the parks of that day was built first and foremost for playing baseball. Each had a distinctive character. Some had shorter fences in right field than in left, some had the converse; some were double-deckers, some single-deckers. The parks served as important repositories of collective memories; their presence evoked a shared past of heroic deeds and monumental blunders. As standing symbols of continuity, few if any other public structures in the nation were as effective as baseball parks in connecting the past and the present.

◻ ◻ ◻

As important as symbols, myths, and awe-inspiring parks were in creating baseball's special place in the American psyche, how the game was played and who played it contributed even more to the sport's coming of age. The first two decades of the twentieth century witnessed the performances of sterling pitchers Walter Johnson and Christy Mathewson, of great batsmen Honus Wagner and Ty Cobb, and of peerless managers John J. McGraw and Connie Mack. It was also the heyday of inside, or scientific, baseball, with its one-run-at-a-time game tactics.

The popularity of conservative offensive maneuvers stemmed in large part from the growing difficulties that teams had in scoring runs. Lengthening the pitching distance to sixty feet and six inches in 1893 at first touched off an offensive barrage. Runs soared to an average of 14.7 per game in the 1894 season before slowly declining during the remainder of the decade as pitchers adjusted to the longer distance. Then came a sudden plunge, a descent that coincided with two key rule changes. One was the decision in 1900 to change home plate from a twelve-inch square to a five-sided figure seventeen inches across. For the typical hitter the new plate added some 200 square inches to the strike zone; pitchers could now work the peripheries of the plate much more effectively than before. The second rule change that adversely affected hitting was the decision of the NL in 1901 and the AL in 1903 to count the first two foul balls as strikes. Prior to this, foul balls meant nothing; hitters could foul off innumerable pitches without worrying about striking out.

With a larger strike zone resulting from the bigger plate and the new foul-ball rule, strikeouts jumped more than 50 percent, while batting averages, home runs, slugging percentages, and runs per game sank to all-time lows. The entire NL averaged only 6.7 runs per game by 1908, less than half of the figures for 1894. AL pitchers hurled six no-hitters in 1908, a record that stood until 1990. The seasons of 1911 and 1912 saw improvements in offense in both leagues, but then run production fell again. Not until 1921 did the average runs per game (9.7) approximate the turn-of-the century averages.

The enlarged strike zone and the new foul-ball rule were not alone accountable for the decline in hitting. Hitters complained about the use of soft, discolored balls, leading baseball historians to label the age as the "dead ball era." Apparently, by about 1904, the practice of players deliberately soiling the ball with tobacco juice and dirt had become a more common practice, thereby making the ball more difficult to see than earlier. Nevertheless, the ball was no less resilient in the first two decades of the new century than it had been in the 1890s. The replacement of a rubber ball with a cork-centered ball in 1910 apparently was responsible only for a short-term, minor improvement in run production.

Some of the hitting drought may also be attributable to more reliance on relief pitching and improved fielding. For the 1901 through 1904 seasons, starting pitchers completed more than 85 percent of their games; after 1904, led by John J. McGraw's more frequent use of the bullpen, the percentage began to fall, reaching slightly less than 54 percent for the 1913 through 1917 seasons. Still, no team in those days had the equivalent of today's full-time career relief specialists. The prevailing managerial philosophy was that if your team was in the lead, leave the starter in. If he was too tired to pitch any more, bring in another starter rather than trust your lead to a second-rate part-timer. An improvement in fielding also partly explains the decline in total runs. Average errors per team fell from more than 400 for the season of 1894 to 265 by 1908.

The increasing use of "trick" pitches—scuffing the ball or adding external substances (especially spit after about 1904)—has frequently been identified as a major cause for the decline in hitting. By applying saliva to the fingers, the pitcher could remove the natural spin from the ball, causing it to behave in unpredictable ways as it approached the hitter. The term "loading the ball up," as the act of applying spit to the ball was called, had a literal meaning; it added to the ball's weight, making it more difficult to hit hard and for longer distances. Though an exceptionally difficult pitch to master, the spitter greatly improved the performance of several hurlers. After he had learned to throw the spitter, John "Happy Jack" Chesbro of the New York Highlanders saw his mark improve from 21 and 15 in 1903 to 41 and 12 in 1904, and in 1908 Ed Walsh won forty games with the spitter as his main pitch.

Yet the significance of the spitball in explaining the dearth in hitting has been exaggerated. The designation by the major leagues of seventeen players as "legal" spitball pitchers in 1921 provides an opportunity to measure their comparative effectiveness. For the 1909 through 1920 seasons, the seventeen spitballers had a combined earned run average (ERA) of 2.77, whereas major league pitchers as a whole recorded a 2.95 ERA. In other words, the identified spitballers allowed only .18 fewer earned runs per game than did all pitchers. Furthermore, because the spitball, like the knuckleball, was difficult for catchers to handle, the spitball pitchers were more frequently victimized by stolen bases and unearned runs than were the nonspitballers.

Most of the pitching aces of the day were big, strong-armed fastball and curveball specialists rather than spitballers. With the lengthening of the pitching distance in 1893 and the growing practice of placing the pitching slab on a mound of dirt ("the mound"), the sheer size of pitchers began to increase sharply. In 1894 the pitchers were relatively small; they averaged 168 pounds (4 pounds lighter than the hitters) and stood at five feet, ten inches tall, the same height as the hitters. By 1908, however, pitchers (at five feet, eleven inches) averaged an inch and a half taller than the hitters and were an average of 9 pounds heavier (180 pounds versus 171 pounds). Notice also that the pitchers of 1908 weighed a whopping 12 pounds more than the average of their counterparts in 1894.

Perhaps it was little wonder, given the average size of men in that day, that the hitters viewed such star pitchers as Charles "Chief" Bender (185 pounds and six feet, two inches), Walter Johnson (200 pounds and six feet, one inch), Christy Mathewson (195 pounds and six feet, two inches), James "Hippo" Vaughn (215 pounds and six feet, four inches), Richard "Rube" Marquard (180 pounds and six feet, three inches), and Denton "Cy" Young (210 pounds and six feet, two inches) as veritable giants. Statistical cognoscenti will also be interested in learning that a multiple regression analysis indicates that the taller and heavier pitchers in 1908 tended to be more effective than their more diminutive counterparts.

Managers tried to counter pitcher dominance by eking out a run at a time. Hit-and-run plays, base stealing, and bunting, which had been pioneered by the Boston Beaneaters and the Baltimore Orioles in the 1890s, became more popular than ever. "Baseball, year by year, [has] grown more scientific, more a thing of accepted rules, of set routine," declared *Baseball Magazine.*" This slow evolution of the sport displayed itself in batting, in the form of the bunt, the place hit and various [other] manifestations of skills." Exponents of inside baseball completely shunned the long ball. Home runs, which were nearly always of the inside-the-park variety, were so rare that in 1908 the entire Chicago White Sox team hit only three, and in the following year John "Red" Murray of the Giants led the league with seven.

Few hitters any longer held the bat at the end and took a full swing. They shortened the arc of their swing and tried to punch the ball through the infield or over the infielders' heads. Managers would even fine or bench free swingers. To obtain hits, to cause errors, and to sacrifice runners into scoring position, managers frequently used the bunt. Manager Joe McCloskey of the St. Louis Cardinals once required his hitters to bunt seventeen consecutive times. The tactic produced the two runs needed to win the game.

However much they differed from one another in other respects, no two managers were more successful practitioners of the inside game than John McGraw and Connie Mack. Born Cornelius Alexander McGillicuddy, Mack, as part-owner and field manager of the Philadelphia Athletics from 1900 through 1950, built and dismantled two of the most powerful teams in big league history. The first of these won four pennants (1910–11 and 1913–14) and two World Series (both over McGraw's New York Giants).

McGraw, who held the helm of the Giants from 1902 to 1932, captured ten NL pennants and four World Series titles (see table 1).

McGraw and Mack offer a study in contrasts. Although both were of Irish origins, self-made men, and used similar field strategies, Mack, "The Tall Tactician," was of "lace curtain" rather than ordinary Irish stock. He was a lean six feet, one inch and 150 pounds, whereas McGraw, "The Little Napoleon," was a stubby five feet, seven inches and in his latter years decidedly rotund. No one represented Ban Johnson's quest to bring greater respectability to pro baseball more effectively than Mack. Courtly, soft-spoken, and formal, he occupied the dugout in a suit and tie, his stiff white collar spotless and stickpin always in place. He never shouted at umpires or his players and rarely if ever cursed, smoked, or drank. Consistent with his belief that paid ball players should be treated as professional men, he always addressed his own players as "Mister" and expected them to address him as "Mr. Mack." Invariably claiming to be short on financial resources, Mack built his great teams through the early identification, re-

Table 1. Major League Pennant Winners

National League, 1900–1920			
New York Giants	Chicago Cubs	Pittsburgh Pirates	Brooklyn Dodgers
1917	1918	1909	1920
1913	1910	1903	1916
1912	1908	1902	1900
1911	1907	1901	
1905	1906		
1904			

The Philadelphia Phillies (1915), Boston Braves (1914), and Cincinnati Reds (1919) won single flags; the St. Louis Cardinals won none.

American League, 1903–20			
Boston Red Sox	Philadelphia Athletics	Chicago White Sox	Detroit Tigers
1918	1914	1919	1909
1916	1913	1917	1908
1915	1911	1906	1907
1912	1910		
1904	1905		
1903			

Cleveland garnered a flag in 1920, but the New York Highlanders (Yankees), St. Louis Browns, and Washington Senators won no pennants in the 1903–20 era.

cruitment, and nurturing of players with raw talent. Many of his players hailed from the Philadelphia area.

McGraw, on the other hand, approached baseball as a savage struggle for survival. Although he (like Mack) tried to improve the public image of ball players, McGraw believed that the aggressive won and the timid lost. Exceptionally pugnacious, he made life miserable for umpires and opposing teams; he cursed, drank heavily, and subjected his players to merciless reprimands. And, unlike Mack, he was rarely short of financial resources. New York's owners repeatedly allowed him to purchase the experienced players needed to capture championships. Perfectly suited to New York as the nation's center of commerce, high finance, show business, and ethnic diversity, McGraw attracted headlines both on and off the field. Away from the field, he loved parties and highballs and regularly patronized the theater and the track.

⊡ ⊡ ⊡

Professional baseball's cast of players in the early years of the century seemed to offer something for nearly everyone. While blacks remained outside organized baseball and few of the new immigrant stock from southern and eastern Europe had found places on big league rosters, the game was no longer so closely identified with urban, working-class, Irish-Catholic life. Increasing numbers of players came from the Midwest, from the small towns of Ohio, Michigan, Indiana, Illinois, and Wisconsin. Joe Jackson and Ty Cobb were two of the first players to hail from the deep South. Charles Bender, Jim Thorpe, and John Meyers were well-known Native Americans. A few Caucasian Cubans such as Armando Marsans and Adolfo Luque also entered the big league ranks. Black Hispanics, on the other hand, found organized baseball as impenetrable as did black Americans. Baseball men liked to publicize the presence of college players; Steven Riess has found that about a quarter of the players in this era had some college education.

Yet while professional baseball was winning wider support among old-stock, evangelical Protestants and the nation's upper classes than ever before, it fell far short of attaining universal acceptance as a respectable occupation. Many parents of would-be ball players shared the beliefs of Rube Marquard's father, who, on learning that his son was considering a career as a professional ball player, warned, "Ballplayers are no good, and they never will be any good." The players "were considered pretty crude," recalled Sam Crawford in a taped interview with Lawrence Ritter. "[We] couldn't get into the best hotels and all that. And when we did get into a good hotel, they wouldn't boast about having us. Like if we went into the hotel dining room—in a good hotel that is—they'd quick shove us way back in the corner at the very end of the dining room so we wouldn't be too conspicuous. 'Here come the ballplayers!' you know, and back in the corner we'd go." In New York City's Jewish subculture, entertainer Eddie Cantor recalled hearing his grandmother shout at him, "Stop! You-you-you baseball player you! . . . That was the worst name she could call me. To the pious people of the ghetto a baseball player was the king of the loafers."

Unlike today's practices, player recruitment and development were haphazard at best. No teams deployed a bevy of scouts, held regular tryouts, or established an orderly procedure for nurturing a raw rookie into a big league caliber player. In most cases, recruitment began with a minor league manager or owner. For example, Rube Marquard got his break into professional ball in 1906 at the tender age of sixteen, when an older friend who was playing with the Waterloo, Iowa, team wrote to him explaining that his manager needed a left-handed pitcher. Sometimes a manager or owner came to observe a touted semipro sandlotter but left after the game with the contract of a teammate or a player on the opposing team with whom he was equally or more impressed. "It was just my good luck that the one day Bobby Quinn [manager of the Columbus team in the American Association] saw me I had a good day, and the same for when Garry Herrmann [owner of the Cincinnati Reds] saw me," explained Al Bridwell. "They both made snap judgments and took a chance on me." In nearly all instances, the major league teams purchased or drafted their players from the independently owned and managed minor league clubs rather than recruiting them directly off the sandlots.

Rookies sometimes faced formidable obstacles in getting a chance to obtain a starting position. Management had not yet developed a rational procedure for the orderly development of new talent, and veteran players resorted to various stratagems to keep rookies from taking their jobs away from them. "It was practically impossible for a youngster, a rookie, to get up to the plate in batting practice," recalled Fred Snodgrass, a former outfielder of the New York Giants. "A youngster was an outsider and those old veterans weren't about to make it easy for him to take away one of their jobs. Youngsters didn't get much chance to show what we could do. We never really got a proper opportunity during all of spring training." Rookies also had to be able to withstand merciless hazing by the veterans.

Like the popular melodramas of the day, the sport featured a marvelous set of stock characters. Although some of the players were deadly serious about their sport, others approached it with a kind of zany, devil-may-care intensity. "You know, there were a lot of characters in baseball back then," recalled Samuel "Wahoo Sam" Crawford in the 1960s. "Real individualists. Not conformists, like most ball players—and most people—are today." Sportswriters and fans loved to assign nicknames that reflected the idiosyncratic behavior or appearance of their heroes. Nicknames came in a virtual flood. They included Bugs, Babe, the Bald Eagle, Cheese, several Rubes, Wahoo Sam, Mugsy, several Chiefs (Native Americans), Muddy, several Kids, Hod, Dummy (for a deaf mute), Dutch, Stuffy, Gabby, and Hooks, to name a few.

Comical behavior accompanied the players both on and off the field. As reported by Lee Allen, Rube Waddell, a pitching star, accomplished all of the following feats in a single year:

> He began that year sleeping in a firehouse at Camden, New Jersey, and ended it tending bar in a saloon in Wheeling, West Virginia. In between those events he won twenty-two games for the Philadelphia Athletics, played left end for the Business Men's Rugby Football Club of Grand Rapids, Michigan, toured the nation in a melodrama called *The Stain of Guilt,* courted, married, and became separated from May Wynne Skinner of Lynn, Massachusetts, saved a woman from drowning, accidentally shot a friend in the hand, and was bitten by a lion.

This account failed to mention Waddell's drinking binges. *Sporting News* called him "the leading sousepaw" in baseball. Waddell also succeeded in obtaining a special clause in his contract forbidding his bunkmate, Ossee Schrekengost, from eating animal crackers while in bed.

Not so humorous for the New York Giants was the famed "Merkle boner." The dreadful mistake occurred on 23 September 1908 in the midst of a hotly contested pennant race between the New York Giants and the Chicago Cubs. With two outs, the score tied in the last half of the ninth inning, and Giants runners Moose McCormick on third base and Fred Merkle on first base, Al Bridwell lashed an apparently winning single to center field. However, as Giants fans poured onto the field, the jubilant Merkle cut short of second base and ran directly to the clubhouse. In the meantime, Johnny Evers, the Cubs second baseman, alertly stepped on second with a ball that he claimed had been struck by Bridwell. Amidst great confusion, the umpires eventually ruled Merkle out, the score tied, and the game called on account of darkness. McGraw was incensed. "If Merkle was out, then O'Day [the chief umpire] should have cleared the field and resumed the game," he objected. "If not, we won." The game might have been long forgotten had it not been that the Cubs and Giants ended the regular season in a tie. The Cubs then won the playoff game for the NL championship.

Merkle's boner contributed to an even greater tragedy, the death of Harry Pulliam. On being elected president of the NL in 1902, Pulliam, formerly in the front office of the Pittsburgh Pirates, set out to reverse the league's notorious reputation for the unruliness of its players and managers. Unlike his predecessor, Nicholas Young, he tried to back up the decisions of his umpires. The stance won him few friends. Although the owners supported orderliness in principle, they in fact routinely undercut Pulliam's authority by personally paying the fines of their players and managers. In particular, New York owner John T. Brush and his manager, McGraw, carried on a running feud with Pulliam. Pulliam's bitter conflict with the New Yorkers culminated in his decision to support umpire Henry O'Day in the Merkle case. A sensitive man, he suffered a "nervous breakdown" in early 1909. On 28 July 1909 he retired to his room at the New York Athletic Club, put on a dressing gown, stretched out on a sofa, and shot himself through the head.

◨ ◨ ◨

Just as no one could mistake McGraw for Mack, or vice versa, no one could confuse the identities of the game's major heroes on the field of play. Apart from their successes on the mound, the similarities between pitching stars Walter Johnson, nicknamed "The Big Train," and Christy Mathewson, dubbed "Matty" or "The Big Six," stopped at their size; they were both exceptionally big men for their day. From 1907 to 1927, Johnson pitched for the Washington Senators, who were rarely in contention for anything except the league's cellar, while Mathewson hurled for McGraw's mighty New York Giants (1900–1916), who were nearly always in the fight for the league championship.

Relying almost exclusively on a paralyzing fastball, Johnson had 417 wins and only 279 losses for the lowly Senators. For ten seasons in a row he won twenty or more games. He struck out 3,506 hitters and pitched 110 shutouts, the latter an all-time major league mark. His strikeouts are all the more remarkable given that the hitters in the early part of his career carefully guarded the plate rather than swinging freely. In one incredible span he whitewashed the Yankees three times in four days and then after three days' rest won two more consecutive games, for a total of five wins in nine days. Johnson's appeal sprang from more than his performances. Ambling, angular, modest, gentle, given to neither smoke nor drink, and from a farm family, he seemed to embody rural, small-town American virtues.

The tall, blond, and blue-eyed Christy Mathewson, on the other hand, was an urbane, sophisticated version of the muscular Christian athlete. Widely heralded as a college man (though in fact he attended but never graduated from Bucknell), he had, in addition to a fastball that some said was Johnson's equal, a roundhouse curve, his favorite pitch, and a mysterious "fadeaway," which was apparently a screwball. He won 373 and lost only 188 games; he pitched with stunning consistency, earning twenty-two or more victories each season from 1903 through 1914. Mathewson regularly admonished boys against smoking and drinking. Keeping a promise he made to his mother, he never played on Sunday. While serving his country in World War I, he was a victim of poison gas, which eventually contributed to his early death. Apotheosized by the press and held up as an ideal for the nation's youth, no player or manager was more successful in enhancing professional baseball's public respectability. In the words of the video documentary of Lawrence Ritter's *The Glory of Their Times,* "Young ladies could now [safely] ask their escorts to take them to the Polo Grounds to see the college boy play."

John "Honus" Wagner and Tyrus "Ty" Cobb, renowned as the two greatest hitters of the day, also offered sharp contrasts. Wagner played shortstop and hit from the right side, whereas Cobb was an outfielder who swung from the left side of the plate. Of German ethnic stock and nicknamed "The Flying Dutchman," Wagner came from the coal mining region of western Pennsylvania; Cobb, on the other hand, was of old-stock origins and from a small town in Georgia. Wagner was quiet, amiable, and well liked by everyone, whereas Cobb was noisy, combative, and intensely disliked by nearly everyone.

Wagner did everything well. As a member of the Pittsburgh Pirates between 1900 and 1917, the big, barrel-chested, bowlegged Wagner led the NL in batting eight times, in slugging percentage six times, and in stolen bases five times. An idea of his hitting prowess can be gained by comparing his performance with the NL's as a whole. For the eight seasons that he led the NL in batting, Wagner averaged a whopping 97 points above the league average, and his slugging percentage outdistanced the league by nearly 200 points. No shortstop fielded better than Wagner. "He just ate the ball up with his big hands, like a scoop shovel," declared teammate Tommy Leach, "and when he threw it to first base you'd see pebbles and dirt and everything else flying over there along with the ball. It was quite a sight! The greatest shortstop ever. The greatest *everything* ever." Leach exaggerated, but only slightly.

Not in fielding, but with the bat and on the base paths Detroit's Cobb was fully Wagner's equal, if not his superior. In a career that spanned twenty-four seasons (1905–28), "The Georgia Peach" compiled the highest lifetime batting average (.367) and won the league batting championship the most seasons (twelve, nine times in succession) in baseball history. Season after season, he hit more than 100 percentage points above the major league average. Statistics, of course, fail to do Cobb full justice. He had no peer as a master of place hitting. With his spread-handed grip he would bunt if the infield played deep; if the infield tightened up, he would slash the ball through the holes or over the fielder's heads. Though eschewing the long-ball, Cobb led the AL in slugging percentage eight times. His daring on the base paths terrorized opponents. He tried to take an extra base at every opportunity, and he led the league in base stealing on six separate occasions.

Cobb magnified the rugged individualism of the day. He drove himself relentlessly to excel in every facet of the game. To Cobb, baseball was a form of warfare. "When I played ball," Cobb recalled in his autobiography written in 1961, "I didn't play for fun. . . . It's no pink tea, and mollycoddles had better stay out. It's a contest and everything that implies, a struggle for supremacy, a survival of the fittest." Cobb used every weapon at his disposal—his spikes, fists, bat, and his biting tongue—all in an effort to intimidate and defeat his opponents. The other players and fans soon recognized that Cobb was serious, that he was a man so driven by internal demons that his sanity was in doubt. Fans everywhere came out to see the rampaging Cobb, partly in awe of his ability, but also in hopes of seeing him stymied by the local club or witnessing a brawl in which Cobb would be the principal victim.

Instances of Cobb's aggressive behavior off the field were equally legion. Throughout the league he verbally challenged taunting fans; in one instance, he leaped into the stands and struck a fan who happened to be crippled. In 1904, believing that his wife had been insulted by a butcher in an argument over twenty cents' worth of spoiled fish, Cobb went to the

butcher's shop, pulled out the revolver that he always carried, and demanded that the butcher telephone his wife an apology. The butcher naturally
complied, but the butcher's young assistant challenged Cobb to resolve the
issue without the pistol. Cobb, quite willing to accommodate, proceeded
to beat the boy insensate. Cobb was particularly brutal to blacks; on at
least two occasions he struck black women. Nor did Cobb suppress a
deeply entrenched animosity toward Roman Catholics, even though Hugh
Jennings, his longtime manager, was a practicing Catholic.

Cobb evoked fear and respect but rarely affection. On the road, he ate
alone and roomed alone. The depth of the feeling against Cobb by fellow
players was manifested in 1910, when he appeared to have won the AL
batting championship. In the final double-header of the season Napoleon
Lajoie, Cobb's leading contender for the title, made eight hits in eight times
at bat. Six of the hits came from bunts toward third base, which the notoriously slow-footed Lajoie had somehow beaten out. It soon became clear
that the St. Louis Browns had deliberately tried to deny Cobb the crown
(plus a sparkling new Chalmers automobile that went with it) by giving
Lajoie free access to first base. The tactic failed. Cobb retained the title by
less than a single percentage point, and Chalmers subsequently decided to
award both men new cars.

Cobb's ugly behavior and intense drive apparently arose from a combination of circumstances. Born of a proud family in Georgia that had once
owned slaves, Cobb was inordinately defensive of his origins. Teammates,
who were overwhelmingly northerners, soon discovered this sensitivity and,
when he was a rookie, pitilessly hazed him. They called him "Rebel" and,
among other acts, broke his bats, nailed his uniform to the clubhouse wall,
hid his clothes, locked him in bathrooms, and tried to get him into a fight
with the biggest man on the club. Cobb responded violently, eventually
intimidating his teammates.

The bizarre circumstances of his father's death may have contributed to
Cobb's obsession to succeed. "I did it for my father, who was an exalted
man," he explained in his autobiography. "They killed him when he was
still young. But I knew he was watching me and I never let him down."
The mysterious "they" was Cobb's own mother. Suspecting his wife of
unfaithfulness, Cobb's father had gone to her bedroom window to investigate. Apparently mistaking him for an intruder, she fired a fatal shotgun
blast into his stomach. The tragedy occurred just as Cobb was entering
the big leagues. "I had to fight all my life to survive," Cobb later wrote.
"They were all against me . . . but I beat the bastards and left them in the

ditch." In his retirement years, Cobb's symptoms of insanity became more pronounced. He talked frequently of a vague conspiracy to take away his life. When he died in 1961, only three people from organized baseball attended his funeral. Rarely has a more successful, more violent, and more maladjusted personality passed through the annals of American sport.

◻ ◻ ◻

During the first two decades of the twentieth century, professional baseball achieved a new level of maturity and stability as an American institution. The World Series became something of a national holiday, baseball concocted a powerful myth of its uniquely American origins, the concrete and steel parks of the big league clubs became important civic monuments, and the game produced a galaxy of national heroes equaled by few other professions in American life. But then, as the third decade of the new century began, the game had to confront a terrifying challenge to its moral pretensions: the fixing of the 1919 World Series.

8

The Big Fix

In September of 1920 a shocking revelation rocked the nation: The 1919 World Series had been fixed. The worst team ignominy in the history of American sport, soon labeled the Black Sox Scandal or the Big Fix, crowded the Red Scare, the presidential election race pitting James M. Cox against Warren Gamaliel Harding, and every other major story off the front pages of the nation's newspapers. Americans were incredulous. According to baseball legend, a small boy approached "Shoeless Joe" Jackson, one of the conspirators and a star outfielder with the Chicago White Sox. "Say it ain't so, Joe," begged the lad, as tears welled from his eyes. "I am afraid it is, son," Jackson responded.

The wound cut deeply. Boston newsboys condemned the "murderous blow" to the national pastime by the "Benedict Arnolds of baseball." In Joliet, Illinois, an angry fan charged Buck Herzog with being "one of those crooked Chicago ball players." A fight erupted, and Herzog was stabbed, even though he was a member of the Chicago Cubs rather than the White

Sox. The scandal punctured the illusions of future novelist Nelson Algren, then a boy on Chicago's South Side. "Everybody's out for The Buck," he concluded. F. Scott Fitzgerald voiced a similar disillusionment: "It never occurred to me that one man could start to play with the faith of fifty million people—with the singlemindedness of a burglar blowing a safe," reflects a character in *The Great Gatsby*.

If the Cooperstown legend, the building of great baseball parks, the popularity of the World Series, and the enthusiasm for play on the field during the first two decades of the twentieth century had not already done so, the public response to the Big Fix offered conclusive evidence that baseball had achieved a prominent and special place in American life. The fix had practical implications as well. It vividly revealed player grievances, bitter divisions among the owners, and the impotency of baseball's internal governing system. Mobilized by the scandal, the owners scuttled the National Commission. They replaced it with a single commissioner, Judge Kenesaw Mountain Landis, to oversee all of organized baseball.

◫ ◫ ◫

Until the exposure of the big fix in 1920, few Americans dreamed that the ball players might sell their services to gamblers or that the National Agreement of 1903 was about to unravel. Initially, the agreement had functioned reasonably well. It had left in the hands of the individual franchises full "legislative" powers—that is, the owners retained for themselves the authority to decide internal club matters, the power to alter the rules governing the cartel, and the right to make policy for the leagues. "Judicial" powers, on the other hand, were lodged in a three-man National Commission composed of the two major league presidents and a third person chosen by them as chairman. Sometimes hailed as "the Supreme Court of Baseball," the commission interpreted the terms of the National Agreement and decided controversies arising from it. The commission also had limited "executive" powers; it could impose fines and suspensions on those who violated the cartel's rules.

The lengthy service of Ban Johnson, the hard-driving and hard-drinking AL president, and of August "Garry" Herrmann, the major stockholder of the NL's Cincinnati club, lent stability to the commission. Herrmann was acceptable to the AL as the commission's chairman only because he had been a key figure in bringing about the peace between the warring leagues in 1903 and because he was a good friend of Johnson from the days when the latter had been a sportswriter in Cincinnati. But it was Johnson who dominated the commission. Johnson not only had enormous energy, wit, and skills, but his base of power rested on the AL. He ruled the league as a personal fiefdom. As in the past, he, and often he alone, chose new club owners and managers, and they remained his loyal creatures. On the other hand, the faction-prone NL had in the first two decades of the new century four different presidents, all of whom were figureheads.

Through 1910, the most serious challenges confronting major league baseball had little or nothing to do with the commission. One concerned the players. With the conclusion of the Great Baseball War, the Players' Protective Association fizzled out, and the owners, as they had done in the 1890s, slashed player salaries. Baseball wages then slowly drifted upward again, though not proportionately to the rapid rise in owner profits. According to Harold Seymour's careful estimates, by 1910 "established regulars" earned "in the neighborhood of $3,000" per season, a figure much greater than a contemporary steelworker's average annual pay of about $700 or a skilled craftsman's $1,200.

But without a competing league, the players bargained from a weak position. They had only three available responses to owner proposals: play for the salary offered, quit organized baseball, or hold out—refuse to play—until they received more generous terms. Few players explained their intent to hold out quite as graphically or as scatologically as star pitcher Fred Toney did in a letter (discovered by Harold Seymour) to Cincinnati owner Garry Herrmann in 1916. Returning his unsigned contract to Herrmann, Toney wrote, "I see you want to give me a good fucking," he said, but "I'll pick shit with the chickens before I'll play for any less" than $6,000. He would rather quit baseball, the irate pitcher continued, than "be fuck[ed] by no Jew S-B." Toney did continue playing, but no records survive to indicate whether his threat succeeded in winning him $6,000. To counter player holdouts, the owners sometimes used flattery, sometimes appealed to the player's sense of loyalty to his teammates or his manager, and sometimes spelled out the potentially disastrous effects on his family. In the background always lurked the owners' ultimate weapon, the reserve clause. Frank Navin, owner of the Detroit Tigers, even used it to bludgeon superstar Ty Cobb. "You will play for Detroit or you won't play for anybody," Navin warned during a Cobb holdout in 1913.

Discontent stemming from salaries, the draft system, the buying and selling of players, the absence of uniform player contracts, and petty dis-

ciplinary measures, among other grievances, all helped nourish the formation of a new players' union in 1912. Organized by David Fultz, an attorney and a former big league player, the Players' Fraternity grew to 700
members (including minor leaguers). After filing a number of lawsuits
against various clubs for contract violations, in 1913 the fraternity presented the National Commission with seventeen demands, most of which
concerned contract standardization, player releases, and severance payments. Confronted with the possibility of players defecting to the newly
created Federal League, the commission reluctantly granted a few concessions, including the right of big league veterans of ten years to negotiate
with any club they pleased. Except for the last provision, the fraternity
made no effort to challenge the reserve clause or the right of the clubs to
sell and buy players. For several years, the union filed lawsuits on behalf
of both major and minor league players, but the collapse of the Federal
League in 1915 and the lack of adequate player support weakened the
fraternity's bargaining position.

The owners worried much more about the Federal League (FL). In 1914,
James A. Gilmore, a Chicago iron manufacturer, lined up wealthy men in
Chicago, New York, and St. Louis to reorganize the FL into a circuit claiming major league status. Extending generous salary offers, the FL lured
away from their home circuits more than one-third (81) of the big-leaguers
and 140 minor-leaguers (according to the counts of Harold Seymour). The
major league owners responded as they had done during the Players League
war of 1890: They blacklisted players who had deserted organized baseball, obtained court injunctions, and raised player salaries. For example,
Ty Cobb's salary jumped from $9,000 in 1910 to $20,000 in 1915. Overall salary averages more than doubled, climbing from $3,187 in 1913 to
$7,327 in 1915. On the other hand, rather than meet the higher salary
demands, Connie Mack, the parsimonious owner-manager of the 1914
champion Philadelphia Athletics, sold or released all his high-priced stars.

Although the Federal League folded in 1915, its demise was by no means
an unalloyed victory for organized baseball. Low attendance in 1914, rapidly escalating player salaries, and the threat of an FL invasion of New York
drove the major league owners to offer generous terms to the FL's main
financial backers. Three of them, including Harry Sinclair, who was later
to gain notoriety in the Teapot Dome scandal, were invited to buy stock
in NL clubs at bargain prices. In addition, the big league clubs agreed to
pay Sinclair $10,000 annually for fourteen years. On the other hand, the
owners of FL clubs not in direct competition with the majors received lit-

tle or nothing except the revenues from their players' sales. The settlement, which may have cost the majors as much as $5 million, tarnished the image of the owners and offered nothing to the minor league clubs that had had their operations interrupted or been bankrupted by the affair.

When the nation plunged into World War I in the spring of 1917, the owners were unsure how to respond. While noisily proclaiming their patriotism, they eventually tried to carry on play as usual. They neither canceled the 1917 and 1918 seasons nor called on their players to enlist in the armed forces; after all, a massive defection of players to the Army or the Navy would have ravaged team rosters. Instead, the owners made expansive but largely empty gestures. They issued free tickets to servicemen, sponsored military parades through the parks before and after games, and urged the fans to buy war bonds. In addition, in 1917 Ban Johnson ordered AL players to practice daily military drills. Under the supervision of an army sergeant assigned to each team, the fans were treated to the pregame spectacle of the players marching in close-order drill with a baseball bat at right-shoulder arms. The St. Louis Browns, who rarely won anything, carried away Johnson's first prize of $500 for the best-drilled team in the league. *Spalding's Guide* concluded that the drills "anticipated" and "nullified" charges of baseball's "slackerism."

Spalding's Guide was overly optimistic. The draft of 1917 compelled all men between the ages of twenty-one and thirty-five to register, but few players were called up and even fewer volunteered for military duty. In May 1918 Secretary of War Newton D. Baker, reflecting the high emotions of the time, went further; he issued a "work-or-fight" order. It required that all draft-age men, regardless of whether they had been deferred before, must either take an "essential" wartime job or join the armed services. Baker specifically rejected baseball's claim that it was an essential industry. The work-or-fight order soon emptied the dugouts. Some 227 men joined the armed forces, while others fled to such draft-exempt occupations as farming and shipbuilding. For a time (before public exposure prompted them to retreat), shipbuilders openly recruited big league players (among them Joe Jackson) for ostensibly wartime jobs while in fact employing them mainly to strengthen their powerful semipro baseball teams in what a satirist quickly dubbed the "Safe Shelter League." To fill their rosters in 1918, the owners had to turn to under- or overaged players. They also shortened the playing season by a month. Attendance fell. For the minor leagues the situation was even more bleak. Only one circuit, the International League, finished the 1918 season.

◨ ◨ ◨

As professional baseball jubilantly celebrated the return to peacetime, it confronted a new and far more serious challenge than that posed by World War I: the Black Sox Scandal. Even before the opening game of the 1919 World Series, widespread rumors of a fix circulated among players, gamblers, and newspapermen. Suspicions multiplied when the betting odds suddenly shifted from the AL champion Chicago White Sox toward the NL's Cincinnati Reds. Initially, bettors had heavily favored the "invincible" White Sox over the Reds, but by opening day the odds had evened up. The White Sox then lost the nine-game series five games to three, adding to doubts about the series's integrity.

Yet many observers shrugged off their misgivings. "Anything can happen in baseball" was already one of the game's favorite clichés, and the onfield performance of the players provided no conclusive or manifest evidence of a fix. Curiously, perhaps because they had not received full payments as promised, several of the "Black Sox" played as well or better than the "Clean Sox." For example, superstar Joe Jackson, one of the alleged game-throwers, hit a series-leading average of .375, and future Hall of Famer Eddie Collins, who was not in on the fix, hit a mere .226.

In fact, had it not been for a persistent reporter, Hugh Fullerton of the Chicago *Herald and Examiner,* the fix might never have been exposed. The day after the series had been completed, Fullerton, a longtime gadfly to the owners, predicted that seven of the White Sox would not be in uniform when spring training opened for the 1920 season. In responding to Fullerton, White Sox owner Charles Comiskey faced painful choices. If he exposed a fix, he would destroy his ball club and his million-dollar equity in his ball players. If he tried to hide the fix, it was a submission to suspected corruption that, if publicly disclosed, might boomerang. Comiskey decided on a rejoinder that he hoped would protect his ball club while simultaneously creating the illusion that he was doing his best to ferret out wrongdoing. He announced to the press that "I believe my boys fought the battles of the recent World Series on the level, as they have always done," but at the same time he offered, a $20,000 (later reported as $10,000) reward to anyone who could provide a "single clue" implicating any of his ball players in game-dumping.

Initially, Comiskey's ploy seemed to work. "Because a lot of dirty, long-nosed, thick-lipped, and strong-smelling gamblers butted into the World Series," responded *The Sporting News,* ". . . stories were peddled that there

was something wrong with the games. . . . Comiskey has met that by offering $10,000 for any sort of clue that will bear out such a charge . . . [but]
there will be no takers, because there is no such evidence." Describing Hugh
Fullerton as an "erratic writer," *Baseball Magazine*, the game's other leading journal, dismissed a fix as preposterous. Fullerton remained undaunt-
ed: In December 1919 he published a new series of articles demanding an
investigation of the rumors, and he named suspected fixers, including
Arnold Rothstein, the kingpin of the nation's gamblers.

With its exciting pennant races and Babe Ruth's phenomenal fifty-four
home runs, play in the 1920 season temporarily pushed misgivings about
the series into the background. But then news on 4 September 1920 of a
fixed game between the Philadelphia Phillies and the Chicago Cubs rekin-
dled suspicions. Three days after the story broke, a Cook County, Illinois,
grand jury convened to investigate not only the Cubs-Phillies game but
baseball gambling in general. The coverup then began to unravel. A small-
time Philadelphia gambler, Billy Maharg, who was embittered because he
had not received his promised cut of the take from the 1919 fix, provided
damning specifics. To lose the series, Maharg reported, eight Chicago players had been promised $100,000, most of which they never received. A
day later, two of the conspirators called before the grand jury cracked: star
pitcher Eddie Cicotte and outfielder Joe Jackson. During more than two
hours of tearful testimony, Cicotte related in detail how the players had
dumped the series.

Despite its findings, the grand jury in its final report expressed the prevailing faith in baseball. "Baseball is more than a national game," it asserted, "it is an American institution." Reflecting the postwar fears of social
unrest, the grand jury found in baseball a powerful means of social control. "In the deplorable absence of military training in this country," the
report continued, "baseball and other games having 'team play' spirit offer the American youth an agency for the development that would be entirely lacking were it relegated to the position to which horse racing and
boxing have fallen." Specifically, the grand jury claimed, "the national
game promotes respect for proper authority, self-confidence, fairminded-
ness, quick judgment and self-control."

The trial, held nearly a year later in August 1921, was something of a
farce. By then, Cook County had a new prosecuting attorney, and three
of his predecessor's assistant attorneys had joined the defense. Only the
persistence of Ban Johnson, who was determined to embarrass Comiskey,
enabled the authorities to gather enough evidence and witnesses to make

a plausible case against the eight conspirators. No explicit Illinois statute forbade fixing ball games; the judge ruled that the players could be found guilty only of a willful conspiracy to defraud the public. In the meantime, the earlier player confessions—which the players now repudiated—had mysteriously disappeared from the grand jury files. (Later, at a trial in which Joe Jackson sued Comiskey for back pay, the player confessions mysteriously reappeared—in the possession of Comiskey's attorney!) This left the testimony of two small-time gamblers as the only substantial evidence against them. After a few hours of deliberation, the jury acquitted all eight players. The spectators in the courtroom roared their approval, and several jurors joined spectators in carrying the players around the courtroom on their shoulders. That evening the jury and the players retired to an Italian restaurant on Chicago's West Side, where they celebrated into the small hours of the morning.

Their joy was short-lived. Judge Kenesaw Mountain Landis, the newly appointed commissioner of baseball, banished the eight men from organized baseball for life. "Regardless of the verdict of juries," Landis solemnly announced, "no player that throws a ball game; no player that sits in a conference with a bunch of crooked players and gamblers where the ways and means of throwing games are discussed, and does not promptly tell his club about it, will ever play professional ball." Landis held firm to his word. Although several of the conspirators played on semipro teams and in outlaw ball, they never again played on teams under the jurisdiction of Landis or his successors.

Why had the fix happened? In retrospect, the scandal should not have been so surprising. Despite professional baseball's unique place in American life, it had always been a part of a larger world of commercial entertainment. Wagering on ball games had been commonplace since the middle of the nineteenth century. Baseball pools existed in all big league cities. Purchasing a weekly pool ticket for as little as ten cents could result in winnings for picking a team that won the most games, scored the most runs, and so forth. By publishing odds on games and providing weekly totals of wins, hits, and runs, the newspapers cooperated with pool managers. This was just one end of the scale; although the small wagers placed in pools amounted to thousands of dollars weekly, the sums paled beside those bets handled by professional gamblers. Like those engaged in other forms of commercial entertainment, many of the players, managers, and owners had close links to the nation's urban demimonde. They spent much of their spare time at the race tracks, theaters, hotel lobbies, and saloons, where they consorted with publicly known gamblers. Most big league players, including even Ty Cobb, did not hesitate to bet on themselves or their teams.

Dumping the 1919 series was not an isolated instance of game-fixing. According to a list compiled by Bill James, during the 1917–27 era, thirty-eight players were either banished from baseball or at the least had serious charges brought against them for game-throwing. A file drawer full of circumstantial evidence pointed to Hal Chase, a classy first baseman who played for five separate big league clubs, as the king of the fixers. Chase was implicated in trying to dump more than a dozen games, including the 1919 series itself. Terrified that disclosure might undermine public confidence in the game and result in the loss of valuable property (in the form of players), the owners had tried to maintain a cloak of absolute secrecy while suppressing all evidence of game-fixing.

Besides being subject to the game's general moral climate, the White Sox players were especially vulnerable to bribery. Expecting that attendance would continue to slump as it had during the war years, the owners had cut salaries for 1919. Comiskey had been especially enthusiastic about seizing the opportunity to reduce his salary costs. Despite having reputedly the best and most profitable team in baseball, the miserly Comiskey may have paid his players the least. The $10,000 bribe that Cicotte received for his part in throwing the 1919 series was nearly double his regular season salary, and so it was with the bribes promised to nearly all the conspirators.

□ □ □

Even before the Big Fix, internal dissension threatened to wreck the entire structure of organized baseball. Apart from accumulated petty annoyances within its ranks, more serious conflicts arose among the owners over rights to player contracts. As early as 1915, several NL owners, led by Barney Dreyfus of Pittsburgh, began to talk about choosing an outsider to replace Garry Herrmann as chair of the National Commission. That Herrmann had sided with Johnson in awarding George Sisler's contract to the AL's St. Louis Browns rather than to the NL's Pittsburgh Pirates had infuriated Dreyfus. Despite the equal or superior merits of the Browns' claim on Sisler, the decision fed the suspicion among NL owners that Herrmann was a mere puppet of Ban Johnson.

Moreover, Johnson could no longer rule his own league uncontested. Johnson and his longstanding ally, Charles Comiskey, had bitterly parted

ways, and new owners Jacob Ruppert and Tillinghast Huston of the Yankees and Harry Frazee of the Red Sox owed no fealty to Johnson. Unlike
other AL owners, they had bought their way into baseball without the
benefit of Johnson's aid or advice. Regardless of the stance of Johnson, the
wealthy Yankee owners were determined to pour money into making their
team a contender with the Giants for the affection of New York fans.

The sale of Boston pitching ace Carl Mays to the Yankees brought the
conflict between the newcomers and Johnson to a head. The controversy
began on 13 July 1919, when Mays, after having completed the second
inning of a game in Chicago, stalked off the diamond, dressed, and returned
by the next train to Boston. He offered no explanation for his abrupt departure, neither to his teammates nor to his manager. (Mays had a notoriously truculent disposition; earlier in the season he had fired a ball into
the stands at a heckler.) A rumor circulated that he had deliberately provoked the incident in hopes of being traded to the Yankees, who paid more
generous salaries than the Red Sox. Regardless, Johnson ruled that no club
could obtain the pitcher until he had been restored in good standing with
the Red Sox. Ignoring Johnson, Frazee traded Mays to the Yankees for
$40,000 and two second-string pitchers. Enraged by the defiance of his
edict, Johnson promptly canceled the trade and suspended Mays.

The Yankee owners refused to acquiesce. Instead, they stunned Johnson
and the entire baseball world by announcing that, rather than resolve the
issue within the confines of the cartel, they would take it to the courts. On
a request by the Yankees, a New York court issued injunctions restrain-
ing Johnson. In its final ruling, the court concluded that Johnson had no
authority to interfere with contracts between the players and the owners.
Before the year was out, three AL owners threatened to join with the eight
NL teams and form a new National League.

Although the Mays affair opened a giant fissure within the AL, it was
only one of several serious rifts in organized baseball's unity. Earlier in 1919
the minor leagues had pulled out of the National Agreement. While as-
senting to a continuation of the player reservation system, the minors refused to allow the big leagues to continue drafting their players. In the
meantime, Garry Herrmann was swept from office. Supported by the NL
owners, the new president of the league, John Heydler, declined to vote
for Herrmann, whereas Johnson refused to support anyone but Herrmann.
Caught in the maelstrom, Herrmann resigned. The stalemate over the
chairmanship left the National Commission impotent. Johnson remained
as AL president until 1927, but beginning with the Mays affair and cul-

minating with the appointment of Landis as commissioner of baseball in
1921, he was shorn of his once-great powers.

In the meantime, the exposure of the White Sox's perfidy drove the
owners to adopt a far more radical solution to their governance problem
than they would otherwise have done. In 1919, before public knowledge
of the fix, the owners had received a report authored by Albert D. Lasker,
a Chicago advertising man and a stockholder in the Cubs, which called
for a new, more powerful three-man commission to be composed of persons entirely independent of organized baseball. Because the Lasker plan
would have sharply reduced the traditional powers of the owners, it initially received a cool reception, but the grand jury revelations of the fixed
series frightened the owners. Convinced that something substantial had to
be done to restore public confidence in the integrity of professional baseball and anxious to reduce the power of Ban Johnson, several owners revived the Lasker Plan. They also bandied about the names of some of the
most prominent men in American life to head the new commission—former
president William Howard Taft, General John J. Pershing, Major General
Leonard Wood, Senator Hiram Johnson, and Judge Kenesaw Mountain
Landis. In the end, they settled on Landis.

Landis seemed to offer the perfect persona for baseball's problems. Although the tobacco-chewing federal judge was narrowly educated, uncon-
cerned about legal niceties, vain, petty, and profane, he could help relieve
baseball's tainted image. Whereas the owners came from the big cities and
were in several cases of recent ethnic stock, Landis was of small-town,
midwestern, Protestant origins. Even his gaunt, tough, hungry appearance
contrasted sharply with the portly, soft, satisfied look of the owners. His
very name—Kenesaw Mountain—evoked a sense of granitelike solidity.
Landis had a reputation for sternness. As a federal district judge for the
Northern Illinois district, he had dared to fine the mighty Standard Oil
Company a whopping $29 million for illegal rebating practices and had
handed out harsh jail sentences to radicals, socialists, and opponents of
World War I. Moreover, the owners owed Landis, who was an enthusiastic fan of the Chicago Cubs, a large debt of gratitude. By procrastinating
in making a decision in 1915, Landis had protected organized baseball from
an antitrust suit filed by the Federal League. "Both sides must understand,"
he admonished at that time, "that any blows at . . . baseball would be regarded by this court as a blow to a national institution."

Landis exacted an extraordinarily high price for his services. The desperate owners not only agreed to an astronomical salary of $50,000, sev-

en times what Landis received as a federal judge, but they shoved aside the Lasker plan for a three-man commission in favor of making Landis the lone commissioner of baseball. According to the new National Agreement of 1921, Landis essentially duplicated the role within organized baseball that he had enjoyed as a federal judge, including long tenure (seven-year terms), financial security, and sweeping powers. He could investigate anything "suspected" of being "detrimental to the best interests of the national game." If he determined that leagues, individual club owners, or individual players had engaged in behavior harmful to the sport, he could suspend, fine, or banish the guilty parties. The owners even imposed on themselves a combination loyalty oath and gag order, one that required them "to loyally support their commissioner," to "acquiesce in his decisions even when [they] believed them mistaken," and not to "discredit the sport by criticism of him or one another."

Dubbed by the press as the "Czar of Baseball," Landis quickly established an image of himself as the great protector of baseball from all who would assault it. In particular, it was believed that he defended the fans and the players against the rapacious owners. "He was Commissioner of all baseball," wrote J. G. Taylor Spink, publisher of *The Sporting News* and a longtime critic, "he always felt he was the ball player's man and the fan's man on baseball's supreme body." Landis had frequent disagreements with individual owners and even went so far as to order Charles A. Stoneham and John J. McGraw of the New York Giants to divest themselves of their stock in race tracks located in Cuba and New York City. This lent credibility to the belief that the commissioner represented the fans and the players rather than the owners.

Yet the realities of the Landis reign were another matter. It was, of course, the owners who appointed him, who paid his salary, and who could fire him. Although prone to bluster and inflated rhetoric, Landis treated the questionable actions of the owners far more gingerly than he did those of the players. He took no action against Stoneham when the Giants' owner was indicted for perjury and mail fraud in 1923 and 1924. Nor did he prohibit Stoneham's continued fraternization with gambling king Arnold Rothstein; Rothstein regularly watched games in the comfort of Stoneham's personal box at the Polo Grounds. Landis rarely intervened in trades or internal club matters. On the one major issue on which a clear majority of the owners opposed him—the farm system—he ultimately capitulated.

Although Landis's decisions regarding players often seemed inconsistent and arbitrary, if not incomprehensible, economist Clark Nardinelli has concluded that they form a clear pattern. Landis had no mercy in handing down the most severe penalties to any player whose actions or reputation posed even the remotest threat to his personal power or to that of the baseball cartel. Thus, he banished Benny Kauff, for example, not so much for allegedly stealing an auto (a charge for which Kauff had been acquitted by a jury), but because Kauff had had the audacity earlier to jump his contract and play in the Federal League. By the same token, he reinstated players who had been thrown out of the game by the league presidents in order to establish the commissioner as the sole person who enjoyed such authority. In short, Nardinelli concludes, Landis was a "skillful and ruthless cartel enforcer" who acted to protect the owners from each other and from outside foes.

If Landis was professional baseball's moral "savior," it was the United States Supreme Court that furnished him and the owners with the freedom to erect a cartel unencumbered by the threat of intervention based on federal law. All of the Federal League's clubs save Baltimore had dropped their antitrust suits against the major leagues. Having received no remuneration from the peace settlement, the Baltimore owners continued their court action. In 1922, Justice Oliver Wendell Holmes Jr., speaking for a unanimous court, declared that professional baseball games did not constitute a "trade or commerce in the commonly-accepted use of the words." In a rather tortuous definition of terms, Holmes reasoned that the personal effort of ball players was "not related to production" and therefore could not be involved in commerce. Nor was interstate movement essential to their activity, for the movement of ball players across state lines was simply "incidental" to their playing ball.

Whatever the merits of baseball's exemption from the antitrust laws, the decision provided a legal umbrella for the agreements on which the professional baseball cartel rested. As Norman Rosenberg has argued, the 1922 decision, plus the owners' relinquishment of their right to publicly criticize each other or Landis and to appeal his decisions to the courts, permitted professional baseball to establish its own "private self-government." Baseball was (and remains, though by the 1980s encumbered by a new body of legal strictures) the only professional sport to enjoy this special privilege.

❊　❊　❊

Although it incurred some serious damage to its standing as the national game, organized baseball successfully navigated through the perils of player unrest, a competing big league, World War I, factionalism, and the Black Sox Scandal. With the National Agreement of 1921, it instituted a new, more powerful governing structure, and the Supreme Court in 1922 extended legal protection to the cartel. In the meantime, George Herman "Babe" Ruth's mighty home runs drove all such baseball news far into the distant background.

9

The Age of Ruth

The annals of the national game include many awesome giants, among them Albert Spalding, King Kelly, Ty Cobb, Walter Johnson, Kenesaw Mountain Landis, Leroy "Satchel" Paige, Ted Williams, Jackie Robinson, and Henry Aaron, but none of them occupies a place equal to that of Babe Ruth. Ruth pushes aside all contenders; he is the Paul Bunyan of baseball history. "All of the lies about him are true," teammate Joe Dugan once exclaimed. Even in our own age, one that takes a special delight in smashing false idols, Ruth remains the colossal demigod of sports. His home run totals established an undefinable benchmark for outstanding performances in all fields of human endeavor. Moreover, few men have so perfectly fulfilled the American dream of success. Ruth's life story comforted and reassured those who feared that the United States was no longer a nation in which a poor boy could rise from lowly origins to fame and fortune.

Ruth likewise holds a central place in important changes that transformed the national pastime. When supplemented by a booming prosperity, Ruth's exploits, far more than Landis's stern edicts against fixes and fixers, triggered a renewed interest in major league baseball. Attendance in the 1920s reached all-time highs. Ruth was a pivotal figure in establishing the greatest dynasty in baseball history, that of the New York Yankees. During Ruth's career, the Yankees captured three consecutive pennants on two separate occasions (1921–23 and 1926–28) and won yet another flag in 1932. Ruth was also the catalyst for a great revolution in hitting. During his career, the pendulum swung away from the pitchers to the hitters. Beginning with the AL's 1920 season, the hitters went on a rampage that continued through the 1941 season before it finally subsided during the World War II era.

◨ ◨ ◨

The hitting revolution came suddenly and unexpectedly (see table 2). Although no one recognized it at the time, the abbreviated 1919 AL season hinted at the mighty upheaval ahead. In the AL, average runs per game rose from 7.3 to 8.2, and Ruth, in his first season as a full-time outfielder, hit twenty-nine home runs, thirteen more than the AL record set by John "Buck" Freeman in 1903. The 1919 season proved to be a modest beginning for Ruth. In the very next year, he hit an epic 54 home runs (more than any other AL team combined except the Yankees), batted .376, walked

Table 2. The Great Breakthrough in Hitting, 1919–21

American League			
Seasons	Batting Averages	Runs/Game	Home Runs
1901–18 (avg.)	.253	7.9	198
1919	.268	8.2	241
1920	.283	9.5	370
1921	.292	10.2	477
1922–41 (avg.)	.281	9.6	630

National League			
Seasons	Batting Averages	Runs/Game	Home Runs
1901–18 (avg.)	.254	7.8	198
1919	.258	7.3	206
1920	.274	7.9	261
1921	.289	9.2	460
1922–41 (avg.)	.279	9.3	604

148 times (51 more than the nearest competitor in either league), scored
158 runs, knocked in 137 runs, and compiled an astonishing slugging
percentage of .847.

With Ruth at the forefront, the AL's total offensive output for the 1920
season jumped sharply. The AL batting average climbed to .283, ten points
higher than the previous twentieth-century record set in 1911, and seasonal
home run output leaped to 370, 112 more than the previous twentieth-
century high in 1902. The NL lagged a season behind, but in 1921 it also
witnessed a sharp increase in offensive statistics. Except for home runs,
which were to continue a sharp ascent into the 1930s, the breakthroughs
achieved in the 1920 and 1921 seasons became the standards for next two
decades.

Efforts to explain the great breakthrough in hitting in the 1919–21 era
have occasioned one of the sharpest debates in baseball history. Four theories have won rabid adherents as the explanation for the breakthrough: (1)
the introduction of a new, more resilient baseball, or the "rabbit ball" conspiracy; (2) a rule change beginning in 1920 that prohibited all "trick" pitches, including especially the spitball; (3) the use of more baseballs per game
and the reduction in the discoloration of the ball, which was mainly the result
of Ray Chapman's death by a pitch during the 1920 season; and (4) the
increasing popularity of "free swinging," a new batting style inspired pri-
marily by Babe Ruth. (A fifth explanation, the "cozy" ballpark theory, might
be added to this list; Philip Lowry, however, has found that the outfield fences
of this era were much farther from the plate than those of today.)

The rabbit ball conspiracy was, and remains to this day, a popular theory to account for the sudden deluge in hitting. Although the claim was
hotly denied by big league authorities, proponents of the interpretation
insist that the big leagues introduced a "juiced-up" ball as a way of coun-
teracting the decline in attendance after 1910. Recently, however, Pete
Palmer, John Thorn, Bill James, and William Curran have subjected the
lively ball theory to a thorough reexamination and found it wanting. In
the first place, they ask, if the ball had been made more resilient, why should
league authorities bother to deny it? The officials did freely admit that in
1920 the manufacturer of league balls substituted Australian for American yarn; some speculated that because the foreign yarn was livelier or
could be wrapped more tightly, it was responsible for the hitting barrage.

The timing of improved offensive statistics also provides weak support
for the conspiracy theory. When was the lively ball introduced? The leagues
admitted that cork had been substituted for rubber as the ball's center in

1910, but, despite a brief interlude of improved hitting, hitting as a whole after 1910 fell below the previous decade. If a lively ball was first used in 1919, then Babe Ruth was about the only beneficiary of it. If it was introduced in 1920, then the NL failed to take advantage of the new ball. Finally, a test conducted by the Bureau of Standards found the 1920 ball to be no more elastic than its immediate predecessors.

Instead of crediting a new ball, the recent revisionists conclude that a large share of the improved hitting can be attributed to the abolition of the spitball prior to the 1920 season. The timing of the rule change fits perfectly the breakthrough in the AL, but, as previously noted, the NL failed to better its offensive output much until the following season. Furthermore, given that all established spitball pitchers were exempted from the new ban, it does not seem plausible that the stricture could explain the abruptness of the breakthrough. In other words, the seasons of 1920 and 1921 must have witnessed only a slight reduction in the total number of spitballs thrown. That the major leagues in 1921 excused a group of seventeen veteran spitball pitchers from the rule for their entire careers also provides an opportunity to test statistically the long-term impact of the spitter (see table 3). Both before and after the ban, the identified spitballers had better earned run averages than pitchers as a whole, but the spitballers did not escape the terrors of the hitting revolution. Like all pitchers, they too saw their earned run averages soar during the 1920s and 1930s. Finally, an indeterminate number of pitchers, perhaps as many as 20 percent, continued to throw the spitter surreptitiously.

The third theory, that the ban on discolored balls and the use of more new balls per game caused the hitting breakthrough, also has its limitations. In earlier times, at the direction of the stingy owners, the umpires

Table 3. Earned Run Averages for Spitballers vs. All Pitchers, 1909–34

	1909–20	1921–34
All pitchers	2.95	4.15
All identified spitballers	2.77	3.72

Note: These dates represent the seasons in which identified spitballers pitched. It thus compares the pitching performances of one or more of the spitballers during these seasons with those of major league pitchers as a whole. Because the seventeen exempted pitchers were by definition veterans, one might reasonably expect them to be more effective from the 1921 season on than the other pitchers, which always included untried rookies. On the other hand, as the spitballers aged, one would expect their performance to diminish.

had tried to limit the number of balls used per game to two or three. Fans had to return balls hit into the stands. A few innings of play plus the deliberate actions of the players invariably darkened the balls with dirt, grass stains, tobacco juice, and licorice, making them more difficult to see. Furthermore, as the balls were repeatedly pounded by the hitters, they became less resilient.

Although there are no comprehensive statistics on the quantity of balls used during the great breakthrough era, a rule banning any "intentional" discoloration of the ball beginning in the 1920 season and the death of Ray Chapman from a pitch thrown by Carl Mays in August 1920 encouraged the use of more fresh balls in each game. As an explanation for the hitting revolution, however, timing again weakens the argument. The AL hitting barrage was already well under way when Chapman was killed, and as previously indicated, the NL hitting continued to be low until the 1921 season. Nonetheless, the long-term improvement in hitting surely owed something to the practice of using cleaner and newer balls. The 1922 *Reach Guide* reported that the pitchers complained about "the number of new balls thrown constantly into the games by the umpires" and the difficulty of getting "a proper grip on them." In response to complaints about the grip, the umpires were ordered to rub down balls before they were put into play, and the pitchers were given permission to apply small amounts of resin to the balls. In the 1930s, when team profits declined because of the Great Depression, the owners again succeeded in reducing the number of balls used, which may account for some decline in offense during the latter half of that decade.

After a careful examination of the four theories, the evidence points mainly in one direction: that the success of Babe Ruth was the most important reason for the hitting revolution. In the 1890s many if not most of the hitters had taken full, unencumbered swings, but during the first two decades of the twentieth century, the heyday of inside baseball, nearly all the batters choked the bat and swung in a shortened, choplike motion. The conventional wisdom of inside baseball had long held that a shortened swing was far more productive than a full swing, but Ruth's astonishing offensive totals left that truism in serious doubt. Had Ruth been playing every day in Yankee Stadium or an equivalent-sized ball park, as Gary Gillette has observed, he might have inaugurated the home-run barrage well before 1920.

"We are irresistibly impelled to see in Babe Ruth the true cause for the amazing advance in home runs," concluded F. C. Lane as early as 1921 in

Baseball Magazine. Ruth had infected others with the "home run fever," Lane added. "There is a disposition on the part of managers not to hold their men back, but rather to encourage them." Apparently, AL hitters began to imitate Ruth first, followed a season later by growing numbers of NL players. "Almost any batter that has it in him to wallop the ball," wrote Lane in 1923, "is swinging from the handle of the bat with every ounce of strength that nature placed in his wrists and shoulders." So that they could swing harder, most of the sluggers used thinner-handled bats that concentrated more weight in the barrel.

◻ ◻ ◻

Not only did the hitters who copied Ruth's full swings smash out more home runs, but they also hit for high averages. The hitters seemed to be striking the ball more squarely by taking a full swing than they had been able to do with a shortened swing. Confirming this point, during the 1920s and 1930s strikeouts per 100 at bats sank to an all-time low. Ruth himself led the AL in batting in 1924 and was among the top five hitters in the league for eight seasons. Had it not been for the overpowering presence of Ruth, the NL's Rogers Hornsby of the St. Louis Cardinals probably would have been the decade's premier baseball hero. Like Ruth, Hornsby was a slugger who hit for both a high average and a plethora of home runs. For the 1920 through 1925 seasons, Hornsby won six batting titles, exceeded the .400 mark three times, and captured three NL triple crowns, simultaneously leading the league in batting, home runs, and runs batted in.

In the 1920s, all twentieth-century offensive records quickly fell. Whereas only four batters in the first two decades of the century had hit .400 or better, eight hitters achieved this distinction in the 1920s. Whereas the NL as a whole hit only .239, and only five men batted over .300 in 1908, more than fifty exceeded that mark in 1930, and in that same season the league as a whole hit a record-shattering .303. The high marks in the late 1920s may have been abetted by the introduction of a new, cushioned, cork-centered ball in 1925. Regardless, league batting averages returned to the .280s in the 1930s, although home run totals continued to climb well above those of the previous decade.

Even in the face of the sluggers' manifest success in producing runs, no manager, not even Miller Huggins of the New York Yankees, completely abandoned the tactics of the earlier era. In the 1920s and 1930s the sacrifice and the hit-and-run play remained common (and they remain so even today), but base stealing declined sharply, and with increasing frequency managers permitted their hitters to swing freely. Even Ty Cobb began to swing more freely; in 1925 he became the first player in the twentieth century to hit five home runs in two games. Perhaps nothing signified the triumph of the hitting revolution more than the acquiescence to it by Connie Mack and John McGraw, the two reigning patriarchs of inside baseball.

Although publicly contemptuous of Ruth, McGraw quickly recognized that for the Giants to compete successfully in the new game they had to develop more punch at the plate. He went so far in 1920 as to urge the Giants' owners to offer the St. Louis Cardinals $300,000 for Rogers Hornsby, a stunning figure nearly three times what the Yankees had sacrificed to obtain Ruth only a year earlier and one that could have purchased any one of several big league franchises. In 1921 the Giants sent a $75,000 check to Seattle for a hard-hitting prospect, Bill Cunningham, and they obtained the Philadelphia Phillies' Emil "Irish" Meusel for cash and players worth some $100,000. Never again did McGraw rely solely on team speed, clever tactics, and good pitching. His championship team of 1924, for example, stole only 82 bases, far fewer than the 347 thefts of his pennant-winning 1911 nine. For the remainder of his managerial career, McGraw's teams featured powerful sluggers.

Mack's 1929–31 Athletics, considered one of the premier teams in major league history, were even more offensively potent than McGraw's Giants. Only the Yankees of Ruth and Lou Gehrig exceeded the home run totals of the powerful Athletics. Although aided by an excellent pitching staff paced by Robert "Lefty" Grove, sluggers Al Simmons, Jimmie Foxx, and Mickey Cochrane terrorized AL pitchers. By cutting off the sleeves from his uniform, presumably to give his arms more freedom of movement, Foxx revealed the mighty forearms and biceps of a professional wrestler. He was nicknamed "The Beast." As observed by William Curran, Simmons's batting stance reflected the change in thinking that had overtaken big league managers. A right-handed hitter, Simmons hit with "his foot in the bucket," that is, with his left foot planted as near the outside of the batter's box as legally permitted. Before World War I, every manager and coach in baseball would have tried to get Simmons to bat "normally," but by the late 1920s wiser men had learned not to tamper with success.

The hitting barrage soon reached beyond the majors into all levels of baseball. Minor league batting averages and home run totals soared. By 1924 in the International and Pacific Coast leagues, which stood atop the bush league classification system, batting averages climbed to .290 and

.298, while home runs increased to 693 and 930, respectively. At three steps lower, in the Class D Western Association, the Okmulgee (Oklahoma) Chiefs hit .328 as a team and the league smashed out a record-shattering 1,147 home runs. In 1930, an entire league crashed through an imagined barrier when all eight clubs in the American Association hit more than .300.

◻ ◻ ◻

Babe Ruth was much more than simply the quintessential slugger who reigned over the great revolution in hitting. No modern athletic hero has exceeded Ruth's capacity to project multiple images of brute power, the natural, uninhibited man, and the fulfillment of the legendary American success formula. Ruth was living proof that the lone individual could still rise from mean, vulgar beginnings to fame and fortune, to a position of public recognition equaled by few men in American history. His mighty home runs represented a dramatic finality, a total clearing of the bases with one mighty swat.

Ruth saw himself as an exemplar of the classic American success story. "The greatest thing about this country," according to his ghost-written autobiography, "is the wonderful fact that it doesn't matter which side of the tracks you were born on, or whether you're homeless or homely or friendless. The chance is still there. I know." Ruth encouraged the legend that he had been an orphaned child. Although the story had no basis in fact, his early years were indeed grim. His saloon-keeping German-American father and sickly mother had no time for the lad; he received little or no parental affection. By his own admission, he was a "bad kid" who smoked, chewed tobacco, and engaged in petty thievery. When he was seven, his parents sent him to the St. Mary's Industrial Home for Boys, an institution in Baltimore run by the Xaverian order for orphans, young indigents, and delinquents. Except for brief interludes at home, Ruth spent the next twelve years at St. Mary's. There, as a teenager, he won a reputation for his baseball prowess, and in 1914 he signed a contract with the Baltimore Orioles of the International League. In the same year the Boston Red Sox signed him as a left-handed pitcher. Six years later the Yankees purchased him for the then-astronomical sum of $125,000 plus a loan of $300,000.

Ruth never had to struggle for success in baseball. He was born with both pitching and hitting skills. Converted from the best southpaw pitcher in baseball to an outfielder, he initially surprised everyone with his ability to hit home runs. From 1918 through 1934, he led the AL in home runs twelve times with an average of more than forty per season; from 1926 through 1931 he averaged slightly more than fifty homers per season. Ruth was no mere slugger. His lifetime batting average of .342 has been exceeded by few players in big league history.

Ruth's feats and personality ran counter to the dominant world of assembly lines, bureaucracies, and scientific management. Ruth was the antithesis of rationality and science. Whereas Ty Cobb relied on "brains rather than brawn," or as he put it, the "hit-and-run, the steal and the double-steal, the bunt in all its varieties, the squeeze, the ball hit to the opposite field and the ball punched through openings in the defense for the single," Ruth always went for the fences. Ruth, according to baseball writer F. C. Lane in 1921, "throws science to the wind and hews out a rough path for himself by the sheer weight of his own unequaled talents." Ruth embodied the public preference for a hero of brute strength who offered quick, decisive solutions rather than one who methodically used cunning and finesse to achieve his goals.

The public loved Ruth. "He has become a national curiosity," reported the *New York Times* as early as 1920, "and the sightseeing Pilgrims who daily flock into Manhattan are as anxious to rest eyes on him as they are to see the Woolworth Building." New technology in the form of action photography in newspapers and moving pictures brought images of Ruth to millions who never had a chance to see him personally. Even today, the old, grainy, silent black-and-white movies revealing a corpulent Ruth taking a mighty swing, mincing around the bases, and waving at the crowds evoke special feelings. Everywhere in the league, the fans poured out to the ballparks to see the Yankees play, apparently caring little whether the home team won or lost but hoping to see the Babe hammer a pitch out of the park. Even Ruth's mighty swings that failed to connect brought forth a chorus of awed "Ooooooohs," as if the audience realized the enormous power that had gone to waste and the narrow escape that the pitcher had temporarily enjoyed. Each day, millions turned to the sports page of their newspaper to see whether Ruth had hit another home run.

Ruth had a flair for the dramatic moment. Perhaps none in the history of sport equaled his called-shot home run during the 1932 World Series. The setting was perfect. During the first two games of the series held in New York, the Yankees, led by Ruth, had verbally harassed the Chicago Cubs' players for refusing to vote one of their fellows (a former Yankee who had been called up from the minors late in the season) a full share of the series money. The bench-jockeying, especially between Ruth and the Cubs, continued in Chicago.

The boos and hisses of some 50,000 Cubs fans greeted Ruth as he stepped into the batter's box in the fifth inning with the score tied 4-4. The Cubs players taunted Ruth about his ancestry. The first pitch from Charley Root was a called strike. Grinning, Ruth turned to the Cubs dugout and raised one finger on his right hand. Again Root pitched. Strike two! The crowd roared. Ruth waved the excited Cubs back into their dugout and held up two fingers. "I'm going to knock the next pitch right down your god-damned throat," Ruth was overheard to have shouted to Root. Then, according to a legend that grew with each telling, Ruth pointed to the center-field bleachers. He hit the next pitch into the very spot to which he had pointed, the longest home run that had ever been struck in Wrigley Field. As Ruth rounded the bases, in a box near home plate, Franklin D. Roosevelt, who was running for the presidency against Herbert Hoover, threw back his head and laughed uproariously.

Everything about Ruth was extraordinary—his size, strength, coordination, and appetite for all things of the flesh. He transcended the world of ordinary mortals and yet was the most mortal of men. He loved to play baseball, swear, drink, eat, play practical jokes, and fornicate. Despite his gross crudities, wrote Billy Evans, a big league umpire, "Ruth is a big, likable kid. He has been well named, Babe. Ruth has never grown up and probably never will. Success on the ball field has in no way changed him. Everybody likes him. You just can't help it."

Ruth ignored traditional Victorian virtues. He drank staggering quantities of bootleg liquor; despite Prohibition, his hotel suite was always well stocked with beer and whiskey. People watched him eat with awe; he sometimes ate as many as eighteen eggs for breakfast and washed them down with seven or eight bottles of soda pop. Ruth was not only the "Sultan of Swat"; he was also a sultan of the bedroom. In each town on the spring training tours and in each big league city, Ruth always found a bevy of willing female followers. A sportswriter wrote a parody of his escapades. "I wonder where my Babe Ruth is tonight? He grabbed his hat and coat and ducked from sight. I wonder where he will be at half past three? . . . I know he's with a dame. I wonder what's her name?" Ruth probably did not know her name, for he had a notorious reputation for being unable to remember the names of even his closest friends.

Ruth's uninhibited behavior sometimes got him into serious trouble. Several women sued him for paternity and child support costs. The Yan-

kee management suspended him five times during the 1922 season for a
variety of offenses. "Your conduct [is] . . . reprehensible," American
League president Ban Johnson wrote to him, ". . . shocking to every
American mother who permits her boy to go to a game. . . . It is a leading question as to whether it is permissible to allow a man of your influence and breeding to continue in the game. . . . The period has arrived
when you should allow some intelligence to creep into a mind that has
plainly been warped." Fortunately for Ruth's heroic image, the sportswriters did not reveal to the public Ruth's—or any other player's—private peccadillos.

In 1925, Ruth's excesses caught up with him. On the way north from
spring training, he collapsed from what the club called acute indigestion—
"the stomach-ache that was heard around the world." (Privately, several
of the sportswriters and Ruth's teammates thought that he was suffering
from a sexually transmitted disease.) Removal of an intestinal abscess temporarily laid him low, but he soon returned to his old ways of staying out
all night and drinking heavily. Miller Huggins, the usually tolerant manager of the Yankees, could no longer abide Ruth's indulgences. He slapped
him with a $5,000 fine—few players made that much in a full season of
play—and suspended him from the club. Ruth had a poor season, but some
of his best years lay ahead.

Ruth had his more endearing sides. He won a deserved reputation for
loving children. Everywhere he went, children flocked to him, simply to
see the great Bambino and perhaps to touch his uniform and obtain his
autograph. Ruth enthusiastically welcomed their attention. He regularly
visited hospitalized children. A legend that has some basis in fact added
immeasurably to Ruth's popularity. In its simplest version, Ruth visited a
boy who was dying. He promised the lad that he would hit a home run
for him that afternoon. He did, which so inspired the youth with the will
to live that he miraculously recovered.

The public also adored Ruth's crude egalitarianism. He deferred to no
one. Introduced to President Calvin Coolidge, he responded, "Hi, Pres.
How are you?" According to another probably apocryphal legend, while
Ruth was holding out for a higher salary in 1930, someone pointed out
to him that a depression existed and that he was asking for a salary higher than President Herbert Hoover earned. "What the hell has Hoover got
to do with it?" demanded Ruth. "Besides, I had a better year than he did."

Ruth's huge earnings added to his heroic stature. Recognizing his talents and fearful that he might be seduced by the Federal League, in 1914

the Red Sox gave him a generous three-year contract worth $3,500 annually. Although in some respects an innocent, Ruth became a tough salary negotiator, threatening repeatedly to hold out or quit baseball if his demands were not met. When he was sold to the Yankees in 1920, he asked for a part of the sale price, and he received $41,000 for the 1920 and 1921 seasons. In 1922, he signed a five-year package for $52,000 annually and then, in 1927, a three-year pact for $70,000. No other player approached Ruth's earnings. Lou Gehrig, his star teammate and probably the second highest paid player in the game, received for most of his career less than half of Ruth's pay.

From the time Ruth set his first home run record in 1919, he was besieged by commercial opportunities outside baseball. Since the early days of the game, star players had supplemented their salaries with product endorsements, vaudeville acts, and personal appearances, but no player enjoyed the opportunities that became available to Ruth. In the winter of 1921, Christy Walsh, a sports cartoonist turned ghost writer, convinced Ruth to permit him to handle the demand by newspapers for Ruth's "personal analysis" of each home run that he hit. For fifteen years Walsh employed a stable of ghost writers, among them Ford Frick, a future commissioner of baseball, to write pieces allegedly by Ruth for newspapers and magazines. Ruth "covered" every World Series from 1921 through 1936, and eventually Walsh's syndicate offered writing services to a large number of other athletes and assorted public celebrities.

Walsh marketed Ruth in other ways. In 1921 he signed him to a vaudeville tour, the first of several, which was said to pay Ruth $3,000 weekly for twenty weeks, a record-shattering sum for a vaudeville performer. Walsh also assembled a list of commercial products with which his client could be associated and set out to convince the manufacturers of the benefits to be gained by Ruth's endorsements. In time, Ruth promoted hunting and fishing equipment, modish men's wear, alligator shoes, baseball gear, and sporty automobiles. In Boston he might trumpet the virtues of Packards, in New York Cadillacs, and in St. Louis Reos. He received between $250 and $10,000 for appearing at banquets, grand openings, smokers, boxing and wrestling matches, and celebrity golf tournaments. Although Ruth was a hopeless spendthrift, Walsh eventually convinced him to put enough of his income in untouchable annuities so that he was able to live comfortably during his retirement.

⊡ ⊡ ⊡

Of all America's legendary individuals, Ruth remains the country's preeminent athletic hero; none except perhaps Muhammad Ali is better known. In 1999 the Associated Press named him Athlete of the (Twentieth) Century. As the carrier of so much of baseball's most exciting history, he is irreplaceable. As with no other American athlete, the very words "Ruth" or "Ruthian" evoke images of power, glory, and nearly unbroken success. Indeed, Ruth mirrored the conception that Americans have held of themselves and their own potential.

Union soldiers playing baseball in the Confederate prisoner camp at Salisbury, North Carolina. Notice the positions of the fielders, spectators, and umpire seated beside the catcher. *Source:* William Clements Library.

Henry Chadwick (1824–1908). Known as the "Father of Baseball," Chadwick was a pioneering baseball journalist and promoter. *Source:* National Baseball Library, Cooperstown, N.Y.

William A. Hulbert (1832–82). A baseball executive in Chicago, he was the principal founder and an early president of the National League. *Source:* National Baseball Library, Cooperstown, N.Y.

Albert G. Spalding (1850–1915). A star pitcher for the Bostons, he later became a dominant figure in the management of the National League and a highly successful manufacturer of sporting goods. *Source:* National Baseball Library, Cooperstown, N.Y.

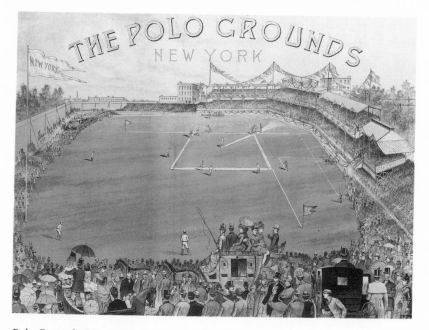

Polo Grounds, New York City, 1887. Notice the position of the players and spectators. *Source:* Warshow Collection, Prints and Photographs Division, Library of Congress.

Michael "King" Kelly (1857–1914).
Considered by many of the fans as the
greatest player of the 1880s, he was
hailed as the "King of Base Ball." *Source:*
Boston Public Library.

Boston Rooters, sometime during the 1890s or early 1900s. These rabid fans sometimes even accompanied their team for games in New York City. *Source:* Boston
Public Library.

Street game, late nineteenth or early twentieth century. *Source:* National Museum of American History, Smithsonian Institution.

John "Honus" Wagner (1874–1955).
One of the game's premier players dur-
ing the early twentieth century, he played
shortstop for the Pittsburgh Pirates.
Source: National Baseball Library,
Cooperstown, N.Y.

Tyrus "Ty" Cobb (1886–1961). This photo reflects Cobb's determination. *Source:*
National Baseball Library, Cooperstown, N.Y.

Connie Mack (1862–1956). The longtime manager-owner of the Philadelphia
Athletics, he projected an image of respectability both on and off the field.
Source: Warshow Collection, Prints and
Photographs Division, Library of Congress.

Spectators at the World Series, 1907. Notice that there are few women present and
that everyone is formally dressed. *Source:* Warshow Collection, Prints and Photographs Division, Library of Congress.

Christy Mathewson (1880–1925), star pitcher for the New York Giants, standing alongside John J. McGraw (1873–1934), his manager. Whereas Mathewson helped bring respectability to professional baseball, McGraw personified the tumultuous, working-class, ethnic character of the game. *Source:* Warshow Collection, Prints and Photographs Division, Library of Congress.

Assistant Secretary of the Navy Franklin D. Roosevelt leading the Washington Senators in military drill during World War I. *Source: The Sporting News.*

Kenesaw Mountain Landis (1866–1944).
Known for his staunch integrity and
forceful personality, Landis served as
commissioner of baseball from 1920 to
1944. *Source:* Chicago Historical Society.

George Herman "Babe" Ruth (1895–1948) and Jacob Ruppert (1867–1939). Ruth,
the game's towering hero in the 1920s, prepares to sign a contract offered by Ruppert,
the executive who inaugurated the New York Yankee dynasties. *Source:* National
Baseball Library, Cooperstown, N.Y.

Jack Dunn (?–1928). As owner of the
Baltimore Orioles, Dunn in the 1920s
built the strongest minor league dynasty
in baseball history. *Source:* National
Baseball Library, Cooperstown, N.Y.

Leroy "Satchel" Paige (1906–82).
From the late 1920s into the 1940s, this
star pitcher towered over black baseball.
Source: National Baseball Library,
Cooperstown, N.Y.

The Pittsburgh Crawfords, champions of the Negro National League, 1934. *Source:* National Museum of American History, Smithsonian Institution.

Branch Rickey (1881–1965). Developer of the farm system as general manager of the St. Louis Cardinals, as general manager of the Brooklyn Dodgers he also embarked on the "Great Experiment" of racially integrating organized baseball. *Source:* National Baseball Library, Cooperstown, N.Y.

Joe DiMaggio (1914–99). Dubbed "The Yankee Clipper," DiMaggio not only represented the arrival of new ethnics from southern Europe into the big leagues but was perhaps the game's premier attraction from the late 1930s through the 1940s. *Source:* National Museum of American History, Smithsonian Institution.

James Roosevelt "Jackie" Robinson (1919–72), the first African American to play in the major leagues in the modern era, in his Brooklyn Dodgers uniform. *Source:* R. L. Wentworth.

The Grand Rapids Chicks, a team from the All-American Girls Professional Baseball League. *Source:* Northern Indiana Historical Society.

The South Bend Blue Sox, of the All-American Girls Professional Baseball League. This photo was taken sometime around 1949. *Source:* Northern Indiana Historical Society.

Charles "Casey" Stengel (1890–1975).
As manager of the powerful New York
Yankees from 1949 to 1960, no manager
equaled his success. *Source:* National
Museum of American History, Smithso-
nian Institution.

Walter F. O'Malley (1903–79). The longtime executive of the Brooklyn and Los
Angeles Dodgers, he led major league expansion to the West Coast and was said
to be the most influential club owner in
the expansion era. *Source:* Los Angeles
Dodgers, Inc.

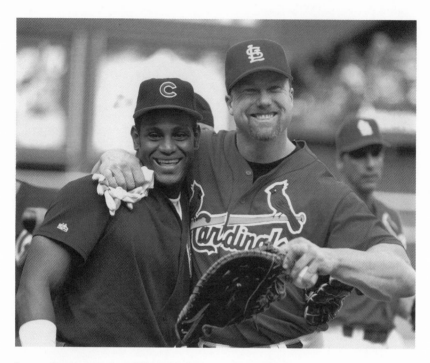

Sammy Sosa (1968–) and Mark McGwire (1963–). The home run feats of Sosa (with 66) and McGwire (with 70) in the 1998 season signaled the arrival of a new era in baseball history. *Source: The Sporting News.*

10

An Age of Dynasties

The stage was set for one of those classic moments for which the game of baseball is so well suited. The St. Louis Cardinals led the New York Yankees 3-2 in the seventh inning of the seventh and final game of the 1926 World Series. With two outs, the Yankees had filled the bases. Tony Lazzeri, the Yankees' dazzling rookie, stepped up to bat. St. Louis player-manager Rogers Hornsby then made a surprising move. He waved in from the bullpen the venerable Grover Cleveland "Old Pete" Alexander. An epileptic and a drinking man who had come to St. Louis in midseason, Alexander had earlier in his career won thirty games or more in three seasons with the Philadelphia Phillies. After moving to the Cards, he had helped them capture the NL flag by winning nine games. In the World Series, he subdued the mighty Yankees twice, 6-2 in the second game and 10-2 in the sixth game, evening the fall classic at three games each. Not expecting to pitch in the final game, he had gone out the evening after the second victory for celebratory drinks. As he strolled to the mound to face the heart of the Yankee batting order, Old Pete was (according to legend) suffering from a monumental hangover.

There they stood, the thirty-nine-year-old veteran confronting the twenty-three-year-old rookie. Lazzeri took a called strike. On the next pitch Lazzeri hit a long, high drive that landed deep in the left-field seats, only a few feet foul. Alexander pitched again—and Lazzeri went down swinging. Old Pete easily glided through the eighth inning. Then, with two outs in the ninth, Babe Ruth stepped up to the plate—and walked. With hard-hitting Bob Meusel at bat and Lou Gehrig on deck, Ruth suddenly and unaccountably broke for second base. The catcher's throw cut him down, ending the inning and the series with a Cardinals victory.

The 1926 series contestants represented two of the longest dynasties in the history of major league baseball. From 1921 through 1943 the Yankees won fourteen pennants—virtually two-thirds of all AL flags for the era—and ten World Series. After World War II the dynasty continued, with the Yanks capturing fifteen additional flags between 1947 and 1964. From 1926 to 1946 the Cardinals collared nine NL championships and finished in second place six times. Initially, the Cardinals and the Yankees epitomized diametrically opposed strategies for achieving success. To obtain talent, Edward G. Barrow, general manager of the Yankees, turned to the club's lush financial resources to purchase players from the minors or other big league clubs, whereas Branch Rickey, general manager of the Cardinals, erected an elaborate farm system. Then, in the mid-1930s, Barrow also added a farm system to the Yankee program of player acquisition.

The contrast between the dynasties extended beyond the methods of Rickey and Barrow. The Yankees became the quintessential representatives of the big city, of urban America with its sophistication, cosmopolitanism, and ethnic and religious heterogeneity, whereas the Cardinals were the quintessential representatives of the small towns and the farms, of rural America with its simplicity, rusticity, and old-stock, Protestant homogeneity. Even the clean, understated elegance of the pinstriped Yankee uniforms contrasted sharply with the images of the dust-covered, baggy uniforms of the Cardinals' Gas House Gang. Players bearing the names of recent immigrants—Tony Lazzeri, Frankie Crosetti, and Joe DiMaggio—dotted the New York lineup, while St. Louis featured its old-stock, country boys—Dizzy Dean, Pepper Martin, and Ripper Collins.

The teams reflected the changing ethnic and geographic origins of the big-leaguers. Substantial numbers were now coming from the families of the more recent arrivals from southern and eastern Europe (Italians, Poles, and Jews, for example), and the numbers coming from German and Irish stock were declining. "Except the Ethiopian" (i.e., black), boasted *The Sporting News* in 1923, "the Mick, the Sheeney, the Wop, the Dutch and the Chink, the Cuban, the Indian, the Jap or the so-called Anglo-Saxon— his nationality is never a matter of moment if he can pitch, or hit, or field." Players from the new stock frequently encountered other ethnic slurs. For example, bench jockeys charged slugger Hank Greenberg and other players of Jewish origins with being "Christ-killers," and newspapers casually referred to Joe DiMaggio and others of Italian ancestry as "Dagos." For the first time, a majority of the players were of small town or rural origins, and a third of them came from the South. Except for African Americans and Hispanics, baseball mirrored the upward mobility of American ethnic groups.

⊡ ⊡ ⊡

With the glaring exception of the Cardinals, from 1921 through 1946 the big league clubs in the larger cities tended to have better records than those in the smaller cities. The Giants, Dodgers, Yankees, Cubs, and White Stockings, the five clubs located in New York and Chicago, which comprised two-thirds of the population served by the big leagues, won twenty-seven of the fifty-two possible pennants in the era. At the same time, the smaller cities of Cleveland, Boston, Cincinnati, and Washington won only six pennants among them (see tables 4 and 5).

Obviously, the size of a city's population alone did not predict the success or failure of its team on the playing field. Although both the Comiskey family in Chicago and Connie Mack in Philadelphia had franchises in the second- and third-largest potential markets, respectively, their complete dependence on baseball for income made it difficult for them to compete effectively in player markets. Even though Mack managed to assemble powerful pennant-winning teams in 1929, 1930, and 1931, the arrival of the Great Depression in the 1930s plus the continuation of a statewide Pennsylvania ban on Sunday games until 1934 caused attendance and income to fall so much that the miserly Mack sold off his team and started rebuilding again from scratch. Nor was he the only owner to sell his stars; first William Baker and then later Gerry Nugent, owners of the Philadelphia Phillies between 1913 and 1942, made it a practice to sell off their superior players. On the other hand, wealthy Thomas Yawkey of the Boston Red Sox spent enormous sums in the 1930s and 1940s to acquire

Table 4. American League Pennant Winners, 1921–46

New York	Chicago	Detroit	Philadelphia	Cleveland	Boston	Washington, D.C.	St. Louis
1943	1945	1931		1946		1933	1944
1942	1940	1930				1925	
1941	1935	1929				1924	
1939	1934						
1938							
1937							
1936							
1932							
1928							
1927							
1926							
1923							
1922							
1921							

Note: Cities are listed, from left to right, in order of average population adjusted to the number of teams located in the metropolitan area.

Table 5. National League Pennant Winners, 1921–46

New York	Brooklyn	Chicago	Pittsburgh	Philadelphia	Boston	Cincinnati	St. Louis
1937	1941	1945	1927			1940	1946
1936		1938	1925			1939	1944
1933		1935					1943
1924		1932					1942
1923		1929					1934
1922							1931
1921							1930
							1928
							1926

Note: Cities are listed, from left to right, in order of average population adjusted to the number of teams located in the metropolitan area.

outstanding veterans, only to bring home but one flag for all his lavish spending. The innovative entrepreneur represented a striking exception of yet another kind. Branch Rickey's farm system enabled a small-city franchise, the St. Louis Cardinals, to compete successfully with clubs located in the larger cities.

Yet a salient fact remained: A larger population base presented a franchise with a decided advantage. More people meant that a club could potentially attract more fans and therefore more revenues than could the teams located in smaller cities. Since the nineteenth century, the owners had partly offset market size by giving 50 percent of the base admission price to visiting teams, but any revenues collected from seats that exceeded the base price, such as box or reserved seats, went to the home club. In 1892 the visiting team received about 40 percent of all gate receipts; by 1929 their share had dropped to only 21 percent. With the additional revenues flowing from their size, the bigger city franchises could spend more for player procurement. Because of their superior drawing power, a star player was typically worth far more to a New York franchise, for example, than he was to St. Louis club owners.

Well before the Yankees won their first pennant in 1921, their crosstown rivals, the New York Giants, had already demonstrated that a blend of a large market area, free spending, and wise decision making could deliver pennant winners. John J. McGraw, who in effect served as both the Giants' field and business manager, brought from Baltimore an acute knowledge of the game, while the new owner, John T. Brush, brought from Cincinnati a generous pocketbook. The combination produced seven Giants pennants between 1904 and 1917. After Charles Stoneham assumed the club's presidency in 1919, the same formula produced a record-shattering four consecutive pennants (1921–24) before McGraw's talents for spotting good players and negotiating strategic trades seemed to diminish.

Until Jacob Ruppert Jr., a patrician brewer and realtor allegedly worth $75 million, and Tillinghast Huston, a self-made engineer, purchased the Yankees in 1915 for $450,000, that club had a mediocre record. Improvement came slowly at first, but a flurry of decisions between 1918 and 1920 reaped a rich harvest. By offering to double his salary, Ruppert lured Miller Huggins away from the St. Louis Cardinals; the diminutive, relatively easygoing Huggins managed the high-spirited Yankees from 1918 until his untimely death in 1929. (Enraged at the appointment of Huggins, Huston and Ruppert parted ways, with the former eventually selling out to the latter.) During the 1919 season, the club purchased from the Boston Red Sox the controversial pitcher Carl Mays, a fastballer who posted a 79-39 career mark while with the Yankees. Then came Babe Ruth from Boston for $125,000. Until the early 1930s, when his skills began to wane, Ruth peerlessly manned the Yankee offense.

But the raids on Boston were not over. In late 1920 the Yankees employed former Boston field manager Edward Barrow as their business manager. Besides possessing good judgment, Barrow had a wealth of baseball experience. He had managed the Red Sox to the AL championship in 1918, had been responsible for converting Ruth from a pitcher into an outfielder, and had served as a minor league field manager, business manager, club president, and league president. It was Barrow, with the generous funding provided by Ruppert and Huston, who continued the dismantling of the once powerful Red Sox, the team that had won pennants in 1915, 1916, and 1918. Invariably short of the liquid capital needed to finance his expensive Broadway shows, Harry Frazee, the Boston owner, sought help from his wealthy New York friends. So long as they could obtain good ball players in return, they were delighted to send money to Frazee. By 1923, eleven individuals on the twenty-four-man Yankee roster had formerly played with Boston. In 1922 the hapless Red Sox sank to the AL cellar, where they languished for eight of the next nine seasons.

Success on the field brought with it record-shattering Yankee attendance. With New York's legalization of Sunday baseball in 1919 and the acquisition of Ruth in 1920, the Yankees regularly drew more than a million fans a year, a figure representing nearly one-quarter of all American League attendance. Initially, the Yankees had played in the Polo Grounds, which was owned by the Giants, but in 1923 they completed the construction of Yankee Stadium. Appropriately for baseball's best team located in the nation's largest city, Yankee Stadium was baseball's most colossal park. Dubbed "The House That Ruth Built" by sportswriter Fred Lieb as a parody of a popular nursery rhyme, the triple-decked stadium seated about 65,000 fans, some 10,000 more than the next-largest facility—the Polo Grounds—and nearly 40,000 more than St. Louis's Sportsman's Park, the smallest of the big league fields.

Although pitcher Herb Pennock and outfielder Babe Ruth, two ex-Boston players, remained keys to the great Yankee teams of 1926, 1927, and 1928, Barrow obtained important replacements from elsewhere. He dipped into the minor leagues and paid $50,000 each (huge sums for that day) to acquire Earle Combs, Tony Lazzeri, and Mark Koenig, all polished players ready to step into the starting lineup. But the most important addition was Lou Gehrig, who was signed directly from the campus of Columbia University. Although Gehrig at first played in the long shadow cast by Ruth and then later in that by Joe DiMaggio, he became one of the game's all-time great sluggers. He led the league in slugging percentage four times, runs scored four times, and runs batted in five times. No player was more consistent in bringing runners home; he drove in 100 or more runs for twelve consecutive seasons. Gehrig and Ruth, who between them banged out 107 homers in 1927, composed the heart of the famed Yankee "Murderer's Row" team that won 110 games and swept the Pittsburgh Pirates in four games for the world championship. In 1969 the Baseball Writers Association voted the 1927 Yankees the greatest baseball team of all time.

After having won three flags in succession twice in the 1920s the Yankees won only one pennant between 1928 and 1935 before they launched into a new reign over the AL. In terms of dominance beyond a single campaign, the Yankees of the 1936 through 1939 seasons were even better than their predecessors. Ruth, who coveted the Yankees managership, played his last season as a Yankee in 1934, but Gehrig continued to hammer the fences in 1936 and 1937 before his performance tailed off in 1938 as a result of the ravages of a rare neurological disorder. In the meantime, Barrow had hired a hard-driving perfectionist, Joe McCarthy, as his field manager. McCarthy brought the Yankees a flag in 1932 and three consecutive second-place finishes before the surge of 1936. For fresh personnel, Barrow again turned to the minor leagues. He acquired catcher William Dickey from Buffalo and purchased from the San Francisco Seals pitcher Vernon "Lefty" Gomez, shortstop Frankie Crosetti, and outfielder Joe DiMaggio. With the Seals in 1936, DiMaggio had compiled a batting average of .398 and hit safely in sixty-one straight games. By obtaining hits in fifty-six consecutive games in 1941, he would establish the big league mark as well.

Not only did these players lead the Yankees to four consecutive league flags and World Series titles, but for four seasons in a row they topped the AL in home runs, slugging percentage, and runs scored. In each of the four seasons they scored more than a run and a half above the average of the other AL clubs. The less spectacular pitching staff had an even better long-term record. In 1939, for the sixth straight season, Yankee pitchers put together the league's stingiest earned run average. For sustained performance over four seasons, no team in baseball history, unless one goes all the way back to Harry Wright's National Association Boston club of the 1870s, approached the Yankees of the 1936–39 era.

⊞ ⊞ ⊞

"No man in baseball in the last quarter century, with the possible exception of Judge Landis and Babe Ruth, has left so deep an impress on the game as Branch Rickey," wrote sportswriter Fred Lieb in 1945 (and this was before Rickey had signed Jackie Robinson). This impress was not due to majestic home runs or lofty decisions from on high; rather, it came from

Rickey's remarkable record of success as the general manager of the St. Louis Cardinals. Although handicapped by being located in the smallest population base in the NL (when the average population of the St. Louis metropolitan area is divided with the AL's Browns), after the Yankees, the Cardinals between 1926 and 1946 had the best record in baseball, as well as, apparently, the highest earnings.

Rickey brought to the Cardinals a strange blend of rich experience, sheer genius, and Methodist moralism. By teaching at a one-room school and later coaching sports, he had worked his way through Ohio Wesleyan College and then the University of Michigan law school. Reared in a strict Methodist home, he made a promise to his mother never to attend Sunday games, although he never hesitated, as his critics frequently observed, to listen to Sunday games on the radio or to take profits on the Sabbath. A prohibitionist, he never drank, although he smoked cigars and surrounded himself with hard-drinking, highly talented employees. He sprinkled his conversations and speeches with biblical allusions and polysyllabic words, leaving his listeners not quite certain of what they had heard. In 1942 sportswriter Tom Meany nicknamed him the "Mahatma," after Indian independence leader Mahatma Gandhi, whom John Gunther had once described as "a combination of God, your father, and Tammany Hall leader." The nickname was so suitable that it stuck.

Perhaps influenced by his own extensive formal education or perhaps by the principles of scientific management that were so popular in the early twentieth century, Rickey approached player training more systematically than anyone else in the game. "He is a Professor of Baseball," reported a sportswriter at the start of Rickey's managing career in 1914. "His efficiency courses in sliding, baserunning and batting mark a new departure in the game." He later set up a preseason "Baseball College" for instruction in fundamentals and introduced such paraphernalia as sliding pits and batting tees that are today taken for granted.

By far the most important of Rickey's innovations, however, was the St. Louis farm system. Long before Rickey, big league clubs had on occasion signed bright sandlot prospects and optioned them to minor league clubs for additional seasoning. When a player was deemed ready to play big league ball, he would then be recalled. Furthermore, prior to Rickey, major league clubs or their owners had sometimes owned or had affiliations with minor league clubs. Technically, such franchises operated completely independently of the parent club, but because big league clubs had limits on the number of players they could carry on their rosters at any given time, they frequently resorted to the subterfuge of sending excess players to minor league clubs with the understanding that they could retrieve such players when they saw fit. Nonetheless, Rickey was the first to build a large empire of farm teams with the express purpose of recruiting and nurturing an entire stable of new talent.

Prior to Rickey, conventional wisdom had held that such a system would not be cost-effective. It was far more economical to leave recruitment of new players mainly in the hands of the lower-level, independently owned minor league franchises. Then, neither the major league nor the high-level minor league club need employ a bevy of scouts or take the risks of investing in dozens of players who never would make it to the higher echelons of baseball. A player who had proven his potential in minor league competition could then be purchased; if the minor league franchise set the price too high, the player would eventually become subject to the draft (at a set price) by a club higher in organized baseball's hierarchy.

Had it not been for the near collapse of the draft system in the 1920s Rickey probably would never have broken with the traditional mode of player acquisition. In 1919 the National Association of Professional Baseball Leagues, the minor leagues' umbrella organization, pulled out of the National Agreement. This ended the draft, although both sides tacitly agreed to respect each other's reserve clauses. The new National Agreement of 1921 raised the draft price to $5,000 a class AA player, $4,000 for an A man, and on down the line to $1,000 for a class D player. The majors could select only one man per season from each of the AA and A clubs. Furthermore, the pact provided that any minor league could completely exempt itself from the draft if it relinquished its own right to draft players from teams in the lower echelons of the minors. Five minor leagues—the three AA leagues (Pacific Coast, International, and American Association), the class A Western Association, and the B Three-I League—chose to do so.

The agreement of 1921 ushered in an era of unprecedented prosperity for the high-level minor leagues, at least for the franchises that were effective in recruiting and developing talent on their own. Although now denied the privilege of drafting from the lower minors, the minor league executives could hold on to their star players indefinitely or sell them for market prices to a major or other minor league franchise. "At the slightest mention" of restoring the draft, reported the *New York Times,* Jack Dunn, owner of the Baltimore Orioles of the International League, "runs away for two miles and then kicks in the side of a barn." Instead of selling his stars, Dunn generally kept them.

In Baltimore, Dunn proceeded to build a minor league dynasty equivalent to that of the Cardinals and Yankees in the major leagues. As early as 1920 the *Reach Guide* reported that "the Baltimore team was universally regarded as of real major league caliber." Between 1919 and 1925 the Orioles won seven consecutive pennants while compiling a won-lost record of 779-354, for a winning percentage of .688. In five of these seasons, the powerful Orioles won 113 or more games, and in none did they win fewer than 100 games. Hailed by Bill James as "the greatest minor league team of all time," the Orioles were stronger than several of the big league teams of their day.

The key to the Orioles' success rested with one person: Jack Dunn, who personified the Horatio Alger success formula, moving up from merely playing on a professional club to owning one. After having served as a pitcher and an outfielder for several major league teams from 1897 to 1904, Dunn first managed the Providence Clamdiggers before moving to Baltimore in the 1907 season. He guided the Orioles to the International League pennant the following season. No club official, not even Branch Rickey, had a superior aptitude for finding promising players. He spotted Merle "Doc" Adams, who was to win twenty or more games in three separate seasons, among the medical students at Johns Hopkins University, and on the other side of the tracks he located Babe Ruth among the incorrigibles of St. Mary's School for Boys. Direct competition with the Federal League's Baltimore Terrapins in 1914—the same year that he signed Ruth—just about bankrupted Dunn. He had to sell his best players, including Ruth, and in 1915 he moved his club to Richmond, Virginia.

Few if any big league clubs had a stronger pitching staff than the Orioles. Leading their corps was six-foot, three-inch Robert Moses "Lefty" Grove, who was, in the opinion of Bill James, "only the greatest pitcher to ever heave a horsehide." Grove's seasonal records with Baltimore stood at 12-2, 25-10, 18-8, 27-10, and 27-7. From 1921 through 1924, he paced the league in strikeouts as well, posting seasonal totals ranging from 205 to 330. Eventually, Dunn was no longer able to resist big league efforts to obtain Grove. In 1925 he sold him to the Philadelphia Athletics, reportedly for either $160,000 or $106,000, which in either case was a record sum. With the Athletics and later the Boston Red Sox, Grove proceeded to lead the AL in strikeouts seven times and in earned run average nine times. Four other Baltimore pitchers captured twenty or more seasonal victories.

The willingness of the International League to accept a modified draft system in 1924 signaled the demise of the Baltimore dynasty. Faced with the prospect of eventually being forced to dispose of his men for the mere $5,000 draft price, Dunn began to sell his star players. While watching his beloved hunting dogs at a field meet in 1928, Dunn was struck down by a heart attack. He left behind an estate valued at more than a million dollars. Other minor league dynasties arose, in particular the Newark Bears of the 1930s and 1940s, but none equaled the success of the Baltimore franchise.

Minor league baseball would continue to prosper after 1924. In fact, Neil J. Sullivan, in his history of the minors, aptly describes the 1920s and 1930s as the "golden age" of minor league ball. Regardless of the frailty of professional baseball below the big leagues, millions of fans, far more than ever attended the majors, found in their games entertainment, repetition of a familiar ritual, and a deeper sense of community. With the establishment of the farm systems in the 1930s, however, the minor leagues increasingly became agencies for the development of big league players rather than enterprises shaped by their own ends.

Because they were unable after 1921 to draft prospects from the high-level minors at a set price, the major league teams' costs of player procurement suddenly escalated. In particular, Jacob Ruppert of the Yankees, Charles Stoneham of the Giants, and chewing-gum magnate William Wrigley of the Chicago Cubs embarked on unprecedented spending sprees. In 1921, for example, the Giants went into the minor league market to purchase Jimmy O'Connell from San Francisco for $75,000 (remember that Ruth had cost only $125,000 the year before), and in 1922 they bought Jack Bentley from Baltimore for $100,000; meanwhile, the Yankees spent $50,000 each for Earle Combs, Mark Koenig, and Tony Lazzeri.

Unable to compete in these bidding wars with the more affluent club owners located in the larger cities, Rickey and Sam Breadon, the Cardinals president, slowly inched their way toward the creation of a farm system. Only three minor league affiliates furnished eight of the regulars on the Cardinals 1926 championship team, and as late as 1929 the entire St. Louis farm system consisted of a mere five clubs, but changes in the minor league draft in 1930 and the Great Depression of the 1930s were to trigger the construction of the full-scale farm empire. In 1930 the majors restricted the AA league draft to athletes who had completed a minimum of four years of play at that level. This provision permitted clubs to protect from the draft their investment in a player assigned to one of their farm teams until they could be more certain of his potential. With the widespread unemployment accompanying the depression, the salary costs for an average minor leaguer sank to a mere $300 per season. Rickey seized these advantages to expand the Cardinal system to include twenty-eight teams by 1936. By then, Rickey had scouts holding three-day tryouts across the country and was signing dozens of raw recruits each year.

The larger the pool of players controlled by the parent club, Rickey reasoned, the greater the probability of potential big leaguers in their midst. Therefore, the Cardinals' farm system called for the signing of great numbers of athletes at minimal salaries to play at the base of the farm system's pyramid, on one of their more than twenty class D clubs. Scouts were told to look for young men who could throw hard and run fast. It was hoped that if a recruit had these natural attributes, his hitting, fielding, or pitching skills could be improved with proper guidance and more experience. Nonetheless, each of the prospects faced a savage winnowing process. Only a few successfully climbed the ladder to the class C or B clubs, then even fewer to the AA clubs, and if indeed fortunate, a player obtained the opportunity to play on the parent club itself.

Not even Rickey dreamed of the spectacular successes of the St. Louis farm system. It produced a steady supply of new talent. Nearly all the Cardinals players came from their farm chain, including such superstars as Dizzy Dean and Stan Musial. Indeed, according to an estimate by Harold Seymour, the system furnished about three times more big league caliber players than was needed by the parent club. Consequently, the Cardinals were able to profit repeatedly by selling off their established stars at the peak of their careers—or just beyond it—at premium prices while maintaining the quality of the team with new additions from the farm clubs. They also sold dozens of their best minor league prospects to other big league clubs; in one year alone, they had sixty-five players who were products of their farm system playing on other big league clubs. Furthermore, the superiority of Rickey's nationwide recruiting system over the more haphazard methods of the independent minor league clubs resulted in the Cardinals farm teams usually outperforming their opponents. With winning records, the Cardinals affiliates drew more fans, generated more revenues, and thereby reduced the costs of the farms to the parent club.

Even though the prices of minor league prospects had skyrocketed in the 1920s, initially all the other clubs continued to operate as they had in the past. For example, the 1926 Yankees had only one player, Lou Gehrig, whom they had signed directly. By 1929, however, Jacob Ruppert told his fellow owners that because of the escalating prices of minor league players he was "going to be forced into owning minor league clubs, and so [was] every other major league owner." The Yankees already owned a franchise in the class D Blue Ridge League, and in 1931 they purchased Newark of the International League. Shortly thereafter, the Yankees hired George Weiss from Baltimore to develop a complete farm system that eventually came to rival that of the Cardinals.

Nonetheless, the heyday of Rickey's broad-based farm system actually was a short interlude in baseball history. It was the product of special circumstances: the loopholes in the 1920s draft, changes in the draft rules made in 1930, and the Great Depression. Farming encountered the impassioned opposition of Kenesaw Mountain Landis; he insisted that it was an infringement on the right of players to move smoothly up or down baseball's hierarchy and that the system breached emotional bonds between the minor league fans and their teams. Even in the midst of tight pennant races, the big league club might spoil its affiliates' chances for a flag by calling up one or more players from their rosters. Based on highly technical violations of the cartel's rules, Landis in 1938 granted free agency to seventy-four St. Louis minor-leaguers and in 1940 to ninety-one Detroit farm hands. Rickey himself recognized that a club could have too many farm teams, that at some point diminishing returns set in, and that at that point a farm system was no longer cost-effective. He had even begun to cut back the size of the St. Louis empire before his departure to the Brooklyn Dodgers in 1942. After World War II new rules on player acquisition and the changing fortunes of the minor leagues resulted in the eventual disappearance of Rickey-type farm systems altogether.

Of course, pro baseball, whether in the big leagues or the minors, represented only the tip of baseball's iceberg in the 1920–50 era. Below the surface of full-time, paid players was a teeming world of semipro and amateur baseball. In Boston, New York, and Chicago, indeed, in every city and town in the nation, boys continued as never before to play bat and ball games on empty lots, on school grounds, and in the streets. They sometimes used empty barrels, discarded planks, or even fire plugs as bases. It was the same on the windswept prairies of the Dakotas, William Jennings Bryan's Nebraska, and Dorothy and Toto's Kansas. There, on their dusty one-room school grounds, both girls and boys spent their lunch hours and recesses playing ball. When the great thunder clouds rolled in from the Southwest, many a young school mom shouted, "Time to come in, children, before it rains!"

And then there was the world of sandlot baseball, of amateur and semi-pro adult baseball—of both white and black teams. Each city had Sunday and twilight leagues. In the twilight leagues the men played after work and before it got dark. Large crowds, far more in total than those attending professional matches, came out to watch the men play. "Every town had its own team in those days," recalled Samuel (Wahoo Sam) Crawford, who hailed from Wahoo, Nebraska. The town teams usually played on Saturday and Sunday afternoons. Even the Great Depression did not dampen the enthusiasm for amateur and semipro baseball. Indeed, newspaper reports suggest that in the 1930s sandlot versions of the game reached yet another peak in popularity.

For teenage boys, nothing equaled the importance of American Legion ball. Anxieties arising from the Russian Revolution in 1917 and the arrival of floods of immigrants from southern and eastern Europe in the prewar years led the World War I veterans to launch a nationwide crusade on behalf of what they called "Americanism." As part of their larger campaign to curb the perceived threat of radicalism and alien cultures to traditional values and behaviors, in 1926 the legionnaires organized a nationwide baseball program for teenage boys. Winning enormous support in local communities and among the veterans themselves, within four years more than 100,000 boys in all forty-eight states were playing legion ball. Aided with funds furnished by the big leagues, the legion sponsored an annual "World Series." But, as Kent Krause has shown, a winning-at-all-costs ethos soon supplanted the legion's earlier ideological goal of using baseball to encourage patriotism, religiosity, and old-fashioned virtues. By then, legion baseball had also become a major training ground for future professional players.

▣   ▣   ▣

While the Yankees and Cardinals were capturing headlines on the sports page, organized baseball as a whole had to cope with one of the gravest challenges in American history: the Great Depression of the 1930s. Like the economy, baseball had prospered enormously in the 1920s. Big league attendance topped nine million in 1930 for the seventh straight year, but then began the plunge downward as the nation fell into the trough of the Great Depression. "Whereas in July, 1930, it was a case of scaring up four bits for a bleacher seat at the Stadium," reported the *Literary Digest,* in 1932 "it [was] a matter of getting enough for a cheap meal." In the next year, 1933, the economy reached bottom; the Gross National Product stood at half of the 1929 figure, at least a quarter of the work force was unemployed, and big league attendance fell to 6.3 million. For both the economy and baseball, recovery was painfully slow, not reaching 1929 figures again until 1940 and 1941, when World War II began to induce a new cycle of expansion. Nearly all the franchises lost money; only the Cardinals and the clubs located in the larger cities that had consistently winning records earned profits during the grim decade. For fans who could somehow manage to buy tickets, however, another concern, namely Prohibition, was sometimes more paramount than jobs. When President Herbert Hoover entered Shibe Park in 1931 to watch a World Series contest between the Philadelphia Athletics and the St. Louis Cardinals, the fans initially greeted him with boos and then, rather than demanding jobs, began to chant "We want beer! We want beer!"

Unlike the bold, experimental programs of Franklin D. Roosevelt's New Deal, the major leagues' responses to the ravages of the Great Depression were cautious. "This is a new era," warned *The Sporting News* in 1932, ". . . baseball must get in step with the times. Talking about innovations as being 'bad for precedent,' that they hadn't been 'attempted before' and that what was 'good enough yesterday is good enough today,' won't get the game anywhere." But the major leagues ignored the warning. They introduced no rule changes that significantly affected the way the game was played, rejected Bill Veeck Sr.'s proposal for interleague play in the "dog days" of July and August, and refused to cut ticket prices.

Not surprisingly, the owners of richer clubs promptly voted down a profit-sharing plan proposed by the poorer franchises. "I found out a long time ago that there is no charity in baseball," explained Jacob Ruppert, owner of the Yankees, "and that every club owner must make his own fight for existence." Without relief from their fellows, the more indigent franchise owners had to resort to whatever desperate measures they could take on their own. One was to sell their better players to the richer clubs. Connie Mack, for example, completely dismantled his AL championship teams of 1929–31, selling off all his stars to richer owners. But such a strategy triggered a vicious cycle because a team with no stars lost more games. Attendance then fell further, revenues declined, and the franchise faced the grim prospect of selling still more players.

The owners even approached the promises of new technology with excruciating wariness. Whether to broadcast games on radio had been controversial since the airing of the first game by Harold Arlin on station

KDKA in Pittsburgh in 1921. Rather than going to the parks to see games, the owners feared, fans might stay at home and listen to the radio accounts. In the 1920s only the Chicago Cubs permitted the broadcast of all their games. With the advent of the Great Depression, fears of radio mounted even further. At nearly every winter meeting the club owners considered a complete ban on radio broadcasts. Although no one could measure precisely the impact of radio on attendance, the experience of the St. Louis Cardinals suggested that game broadcasts might create more interest in the team and actually bring more fans into the parks. St. Louis prohibited broadcasts of the 1934 season, the season that featured the exciting Gas House Gang and an NL pennant. Though no doubt affected by the depression as much as by the absence of radio broadcasts, Cardinal attendance fell 283,000 below the figures for the 1931 championship team. The Cardinals promptly restored radio broadcasts. Nonetheless, in 1934 the three New York teams signed a pact calling for a complete radio ban that remained in effect until 1939, when Larry MacPhail, the new Brooklyn general manager, refused to renew it.

Nor did the tradition-bound owners seize the full opportunities for profit presented by night baseball. Although baseball had been played occasionally under artificial lighting as early as the 1880s, it was not until the 1930s, with technical improvements and the onset of the Great Depression, that night ball made significant headway. Beginning with the demonstrable success of the black, barnstorming Kansas City Monarchs' portable lighting system in 1929, the minor leagues rushed to install lights in 1930. Although minor league attendance in the 1930s reflected the tides of the economy, night ball staved off the full impact of the depression. In 1932, relying heavily on night games, Larry MacPhail's American Association club of Columbus, Ohio, even outdrew the parent Cardinals. "Men are not going to quit their tasks during the week to go to ball games," concluded *The Sporting News*, ". . . but a vast majority of them would welcome a chance to go in the evenings to relax."

The financially desperate Cincinnati Reds finally broke though the big league ban on lights. In 1934, the Reds' new general manager, Larry MacPhail, and their new owner, Powel Crosley, convinced the NL to permit them to play seven night games in 1935. "A cowardly surrender to commercialism," howled one critic. "The National League has become a burlesque circuit," charged Washington Senators' owner Clark Griffith. Nonetheless, at least in terms of attendance, the first nocturnal game played on 24 May 1935 proved an instant success. More than 20,000 fans came, ten times above the average weekday attendance of the lowly Reds, and both fans and players dismissed fears arising from difficulties in seeing the ball.

Contrary to a popular impression, however, the 1935 game by no means heralded the wholesale conversion of the big leagues to night baseball. Indeed, no club except Cincinnati installed lights until three years later, and as late as 1941 seven parks remained without lights. A limit of seven night games per season remained in effect for each club until 1942, when, as a concession to wartime conditions, it was expanded to fourteen of the normal seventy-seven home games. By then, Clark Griffith had completely reversed himself to become the leading proponent of unlimited night ball, but he encountered the opposition of Commissioner Landis, who in a showdown vote sided with the NL to retain the fourteen-night-game limit.

Although they agreed on little else, the owners achieved unanimity on at least one strategy for responding to the Great Depression. That was to reduce their operating costs by slashing player salaries. As they had done during the 1890s, the owners called on the players to bear the brunt of the economic catastrophe. Although the owners did not follow the minor league example of imposing a salary ceiling, total payrolls dropped from $4 million in 1930 to $3 million in 1933; by 1933, the average player salary had plummeted to $4,500. That figure disguises wide disparities between teams. The payroll of the Yankees, for example, was about five times that of the St. Louis Browns. Anticipated widespread player holdouts never occurred. "The ball player . . . is a fortunate man," said pitcher Burleigh Grimes. "In other occupations, there has been a shrinkage in salaries and a lack of employment. . . . [But] the ball player . . . has gone on [working] daily and been paid in full."

Organized baseball also adopted several symbolic acts that incited greater fan interest in the game. Although a tradition of all-star games extended back to the 1858 series between the "picked nines" from Brooklyn and New York, the current All-Star series originated with Arch Ward, the sports editor of the *Chicago Tribune*, who convinced the reluctant owners to stage a game between stars of the AL and NL during Chicago's Century of Progress Exposition in 1933. For the first two games, the managers shared with the fans the selection of the players, but from 1935 through 1946 the managers chose the entire squads. In 1947 fans began to choose the starting lineups except for the pitchers, who continued to be selected by the managers. In the early years the AL dominated the series, winning twelve games and losing only four through 1949. Individual player awards likewise had a long history, but the Baseball Writers Association of America created the modern annual Most Valuable Player Award in 1931. For the first season Frankie Frisch took NL honors and Lefty Grove captured the AL award.

Other steps reflected a more general American preoccupation with trying to preserve traditional virtues and values in the midst of the depression. Baseball made its most important symbolic gesture to continuity with the founding of the Hall of Fame in 1936 and, three years later, its official opening in the bucolic village of Cooperstown, New York. In 1936, the sportswriters chose as charter members to the Hall of Fame Ty Cobb, Babe Ruth, Honus Wagner, Christy Mathewson, and Walter Johnson, thereby entirely ignoring not only baseball's nineteenth-century performers (a slight rectified in time for the opening of the Hall of Fame in 1939) but also, of course, all black claimants to the honor.

None of the baseball rituals introduced in the 1930s evoked as much pathos or sentimentality as the all-too-real illness and tragic death of Lou Gehrig. Suffering from a rare neurological disorder that subsequently became known as Lou Gehrig's disease, the great slugger took himself out of the lineup after having played a record-shattering 1,130 consecutive games. On 4 July 1939 at Yankee Stadium, a host of dignitaries, including Babe Ruth, honored him. In front of 70,000 somber fans, Gehrig hobbled to the microphone at home plate and said that he considered himself "the luckiest man on the face of the earth." He died less than two years later. Gehrig's apotheosis was completed in 1942 with the release of *The Pride of the Yankees*, a movie in which a miscast Gary Cooper played Gehrig.

◻ ◻ ◻

As the 1940s opened, it was evident that organized baseball had weathered the Great Depression, and it seemed equally clear that the Cardinal and Yankee dynasties would not be dislodged easily. Although hundreds of players entered the armed services in World War II, the respective farm systems of the Cards and Yanks continued to feed those teams a fresh stream of new talent. Between the two franchises, they won six of ten wartime flags. What no one could foresee in 1940 was a continuing drama orchestrated by Branch Rickey. In 1942 Rickey transferred from the Cardinals to the Brooklyn Dodgers, and four years later he startled nearly everyone by successfully ending organized baseball's longstanding ban against players of African descent.

11

Baseball's Great Experiment

On 28 August 1945, only thirteen days after the guns had ceased firing in World War II, Clyde Sukeforth, a Brooklyn Dodgers scout, ushered Jackie Robinson into the office of Branch Rickey, the Dodgers' president. The bushy-browed Rickey initially said nothing. He just sat and stared at the broad-shouldered black man who sat in front of him. His piercing eyes made Robinson "almost feel naked," as the younger man later recalled. But Robinson did not cower. "Jack stared right back at him," Sukeforth remembered.

Then, as was his wont, Rickey launched into a long monologue. He recounted how he had conducted a thorough investigation of both Robinson's personal life and his baseball career. He had concluded that Robinson was the man to crack organized baseball's ancient color ban. Although Robinson had sensed beforehand that a plan to breach baseball's rigid segregation had occasioned this meeting, the actual description by a white executive of how it was to be done stunned him. He and fellow black players had long dreamed of this day, but the reality of it was another matter. For Robinson, it was an emotionally wrenching moment.

For three hours, Rickey lectured Robinson on the grave responsibilities that would rest on his shoulders. He dramatized the problems Robinson would confront. Mixing his remarks with racial slurs, Rickey even acted out the roles of insulting opponents, abusive teammates, and hostile fans. "His acting was so convincing that I found myself chain-gripping my fingers behind my back," Robinson later wrote.

Finally, Robinson could take it no longer. "Mr. Rickey, do you want a ballplayer who's afraid to fight back?" he blurted out. "I want a player with guts enough not to fight back," Rickey bellowed in response. Robinson, a proud, high-spirited young man, did not immediately accept the challenge. It was not in his nature to retreat from confrontations. As an army lieutenant in World War II, he had been court martialed for refusing to sit in the back of a bus in the seats reserved for the "colored people." After what seemed to Sukeforth a full five minutes, Robinson finally said, "I think I can play ball in Brooklyn. . . . If you want to take this gamble, I will promise you there will be no incident."

This fateful meeting not only heralded the reversal of organized baseball's long-term ban against black players but signified the beginning of a new era of white-black relations in the United States. Because baseball enjoyed the distinction of being the national game, racial integration within it was of vast symbolic importance. If it was proper and possible for blacks and whites to play baseball together, then why should they continue to be separated in the armed forces, the schoolrooms, the courtrooms, the workplaces, and the neighborhoods of America? Once the racial wall in the national game had been breached, it seemed indisputable that all other barriers to blacks should be removed as well.

▣ ▣ ▣

For a time after the imposition of complete segregation in the 1890s, blacks had entertained hopes that their exclusion from organized baseball would not be permanent. Exhibitions of outstanding skills by black players, predicted Sol White in 1906, "will open the avenue in the near future wherein [blacks] may walk hand-in-hand with the opposite race in the greatest of all American games—baseball." Unfortunately, White was overly optimistic. Even a subterfuge by one of the cleverest men in the game failed. In 1901 Baltimore Orioles manager John McGraw had been unable to pass off black second baseman Charlie Grant as an Indian whom he named Chief Tokohama. In 1911 the Cincinnati Reds raised black hopes again by signing two light-skinned Cubans. "With the admission of Cubans of a darker hue into the big leagues," commented Booker T. Washington's *New York Age*, "it would then be easy for colored players who are citizens of this country to get into fast company." But the Reds quickly torpedoed such a scenario by publicly certifying that the Cubans were "genuine Caucasians." It is nevertheless possible that a few Hispanics (as well as other) players with a mixed African ancestry played in the majors before Jackie Robinson.

Barred from the organized game's structure, blacks had no choice but to carve out their own separate world of baseball. As in white baseball, countless black sandlot and town teams regularly formed, played briefly, and then disbanded. Until the 1920s not a single black professional league survived a full season. For more than a half century, the black game at its highest levels revolved around barnstorming teams. The Cuban Giants, founded in 1885, established a model and provided a recurrent nickname for other itinerant squads. Apparently to achieve greater acceptance among white fans, the team tried to pass itself off as Cuban, even to the extent of gibbering in a tongue that ignorant spectators might confuse with Spanish.

Successful barnstorming usually included both skilled play and flamboyance. The barnstormers liked to arrive early in the town or city of a scheduled game so they could plaster up signs announcing the contest and call attention to themselves by conspicuously strolling about the streets. As early as the 1890s, the Page Fence Giants, who represented the Page Woven Wire Fence Company of Adrian, Michigan, promoted upcoming games by riding bicycles through the streets, whereas the All-American Black Tourists team arrived in host towns decked out in full dress suits, opera hats, and silk umbrellas. For many isolated American communities in which the residents rarely saw blacks, the coming of a traveling troupe of black ball players must have been as exotic and as exciting as the arrival of a circus. Even towns of a thousand or so residents might turn out 500 or 600 fans to watch the barnstormers play a local white semipro team.

The barnstormers frequently clowned during the game, as well as before it. If confident of victory, as they usually could be, hitters might get down on their knees to receive the next pitch after the umpire had called a low pitch a strike, or, on knocking a ball out of the park, a hitter might run the bases backward. A favorite pantomime, versions of which were later made famous by the Harlem Globetrotters basketball team, was to act out a sequence in which an imaginary ball was delivered to the batter, flew off the bat to a player's glove, and then was whipped around the bases. Traveling teams like the Tennessee Rats, the Zulu Cannibals, and the Ethiopian Clowns of the 1930s and 1940s capitalized exclusively "on slap-stick comedy and the kind of nonsense which many white people like to believe is typical and characteristic of all Negroes," observed a black newspaper. Although successful in attracting fans, clowning perpetuated negative black stereotypes.

From 1910 through the early 1920s no person was more important to black baseball than Andrew "Rube" Foster. A big, imposing man—he stood six feet, four inches tall—Foster quickly revealed his multiple talents by rising through the ranks to become first an outstanding pitcher, then one of the game's most successful field managers, and finally a club owner, league organizer, and league president. In 1911, with the financial backing of a white Chicago saloon keeper (a son-in-law of Charles Comiskey), Foster became the leading booking agent for black teams in the Midwest and formed the Chicago American Giants, which soon became the nation's premier black nine. To counter the power of competing white booking agents in scheduling the contests of black quads and to bring a semblance of order to black baseball, Foster proposed the creation of two black circuits patterned after the white major leagues. After having failed to obtain support from the East, he went ahead and organized the Negro National League (NNL) in 1920. Consisting initially of barnstorming teams based in Chicago (two), Detroit, Indianapolis, St. Louis, and Kansas City, all the clubs except the Kansas City Monarchs were controlled by blacks. In the 1920s several other black leagues, including the Eastern Colored League, the Southern Negro League, and the Texas Negro League, none of which were as successful as the NNL, rose, struggled briefly, and expired.

The Negro National League always operated on the edge of extinction. Although some financial data published in 1923 indicate that the NNL averaged about 1,650 fans per game, a respectable figure when compared to the upper-level minor leagues of that day, the black ghettos simply did not have enough people or discretionary income to support a full summer of league play. Neither did the black league attract many white fans; as Effie Manly, an owner of the Newark franchise, observed, "it was next to impossible to get much space [for black baseball] in the white metropolitan dailies." Blacks, on the other hand, frequented white major and minor league ballparks. While "scores of people in Harlem . . . do not know there is a colored baseball club in the city," charged the *Amsterdam News* in 1929, Harlemites avidly followed the exploits of New York's white major league teams.

Of the more than 200 games typically played in a year by the black clubs, only a third were league games. They played the remaining two-thirds of their games against a motley array of pro and semipro teams, white and black, while touring towns both small and large throughout the United States, Mexico, Central America, and the Caribbean. When clubs could make more money by playing nonleague foes or by making barnstorming forays, they might simply refuse to schedule or play league games. Furthermore, because few of the black clubs owned a playing field, they were at the complete mercy of white club owners. This meant they could play in major or minor league parks only when the white clubs were not playing there. Because of the allure of nonleague games and problems with finding playing fields, the black clubs never played the same number of league games in a season, a fact that greatly reduced the potential excitement of pennant races.

The Great Depression of the 1930s ushered in a new age of league baseball, one that Jules Tygiel has labeled "the reign of the numbers men." Earlier, in 1926, Foster had grown ill, depriving the Negro National League of its leadership. Two years later the Eastern Colored League collapsed, and in 1931 the NNL disbanded, leaving black baseball without an organized structure. White booking agents and black numbers men stepped into the gap. In Pittsburgh, Gus Greenlee, the "Mr. Big" of the Northside numbers rackets, took over the local Crawfords, on which he lavished $100,000 to build a new stadium and to woo star players from other teams.

In 1933 Greenlee brought together numbers racketeers in Harlem, Newark, and Baltimore to rejuvenate the NNL. Four years later the formation of the Negro American League, comprising cities in the Midwest and South and dominated by the Kansas City Monarchs, permitted the playing of an annual "World Series." Nonetheless, the premier event in black baseball was not the World Series but rather the annual East-West All-Star Game, which was introduced by Greenlee in 1933 and played in Chicago. By 1939 popular players received as many as a half-million fan votes, and large crowds attended the All-Star Games. Negro league ball reached the apex of its popularity in the war years. In 1942, two million fans watched its games, and the East-West game attracted 51,000 spectators.

By then, black pro baseball had become an integral part of northern urban ghetto life. Despite being victimized by discrimination, prejudice, and an inferior share of the fruits of America's economic productivity, urban blacks were able to build some community structures. Among these were the services provided by black professionals, newspapers, small businesses and racketeers, voluntary associations such as churches, lodges, and athletic clubs, and the agencies of commercial entertainment such as the local professional and semipro baseball teams. As among urban whites, the teams frequently deepened a sense of community. "The Monarchs was Kansas City's team," bragged bartender Jesse Fisher. "They made Kansas City the talk of the town all over the world." The "Monarchs have done more than any other single agent in Kansas City," added the *Kansas City Call*, "to break the damnable outrage of prejudice that exists in this city."

Although, like other black entertainers, the ball players held esteemed positions in their communities and earned incomes far above the average for African Americans, life was not always easy for them. They regularly confronted America's overt racial discrimination, perhaps more than most blacks. Barred from white hotels and restaurants, they frequently had to sleep in private homes, black flophouses, or even on the team bus. Life on the road was difficult in other ways. "Rarely were we in the same city two days in a row," recalled Roy Campanella of the Baltimore Elite Giants. "Mostly we played by day and traveled by night."

◫ ◫ ◫

Apart from clowning, the black style of play differed in other ways from white baseball. With the hitting revolution of the 1920s, the emphasis in white baseball had shifted to power, especially to the home run. Although black baseball had its sluggers as well, it was more opportunistic, improvisational, and daring than white ball. It resembled more the inside baseball of an earlier era, that of the Baltimore Orioles of the 1890s and of John J. McGraw's Giants in the first two decades of the twentieth century.

Nothing summed up the uniqueness of black baseball more than its sheer speed. When combined with the bunt, the hit-and-run play, the stolen base, and taking the extra base, team speed often confounded white opponents. Center fielder James "Cool Papa" Bell, who personified black speed, was so fleet-footed, marveled rival third baseman Judy Johnson, that "you couldn't play back in your regular position or you'd never throw him out." The best story of Bell's swiftness came from a master of hyperbole, Leroy "Satchel" Paige. Bell was so fast, Paige said, that "he could flip the switch and get into bed before the room went dark." Bell's remarkable speed allowed him to play shallow in center field, catching drives that would otherwise drop in for base hits, while successfully patrolling the deepest reaches of the outfield.

Dozens of individual black players were equal or superior to the white big-leaguers. Pittsburgh's Homestead Grays teammates Josh Gibson and Buck Leonard were justifiably hailed as the Babe Ruth and Lou Gehrig of the black leagues. The duo led the Grays to nine consecutive NNL titles. Beginning in 1927 and continuing for nearly two decades, Gibson launched prodigious home runs while playing on the sandlots of Pittsburgh, in the black leagues, and on barnstorming tours. Witnesses claim that the distances of shots that he hit in Forbes Field and in Yankee Stadium have never been exceeded by any other player in baseball history. Sadly, only a few months before Jackie Robinson played his first game in a Brooklyn Dodgers uniform, Gibson died from a brain tumor at the age of thirty-five.

Only one other black player was better known or more popular than Gibson: the legendary pitcher Leroy "Satchel" Paige, who figuratively and to a substantial degree literally towered over the world of black baseball. Like Ruth, who had so dominated major league baseball earlier, the long and lean Paige uncontestedly occupied the center stage of black baseball in the 1930s and 1940s. Like Ruth, he possessed awesome skills. An aura of excitement always hung about him, an anticipation that he might perform the unexpected or do the impossible. "Just the sight of [Paige] strolling languorously toward the mound—an improbable figure rising high on pencil-thin legs," Robert Peterson has written, "was enough to send waves of excitement coursing through the ballpark."

Like that of Ruth, the Paige legend began with his struggle to surmount poverty. He was born the seventh of eleven children in a Mobile, Alabama, ghetto. Contrary to popular opinion, it was not his size-twelve feet but the toting of satchels at the Mobile train station as a lad of seven that provided Paige with his colorful nickname Satchel. Five years later, stealing rings at a local store landed Paige in the Mt. Meigs reform school, where he spent the next five years learning to read and write (barely), growing to six feet, three and one-half inches and 140 pounds. In 1924 and 1925 he pitched for the local Mobile Tigers semipro team. The next season he joined the Chattanooga Black Lookouts of the Negro Southern League, and two years later he switched to the Birmingham Black Barons of the Negro National League. By 1930, his blazing fastball, pinpoint control, and showmanship had already made him a legend in the South. "Everybody in the South knew about Satchel Paige, even then," recalled Jimmie Crutchfield. "We'd have

8,000 people out—sometimes more—when he was pitching, which was something in Birmingham."

In the 1930s the Paige legend reached epic proportions. During his stormy association with Gus Greenlee's powerful Pittsburgh Crawfords between 1932 and 1938, not only did Paige pitch sensationally, but Greenlee regularly hired him out to semipro clubs on a per-game basis. Feuding frequently with Greenlee over his salary, Paige on several occasions jumped his contract. In 1934, for example, he finished out the season with a white Bismarck, North Dakota, semipro team, and in 1935, when he was banned from the NNL, he pitched the club to the national semipro championship. In addition, in the autumns of 1934 and 1935, he toured the nation with his "Satchel Paige All-Stars" pitted against Dizzy Dean's white big league "All-Stars." Surviving records indicate that Paige's team won two-thirds of these games. In 1937 he hurled a team sponsored by dictator Rafael Trujillo to the championship of the Dominican Republic and in the following season pitched in the Mexican League.

Suddenly, in 1938, Paige's pitching career seemed to be over. After having pitched in so many games almost daily on a year-round basis, he came down with a sore arm. The Kansas City Monarchs signed him solely as a gate attraction, to accompany the team and pitch a few innings in each game for their barnstorming second team. Then, just as abruptly as it had left him, Paige's fastball returned. He joined the Monarchs' parent team, for which he hurled between 1939 and 1947. He never pitched better. While aiding the Monarchs in capturing four straight Negro American League pennants, he pitched most of his games on a hired-out basis for semipro clubs and even for other black league clubs. "He kept our league going," recalled Othella Renfroe. "Anytime a team got into trouble, it sent for Satchel to pitch."

The Paige legend arose from more than his pitching prowess; indeed, few if any pitchers in the history of the game have been his equal. Paige was also a consummate showman. In an age before the exploitation of black stereotypes seemed so obnoxious, he used a full arsenal of minstrel show formulas. Some of these are vividly revealed in Tristram Potter Coffin's description of Paige in a barnstorming game played against white opponents at Newark, Ohio:

> Between innings, Paige sat in a rocking chair and sipped from a black bottle. He used all his eccentric pitches, throwing overhand, sidearm, underhand; showed the batters the hesitation pitch, the two-hump blooper,

the fastballs Long Tom and Little Tom. . . . He joked and hammed around, played first base, and even got a hit. It was a minstrel show transferred to the ball field—a show Paige had acted out a thousand times before and which had kept body and soul together for close to half a century.

In addition, the Paige persona included a naturally comic appearance, astonishing stamina and success with women, a decided preference for rest over work, a complete absence of time-consciousness, an enormous fund of country folk aphorisms, and a talent for telling tall tales. He either refused to say how old he was or came up with contradictory dates for his birth, leaving the impression that, "like most Darkies," he could not remember his birth date. He carefully cultivated a reputation for not being in a hurry or on time. When confronted with why, he invariably responded with a folk saying: "My feets told me it was gonna rain, so I didn't think there'd be a game." His rules for remaining youthful included avoiding "fried meat which angry up the blood." "Keep the juices flowing by jangling around gently as you move" and "Don't look back. Something might be gaining on you," he said.

Dozens of tall tales embellished the Paige legend. They included calling in the outfield, deliberately loading the bases, and then striking out the side. Or pretending to throw three Long Toms (fastballs), with the catcher slapping his hand in his mitt after each while the umpire yelled, "Strike One," Strike Two," and "Strike Three." The batter then walked back to the dugout muttering, "Ole Satch is so fast today you can hardly see 'em leave his hand!"

In 1948, as a forty-two-year-old rookie, Paige finally entered the big leagues. With a 6-1 record, he aided Bill Veeck's Cleveland Indians in capturing the AL crown. Released by the Indians at the conclusion of the 1949 season, he barnstormed until 1951, when Veeck, now the owner of the St. Louis Browns, signed him again. As a relief specialist, he pitched in forty-six games in 1952 and fifty-seven games in 1953. Except for a three-inning outing with the Kansas City Athletics in 1965, he pitched the remainder of his career with minor league and barnstorming teams.

◩ ◩ ◩

Until the war years of the 1940s, few blacks dreamed that they might soon crack organized baseball's color ban. They, along with most white Americans, were unaware of the slow, largely silent pressures that were mounting to end America's apartheid. One pressure was simply the sheer number of blacks flooding into northern cities. In the "Great Migration" from the South to the North, more than two million came in the 1910s, one million in the 1920s, 400,000 in the 1930s, and another million in the 1940s. Although strapped by low incomes, the fast-growing pool of blacks living in major league cities represented both potentially new baseball customers and a new political bloc.

Urban blacks soon learned that trading black votes for black rights in the highly contested, two-party states of the North could be an effective tactic for obtaining concessions. In 1942, in New York, a state in which black voters could decisively affect elections, the legislature passed the Quinn-Ives Act to ban discrimination in hiring. In New York City, Mayor Fiorello LaGuardia established a special committee to consider the city's race relations, including the apparent discrimination against blacks by the local Dodgers, Giants, and Yankees. By 1945, the political circumstances in New York City for an assault on segregated baseball had improved.

Ironically, the rise of Nazi Germany and the outbreak of World War II also contributed to the black cause. To sports fans, the victories of track star Jesse Owens at the 1936 Olympic Games held in Berlin and boxer Joe Louis's knockout of Germany's Max Schmelling in 1938 seemed the perfect answer to Nazi racism, but the successes of the black athletes also highlighted the contradictions between official American principles and the nation's actual racial practices. During the 1930s, black newspapers, a few influential white sportswriters, and the American Communist Party seized on the discrepancy between principle and practice to advocate the end of baseball's unofficial color ban. That blacks fought and died for their country in World War II while simultaneously being barred from organized baseball revealed an incongruity of equal proportions. "I can play in Mexico, but I have to fight in America where I can't play," protested Nate Moreland. "If we are able to stop bullets, why not balls?" queried placards carried by picketers at Yankee Stadium.

Blacks hoped that the manifest shortage of good big league players resulting from the war might provide them with opportunities to break the color ban. "How do you think I felt when I saw a one-armed [white big league] outfielder?" exclaimed star black pitcher Chet Brewer. By 1943 rumors circulated that several major and minor league clubs were on the verge of signing black players, but nothing came of them. In the same year, rumors spread that young Bill Veeck, who had recently put together a package for the purchase of the Philadelphia Phillies, was embarking on a

daring plan to stock his new team with Negro league stars. Commissioner Landis quickly squelched Veeck by blocking the purchase. While repeatedly denying the existence of any rule against signing blacks, Landis had
in fact consistently policed the color line. His death in 1944 eliminated a
major obstacle to baseball's integration.

In 1945, in the final year of the war, opposition to baseball's segregation gained additional momentum. On April 6, *People's Voice* sportswriter Joe Bostic infuriated Branch Rickey by appearing at the Brooklyn Dodgers training camp with two black league players in tow, for whom he
demanded a tryout. Outmaneuvered, Rickey had his coaches put the players through a fielding and hitting drill, although he had no intention of
offering them a contract. A week later, pressured by a city councilman and
an influential sportswriter, the Boston Red Sox reluctantly agreed to give
auditions to Sam Jethro, the Negro league's leading hitter, in 1944, as well
as to Marvin Williams and Jackie Robinson, but afterward the players
heard nothing from the Red Sox. Nonetheless, the words of baseball's
newly appointed commissioner, A. B. "Happy" Chandler, former gover-
nor of Kentucky, were far more promising than anything Landis had ever
said. "If a black boy can make it in Okinawa and Guadalcanal," Chandler told a black reporter, "hell, he can make it in baseball."

In the meantime, unknown to baseball's leading proponents of integration, Rickey was putting in motion his own plan for dismantling baseball's
Jim Crow system. Although Rickey later claimed that he had been a sup-
porter of integration since 1904, when an Indiana hotel had refused lodg-
ings to a black player on a college team that he was coaching, he had revealed no interest in racial justice as the longtime general manager of the
St. Louis Cardinals. Apart from moral considerations that may have aris-
en from his devout Methodist upbringing, Rickey admitted that he looked
to blacks as a way of improving the performance of his team. "I don't mean
to be a crusader," he wrote to a sportswriter friend in 1945. "My only
purpose is to be fair to all people and my selfish objective is to win baseball games." Moreover, the notoriously parsimonious Rickey had no intention of remunerating the Negro leagues for their player losses; after all,
he had uncovered a large pool of remarkable talent for which he had to
pay virtually nothing. Finally, Rickey was acutely aware of the political
situation in New York and was no doubt conscious of the potential for
attracting more black fans to Dodger games.

Rickey worked out a careful plan for introducing a black player into the
major leagues. Apparently so that he could scout black talent without being

detected, he announced the formation of an all-black league. He sought a black athlete who could make the club and stand up to the expected abuse from white players and fans. Except for his fiery disposition and some doubts about his playing skills (Robinson was not considered the best of the black league stars by anyone), Jackie Robinson, a shortstop for the Kansas City Monarchs, fit Rickey's requirements perfectly. Robinson had experience in dealing with whites, had been a student at UCLA, had been an army officer in World War II, and was an active Methodist who did not smoke, drink, or womanize. Finally, Robinson was a gifted athlete, perhaps the best all-around athlete in the United States. He had starred in football, basketball, golf, track, and swimming at UCLA. After their tension-ridden interview in 1945, Rickey assigned Robinson in 1946 to play for Montreal, on a Dodger farm club located in a city with a more liberal racial climate than most counterparts in the United States. At Montreal, Robinson won the International League's most valuable player award and moved up to the parent club in 1947. In the meantime, Rickey ignored two requests by the Kansas City Monarchs that the club be compensated for its loss of Robinson.

Robinson was an instant hero of blacks. "When times get really hard, really tough, He [God] always send you somebody," said Ernest J. Gaines's fictional heroine Miss Jane Pittman. "In the Depression it was tough on everybody, but twice as hard on the colored, and he sent us Joe [Louis] . . . after the war, He sent us Jackie." At games in spring training, in the International League, and in the National League, blacks came out in droves to see Robinson play. Partly due to the sheer novelty of a black playing big league ball and partly because Robinson exhibited a daring on the basepaths unequaled since Ty Cobb, many whites came specifically to see him play as well. Thanks largely to Robinson, five National League teams set new season attendance records in 1947. But racial integration spelled disaster for the black leagues. "Negro League fans," as Jules Tygiel has observed, "voted with their dollars decisively in favor of integration." The Negro National League dissolved after the 1948 season, and the Negro American League fielded only four teams in 1953 before finally expiring in 1960.

No uniform white reaction greeted Robinson. Before he arrived in Brooklyn, southern players on the Dodgers circulated a petition demanding that he not be promoted to the parent club, but organized opposition dissipated when Rickey agreed to trade discontented players to other clubs. Although eventually accepted by his teammates as a valuable asset, Robinson, who was by nature a brooding loner, was never popular with them. Apparently, a threat of wholesale suspensions by NL president Ford Frick stopped a rumored plan by St. Louis Cardinals players to boycott games with the Dodgers.

Yet dangers lurked everywhere. Robinson regularly received scrawled notes threatening his life. "Every time daddy went on one of those early trips," his daughter Sharon recalled, "we had fears that he would be assassinated!" At the personal costs of persistent headaches, bouts of depression, and smoldering resentments, Robinson eased the way for his acceptance by publicly ignoring the racial slurs of the players on the other teams. Instead of retaliating directly, he channeled his energies onto the baseball field, where he played magnificently. By the end of 1947 Robinson had won over many whites; in fact, his popularity was so great that he won the Rookie of the Year Award, and a poll ranked him second only to singer Bing Crosby as the nation's most admired man. The poll suggested that pressures to exclude or limit blacks in organized baseball may have arisen more from the owners' fears and prejudices than from the public's.

Regardless, Robinson's successes failed to result in baseball's rapid integration. A few weeks after Robinson joined the Dodger organization, Rickey signed three additional blacks, but no other teams immediately followed his example. At the conclusion of the 1948 season, a full year after Robinson had first played at Brooklyn, only one team (Cleveland) had a black player, and as late as 1953 only six teams fielded black players. Finally, in 1959, twelve years after Robinson's debut, the Boston Red Sox became the last team to employ a black player. Integration was uneven. Throughout most of the 1950s the New York/San Francisco Giants alone had twice as many blacks as the entire American League. Indeed, the NL's far greater number of black players may have been the main reason that it won nine of thirteen All-Star Games in the 1950s.

Blacks quickly demonstrated that they had playing skills equal if not superior to those of whites. In fact, long before the advent of Robinson, black stars had regularly defeated whites in touring "all-star" and exhibition contests; John Holway has found records of black stars winning 269 and losing 169 of these contests between 1887 and 1947. Jackie Robinson himself won the NL's Most Valuable Player Award (MVP) in 1949, had a .311 career batting average, and helped carry the Dodgers to six league flags. Beginning with Dodger catcher Roy Campanella's second award in 1952, black players won the next six NL MVP awards. Blacks also won a disproportionate number of other NL crowns (in terms of their total numbers in the league as well as in the general population). In the 1950s they captured four titles in batting, five in runs batted in, four in home runs, and six in stolen bases. In the following decades, exhibitions of black skills would be equally impressive.

By the early 1950s, many if not all clubs had unwritten understandings to restrict the total number of blacks. Driven in part by the profit motive, the owners tried to calculate whether increasing the number of black players would result in more wins and thereby increase attendance or whether it would adversely affect the identification of white fans with their teams and thereby reduce attendance and revenues. The net effect of such thinking was that blacks had to outperform whites to make team rosters. For example, Gerald W. Scully found that, for the 1966–70 seasons, blacks batted an average of 20.8 points higher than whites.

Other forms of discrimination continued long after the collapse of baseball's color line. Blacks tended to be relegated to certain playing positions and excluded from others, a phenomenon known as "stacking." In 1976, for instance, 52 percent of the major league outfielders were black, 4 percent of the pitchers, 4 percent of the catchers, none of the shortstops, 17 percent of the third basemen, 39 percent of the second basemen, and 50 percent of the first basemen. Sport sociologists speculated that white management discriminated in favor of whites when choosing players for "central positions," those that require more decisions, leadership, and interaction among players. Perhaps the pattern was self-perpetuating, for blacks may have concluded that they could improve their chances of success by preparing themselves for noncentral positions. At any rate, although in the 1980s the incidence of stacking diminished, *Sports Illustrated* reported in 1988 that 78 percent of the black players (not including pitchers) played first base or the outfield.

Nor did blacks obtain equal opportunities in management. No black owned a big league franchise, and few held positions as game officials, managers, coaches, or executives. Until 1961, when the Pittsburgh Pirates appointed Gene Baker to manage their Batavia franchise, no black managed a team at any level of organized baseball. Finally, in 1975, the Cleveland Indians hired Frank Robinson as the first big league black manager, but this precedent did little to expand black opportunities. More than four decades after the collapse of baseball's Jim Crow, only four blacks had managed big league clubs, and surveys taken in 1982 and in 1987 disclosed barriers to blacks nearly as impenetrable for other administrative positions in baseball. A 1987 study revealed that fifteen of the twenty-six major league clubs did not employ a single black in a management position.

On the other hand, racial integration not only allowed blacks to play in organized baseball but also opened the door to a growing number of Latino players. Led by Roberto Clemente, who captured four batting titles, and Juan Marichal, who emerged as the decade's winningest pitcher, Latino stars began to rise to prominence in the 1960s. Adding to Clemente's stature as a folk hero in the Caribbean and in the United States was his death in a 1972 plane crash while carrying supplies to the victims of a Nicaraguan earthquake. Had it not been for the severance in the 1960s of diplomatic relations between the United States and Cuba, American professional baseball would have been the beneficiary of an even greater amount of Latin talent. But the flow of players from Latin America to the big leagues was not simply one of South to North. North American players continued, as they had since the beginning of the century, to trek southward to the Caribbean basin during the winter to play with barnstorming outfits and in professional leagues.

❏   ❏   ❏

Throughout most of its history, baseball mirrored the nation's racial practices. During the same era that the South (and to a lesser degree the North) fastened on the nation a rigid system of racial segregation, organized baseball unofficially excluded blacks from its game. For a shining, sterling moment in its history, however, the sport embarked on a "great experiment" in race relations. Well before any other major institution in the nation had acted to end Jim Crow and a full seven years before the famous Brown Supreme Court decision ending school segregation, baseball terminated its color ban and for a time seemed to be poised for an even larger assault on racism. But the attack never came. In subsequent decades the racial practices of the national pastime reflected the dogged persistence of the nation's racial bigotry.

12

The Last Days of the Old Game

In 1956 the New York Yankees and the Brooklyn Dodgers met in the World Series for the sixth time in ten years. Prior to 1955 the Yankee leviathan had crushed its crosstown rivals four consecutive times. In 1955 the Bums finally won a Series. Hoping to repeat their success in 1956, they took the first two games, but the Yankees bounced back to win the next three. Nothing extraordinary happened until game five, when Yankee pitcher Don Larsen hurled a perfect game. Never before in a World Series had even an ordinary no-hitter been pitched, let alone a perfect game. After that feat, the seventh and final game was anticlimactic. The Yanks won 9-0.

The 1956 Subway Series was the last ever played in New York City between the two great dynastic rivals of the post–World War II era. This was only one indication that organized baseball was in the final chapter of an older game. Never again would the major leagues be limited to ten cities in an area that extended southward only to Washington and westward only to St. Louis, would the players travel only by train, or would a commissioner enjoy an authority equal to that of Judge Kenesaw Mountain Landis. Never again would the game be played exclusively on natural grass by men in flannel uniforms or would the players wear small, floppy gloves that they would leave behind on the outfield grass while taking their turns at bat. And never again (after 1954) would Connie Mack—tall and dignified in his suit and tie—occupy the dugout of the Philadelphia Athletics as he had since 1901. Organized baseball would never again be "lily white," a game that completely excluded Americans of African descent. Nor would sandlot and minor league baseball ever again rule supreme in countless neighborhoods, towns, and smaller cities. Fans would never again be able to read the venerable *Baseball* magazine, and *The Sporting News,* the weekly "Bible of Baseball," would never again devote its pages exclusively to coverage of the national game. A long era of baseball history was passing.

▣ ▣ ▣

Nothing about baseball's response to World War II suggested that the game was about to close its longest chapter. In 1942, at the nadir of Allied military fortunes, Landis queried President Franklin D. Roosevelt, a man Landis passionately despised, about the future of baseball. Landis volunteered to suspend operations entirely if necessary. Responding that play would be good for sustaining morale "even if the actual quality of the teams is lowered by the greater use of older players," Roosevelt urged that the big leagues, within the constraints imposed by the war, carry on as usual. Because of an alleged rubber shortage, baseball in 1943 substituted balata, a rubberlike gum, for the rubber sheathing around the ball's cork center. Whether because of the somewhat softer "bastard" ball or the absence of the sluggers who had departed for the war, offensive output slumped. In 1944, Nick Etten of the Yankees led the AL in home runs with only twenty-two, and in the following season the Yankees' George Stirnweiss led the loop in batting with a mere .309.

One unexpected consequence of the war was the inauguration of one of the game's key rituals, the playing or singing of "The Star Spangled Banner" before each contest commenced. The United States had entered World War I without an official national anthem, but "The Star Spangled Banner" caught on with the fans in the 1918 World Series. After the series, it continued to be played at Opening Day, at the World Series, and on other patriotic occasions when a band was present. In 1931 Congress officially made "The Star Spangled Banner" the national anthem, and by World War II, powerful, sophisticated public address systems let fans hear it sung by vocalists or performed on recordings. By the end of the war in 1945 it had become an accepted practice to have the national anthem performed before each game.

The war, on the other hand, provided an open challenge to the notion of baseball's exclusiveness as America's game and to the game's allegedly unique congruencies with American character. No nation in the world, apart from the United States and perhaps some of the Caribbean republics, took to baseball with more alacrity than Japan, the major partner with Germany in the Axis alliance. American missionaries had introduced the sport there as early as the 1870s, professional leagues eventually formed, and in the 1920s and 1930s Japanese baseball fans cheered such American stars as Babe Ruth and Lou Gehrig as they played on touring nines. American soldiers in the Pacific soon learned of the enemy's familiarity with baseball when they confronted Japanese battle cries of "Fuck Babe Ruth!" After the war, perhaps sensing that baseball might foster democracy, the United States occupational forces quickly assisted Japanese baseball authorities in reestablishing their professional leagues.

The biggest wartime problem for American professional baseball was the loss of players to the armed forces. For opening day of 1944, *The Sporting News* reported that only 40 percent of those who had played in 1941 were still in the starting lineups; all nine of the 1941 Yankee starters, for example, had gone off to war. By 1944, several of the game's greatest stars—including Joe DiMaggio, Hank Greenberg, Ted Williams, and Bob Feller—had already been in the service for a year or two. Clubs filled their rosters with physical rejects or players who were too old or too young for the military draft. The St. Louis Browns, who won their only AL championship in 1944, even employed a one-armed (but able) outfielder in 1945. Stocked by big-leaguers in the armed services, several servicemen's teams fielded stronger nines than the major league clubs.

Wartime player shortages contributed to the creation of a professional women's baseball league. A few women occasionally played baseball as early as the 1860s, but play usually took diametrically opposing forms. Either it was a game played on the secluded grounds of women's colleges, protected from the prying eyes of spectators, or it was a novelty designed explicitly to attract spectator stares for profit. In the 1880s entrepreneurs organized several barnstorming women's teams, whose members as often as not exhibited more talent as showgirls than as ball players. Around the turn of the century a half dozen or more of these barnstorming nines were known as Bloomer Girls, although such teams sometimes included a few boys in disguise as girls. A flyer, circa 1913, advertised "The Original Bloomer Girls" as "Refined and Moral . . . Indorsed by Public Press and Pulpit, [and the] only Female Club Recognized by . . . Reputable Managers," implying that the other girls' clubs fell short of publicly acceptable refinement and morality.

Ultimately, softball was a far more important impetus to female ball playing than the barnstorming baseball teams. Although several modified versions of men's baseball rules had been tried by women—especially shortening the distances between the bases—none of them had won widespread favor. But softball, with its larger ball and smaller diamond, was another matter. Starting from centers in Chicago and southern California, interest in the game had grown so much that by 1933 the Amateur Softball Association scheduled national tournaments for both women and men. Play by defense workers during World War II and the increased use of cheap outdoor lighting furnished an added stimulus to women's softball. An estimate in 1943 placed the total number of women's teams at more than 40,000, nearly one-fourth of all softball teams.

Fearing that professional baseball might be forced to close down during World War II, Philip K. Wrigley, chewing-gum magnate and owner of the Chicago Cubs, hit on the idea of forming a professional women's softball league to play in big league parks. Although the men's game was able to continue through the war without interruption, Wrigley went ahead anyway with a modified version of his plan. In 1943 the All-American Girls Professional Baseball League made its debut with four teams: The Rockford (Illinois) Peaches, the South Bend (Indiana) Blue Sox, the Racine (Wisconsin) Belles, and the Kenosha (Wisconsin) Belles. The league initially used a twelve-inch ball, sixty-five-foot base paths, and underhanded pitching. Its 108-game schedule attracted 176,000 fans, which, according to one observer, was "a higher percentage of the population [in the league cities] than major league baseball ever [drew] in its greatest attendance years."

Wrigley insisted that his players completely dissociate themselves from the prevailing image of the top-flight women softball players. Critics frequently charged the softballers with being "muscle molls" on one hand or with flaunting their sexual attractions on the other. "Give 'em a cud of tobacco," wrote Robert Yoder in the *Saturday Evening Post* in 1943, "and these female softball players would look just like their big-league brothers." Nevertheless, promoters gave their teams such alluring names as the

"Balian Ice Cream Beauties," "Barney Ross's Adorables," and "Slapsie Maxie's Curvaceous Cuties."

Wrigley brooked no compromises with a strict feminine image. In both the 1943 and 1944 seasons, the league required that the players attend a charm school conducted by Helena Rubenstein's famed Chicago-based beauty salon and finishing school. There they learned how to apply makeup properly, fix their hair, and, in the words of Debra Shattuck, "display impeccable social graces." Perhaps because the costs were believed to outweigh the returns, use of the school was discontinued after two seasons, but the league continued to insist on a strict dress and behavior code. "Masculine hair styling, shoes, coats, shirts, socks, T-shirts, are barred at all times," read the dress standards in 1951. Whereas ejection from a game by the umpire could cost a player a ten-dollar fine, a much stiffer penalty of fifty dollars awaited the girl who appeared "unkempt" in public.

The All-American Girls Professional Baseball League continued to prosper in the immediate postwar years. The fans apparently liked the introduction of overhanded pitching, the use of a smaller ball, and an extension of the distance between the bases to seventy-two feet, all measures that moved the sport closer to the men's game. Throwing across the diamond must have been difficult for the women, however, for in 1943 Sophie Kurys was thrown out only twice in 203 stolen base attempts. Attendance peaked in 1948, when the league's ten teams drew nearly a million fans, but then, as Americans became more enthralled by television and other forms of at-home recreation, attendance began to fall. After having provided nearly 500 women with an opportunity to play pro baseball and entertaining several million fans, the league folded in 1954.

▣ ▣ ▣

Just as nothing about baseball's response to World War II suggested that the game was closing a chapter of its history, baseball journalism in the 1940s and 1950s remained much as it had been since early in the century. The modern sports page had begun to take shape in the 1890s but did not become a standard feature in all major daily newspapers until the 1920s. In that decade, the percentage of total space allotted to sports was more than twice what it had been three decades earlier. Baseball took up a disproportionate amount of the sports page; even in the winter fans could read lengthy "hot stove league" reports about the past, present, and future of the game. Rather than having to confront the turmoil and unpredictability of front-page news, many Americans (especially men) turned to the baseball news to find clearcut triumphs and defeats, continuity, and order-liness. "You pulled off the double play the same way for the Richmond County juniors, the Auks or the White Sox," Tom Wicker, a *New York Times* columnist, has written. "Baseball was a common denominator... it was the same one day as the next, in one town as another."

By the 1920s dozens of daily newspapers employed writers who special-ized in sports. Rather than stringing together quotations from participants (too often a characteristic of sports reporting in the age of television), Grant-land Rice, Paul Gallico, Frank Graham, Damon Runyan, Ring Lardner, Westbrook Pegler, Heywood Broun, and Arch Ward, among others, tried to construct an interesting and interpretive story of what had happened or was about to happen. The best of them could weave a story as tight as the strands of a steel cable. Apart from presenting a coherent narrative, they used powerful, often onomatopoetic verbs, colorful figures of speech, and alliterative nicknames. Nicknames came in a virtual flood: the Sultan of Swat (Babe Ruth), the Yankee Clipper (Joe DiMaggio), and the Old Ro-man (Charles Comiskey). They also delighted in using all three names of people involved in sports, such as Grover Cleveland Alexander, Kenesaw Mountain Landis, or George Herman Ruth, thereby conferring upon them a kind of tongue-in-cheek grandeur. Taking it for granted that they should promote the welfare of the national pastime, they rarely exposed to public scrutiny anything negative about the private lives of ball players, manag-ers, or owners. However, this did not exempt them from examining criti-cally the public actions of baseball's personnel.

Radio, which began to have an impact on sports as early as the 1920s, brought a totally new experience to the fan. Now the fans did not have to await their morning newspapers; they could instantly share the drama tran-spiring on the playing field. While remaining loyal to the basic facts, the announcers could add drama by resorting to hyperbole or altering the rhythm and inflection of their deliveries. Radio inspired the imagination. Because listeners could not see what was happening, they were free to take liberties with the content of what they heard on radio. Rather than visu-alizing the shortstop merely stopping a routine ground ball, the listener might imagine that it had been a hard smash, or an ordinary fly ball might be transformed into a long drive.

Until they were upstaged by television in the 1950s, the radio broadcasts of the World Series became an annual rite. The *New York Times* deemed the airing of the 1926 series to be such a pioneering venture that it carried the entire narrative in its sports section. By the mid-1930s, Landis was successfully insisting that radio pay for broadcasting the series. In 1939 the Gillette Safety Razor Company began its thirty-two-year stint as the regular sponsor of the series. Landis himself carefully monitored the content of the broadcasts. When Ted Husing, CBS's premier sportscaster, questioned some of the decisions of umpires in the 1933 series, Landis banned him from the World Series microphone for life.

Radio became a far more important medium for regular season baseball games in the post–World War II era. Between 1945 and 1950 the number of locally operated AM radio stations doubled; these stations often turned to baseball to fill program gaps. For instance, in the 1950s the Mutual Broadcasting Company sent its major league "Game of the Day" to nearly 500 stations scattered across the country. In parts of the West Coast a listener could hear baseball broadcasts from 11:00 in the morning until 11:00 at night. In the late 1940s and early 1950s, the St. Louis Cardinals regional network regularly included some 120 stations spread over nine states. On weekends the arrival of busloads of Cardinal fans from towns several hundred miles from St. Louis furnished visible testimony of radio's capacity to create fan loyalty over a large regional area. On the other hand, the radio broadcast of major league games may have damaged attendance at sandlot and minor league games.

Until the mid-1950s, many broadcasts consisted of "re-creations" rather than live play-by-play coverage. Because sending a crew to a far-off location (not to mention telephone charges) could be excessively expensive, stations re-created games from telegraph reports. Miles from the site of the game, a Western Union operator received a Morse code report of the game and transcribed the dots and dashes into a shorthand version of the contest. The announcer then described the game as though he were actually witnessing it. For a backdrop, sound technicians furnished recordings of crowd noises. Sometimes loud cheering broke out on the recording at an entirely inappropriate time. The announcer responded by quickly inventing a spectacular catch of a foul ball by a fan or perhaps a rhubarb between a manager and an umpire. Sometimes the Western Union ticker broke down; radio fans were then treated to the batter hitting a dozen fouls in succession or a sudden, inexplicable rain shower.

Locally, regular season baseball broadcasters became institutions. To the fans, they were often inseparable from the team and its fate. Mel Allen, the voice of the Yankees, and Harry Caray, the voice of the Cardinals, were masters of the "gee whiz" style of broadcasting, which sometimes elevated ordinary play into the realm of the immortal. Red Barber, on the other hand, relied on precise description to enchant Brooklyn fans. Barber began his career doing Cincinnati Reds games for $25 a week in 1934; by 1954, when he departed from Brooklyn to join the Yankees, his salary had risen to $50,000 annually. All the announcers served at the pleasure of the owners, and when they failed to convey the message desired by their employers, they faced dismissal. Annoyed by Barber's candor, the Yankee management fired him in 1967.

Still, the central attraction of baseball remained the game itself. Few events in American history quite equaled the sheer drama of the final game of the 1951 playoff between the Brooklyn Dodgers and the New York Giants for the NL pennant. The Giants and Dodgers divided the first two games. In the decisive third contest, when the Giants came to bat in the last half of the ninth inning, they trailed the Dodgers 4-1. Alvin Dark led off the epic inning with a single; Don Mueller then slashed a single to right field, putting Giant runners on first and third. Monte Irvin popped up, but Whitey Lockman hit a double to left field, scoring Dark. Charlie Dressen, the Dodger manager, waved in Ralph Branca from the bullpen to replace Don Newcombe, the struggling pitcher. Branca threw a strike past Bobby Thomson. On the next pitch, Thomson drove a fast ball into the lower left-field seats of the Polo Grounds, bringing in three runs with a single blow. The pennant race was over. The Giants had won, 5-4.

That the game in the 1940s and 1950s was played essentially as it had been since the hitting revolution of the 1920s partially disguised a trend toward more one-dimensional offenses (see table 6). Players hit fewer triples, doubles, and singles; they sacrificed less and executed fewer hit-and-run plays than in the past. Whereas thirty-five players compiled seasonal batting averages over .350 in the decade before the war (1932–41), only eight accomplished this feat in the ten years afterward (1946–55). For a time, it seemed that the art of the stolen base was dead. Dom DiMaggio led the AL with a total of fifteen in 1950, and the entire Washington Senators team managed only thirteen stolen bases in 1957. During the first seven years of the 1950s not a single team stole a hundred bases in a season.

Home run production, on the other hand, ratcheted up another notch, averaging 573 more per season than in the prewar era. Sluggers of the prewar era had usually hit for high averages and frequently banged out

Table 6. The One-Dimensional Game, 1946–60

	1930–41	1946–60
Home runs	1,362	1,935
Triples	990	727
Doubles	4,275	3,499
Stolen bases	956	769
Base on balls	8,049	8,954
Strikeouts	8,245	10,569

Note: Figures are averages per season. Because of the disruptions of the 1942–45 seasons due to World War II and the use of the balata ball, data for those years are not included. In 1961, the American League became a ten-team loop, making gross seasonal comparisons impossible. Except for an upturn in stolen bases, the same basic trend continued through the 1968 season.

league-leading totals in doubles and triples, but in the one-dimensional era nearly every team featured a plodding, muscular hitter who specialized solely in clobbering the ball over the fence. Although striking out far more frequently than their predecessors, the postwar sluggers were more likely to ignore all pitches except those that they thought they could lift into the seats. "Home run hitters drive Cadillacs; singles hitters don't," explained Pittsburgh's Ralph Kiner. "At its best," Bill James has concluded, "it was the baseball of the ticking bomb, the danger building up and up and up until somebody finally put one in the seats. At its worst it was station-to-station baseball run amuck, baseball with no threat except the threat of the long ball."

Although baseball cognoscenti fondly recall the names of Ralph Kiner, Hank Sauer, Jim Lemon, Walt Dropo, Vic Wertz, Gus Zernial, and Ted Kluszewski—among others known almost exclusively for their home run prowess—the hitters with the more enduring reputations offered more than the home run. In particular, Ted Williams of the Boston Red Sox and Stan Musial of the St. Louis Cardinals stood out as all-around hitters. Musial, who played from 1941 through 1963, never led the NL in homers, but he averaged thirty-one per season from 1948 through 1957. In addition, he captured the slugging percentage crown six times, doubles eight times, triples five times, and batting average seven times. Williams was the last player to hit .400 or more (1941) and won seven AL batting titles while compiling a .344 lifetime average. Williams's career, which spanned 1939 through 1960, was interrupted by his service as a marine pilot in both World War II and the Korean War, cutting five complete seasons from his prime; nevertheless, he captured the home run title four times and the slugging percentage crown nine times. Only Babe Ruth stood ahead of Williams in career slugging percentage.

Perhaps equally impressive were the all-around performances of Mickey Mantle, Willie Mays, and Henry Aaron. In a career shortened by injuries, Mantle captured six AL titles for runs scored, four for home runs, one for batting, and four for slugging percentage. Known for his spectacular fielding and running as well as hitting, the exceptionally popular Mays led the NL in base stealing four times, home runs four times, and slugging percentage five times, and finished among the game's top all-time home run leaders. In an exceptionally long career spanning 1954 through 1976, Aaron not only led the NL in home runs four times, batting average twice, and slugging percentage four times but with a total of 755 eclipsed Ruth's career home run mark of 714. As he neared Ruth's record, Aaron became the subject of both an immense media blitz and a barrage of hate mail, much of which was blatantly racist.

⊞ ⊟ ⊟

In the postwar era, the correlation between team success and the population area served by each big league club was stronger than ever before (see tables 7 and 8). Located in New York, the nation's most populous metropolitan area, the Yankees accounted for 40 percent of the AL's attendance

Table 7. American League Pennant Winners, 1946–68

New York	Boston	Cleveland	Baltimore	Chicago	Minnesota	Detroit	Philadelphia/ Kansas City
1964	1967	1954	1966	1959	1965	1968	
1963	1946	1948					
1962							
1961							
1960							
1958							
1957							
1956							
1955							
1953							
1952							
1951							
1950							
1949							
1947							

Note: Divisional play began in 1969.

Table 8. National League Pennant Winners, 1946–68

Brooklyn/ Los Angeles	St. Louis	New York/ San Francisco	Boston/ Milwaukee	Cincinnati	Pittsburgh	Philadelphia	Chicago
1966	1968	1962	1958	1961	1960	1950	
1965	1967	1954	1957				
1963	1964	1951	1948				
1959	1946						
1956							
1955							
1953							
1952							
1949							
1947							

Note: Divisional play began in 1969.

and captured an astonishing fifteen flags in eighteen seasons. In the NL, before departing from New York, the Brooklyn Dodgers won six titles and the New York Giants two. At the conclusion of the 1964 season, teams from New York had appeared in thirty-nine of the sixty-one World Series since 1903. The clubs in the NL that had shifted the location of their franchises were also noticeably successful; prior to 1967 the Dodgers captured four crowns in Los Angeles, the Giants one in San Francisco, and the Braves two in Milwaukee.

The foundations for the postwar Yankee dynasty had been laid many years earlier. In the 1920s and 1930s wealthy owner Jacob Ruppert had urged general manager Edward Barrow to spend freely on the purchase of superior players from the minors and other big league clubs. In 1932 Ruppert assigned George Weiss the responsibility of developing a farm system that was to become the equal of Branch Rickey's in St. Louis. After the war, when the Yankees came under the ownership of Dan Topping and Del Webb, who wisely retained Weiss as farm director, the farms continued to supply the Yankees with a large transfusion of fresh talent. Among the best players to graduate from the farm to the parent club were Yogi Berra, Whitey Ford, and Mickey Mantle.

The farm system also furnished Weiss, who became the Yankee general manager in 1948, with a surplus of major league prospects whom he could use as trading bait. Season after season Weiss in effect made two-for-one deals in which he exchanged two or more of his promising minor-leaguers (sometimes plus cash) for a proven big league player needed to fill a particular vacancy in the Yankee lineup. Prior to Weiss's departure from

the Yankees in 1961, pitchers Allie Reynolds, Johnny Sain, Jim Konstan-
ty, Ryne Duren, Bob Turley, Don Larsen, Bobby Shantz, Eddie Lopat, Al
Ditmar, and Ralph Terry, all of whom had been acquired from other clubs,
had as Yankees earned a 553-364 won-lost record and accumulated 177
saves. Veteran hitters Johnny Mize, Enos Slaughter, Gene Woodling, Dale
Long, Irv Noren, and Roger Maris, who were obtained by Weiss from other
big league clubs, performed equally well in the Yankees' pin-striped uniforms. Weiss repeatedly made astute late season deals just in time to aid
the Yankees during their stretch drives for the pennant.

Not the least of Weiss's brilliant moves was to employ fifty-eight-year-old
Charles Dillon "Casey" Stengel in 1949 as the team's field manager. Because
of his garrulity, irascibility, crude practical jokes, and confusing syntax (labeled Stengelese by sportswriters), Stengel was widely regarded as something
of a clown, but behind his rubbery countenance lurked a vast reservoir of
baseball knowledge, an unorthodox but effective capacity for handling men,
and a supreme confidence in his own judgment. Until joining the Yankees,
Stengel, who had played for and learned much from the legendary John J.
McGraw, had enjoyed little success as a big league manager. In his nine years
serving the Brooklyn Dodgers and Boston Braves his teams had never finished
higher than fifth place. "Stengel's jokes got better but the team didn't," explained Harold Parrott. As a minor league manager, however, he had shown
that when he had good players at his disposal he could field winning teams.
He reaffirmed this ability in a spectacular fashion with the Yankees. During
his first five years, the Yankees won five consecutive flags and then proceeded to win five more pennants in the next seven seasons.

Although the influence of McGraw can be detected in his managerial
tactics, Stengel boldly departed from traditional managerial wisdom. Believing that a quick player with a good arm could play at any position, he
encouraged player versatility. Not a single member of the 1960 championship team's infield, for example, occupied the position he had started
in. Stengel used player platooning more than any previous manager in the
game's history. He was familiar with platooning from personal experience;
in the 1920s McGraw had started Stengel, a left-handed hitter, against
right-handed pitchers and a right-handed hitting teammate against southpaw pitchers. Platooning had never been widely used, however, and fell
completely into disfavor in the 1930s and 1940s. As manager of the Yankees, Stengel revived it, regularly platooning one or more starters. By the
mid-1960s several other clubs were copying Stengel's tactics.

Stengel likewise relied more on relief pitching than other managers. Since early in the century, managers had relieved starting pitchers, but only with the greatest reluctance and only when the starter was visibly struggling. Even the hitting revolution of the 1920s brought little change; complete game percentages declined slowly over the next two decades. After World War II, managers turned more frequently to their bullpens, and no manager was quicker to jerk a struggling starter out of the game than Stengel. Despite the Yankees having year in and year out the best offensive output and lowest earned run average in the AL, Yankee pitchers in the Stengel era fell below the league average in completed games.

In the end, the long string of successes masterminded by Weiss and Stengel was not enough to satisfy the Yankee owners. After the Yankees lost the 1960 World Series to Pittsburgh, the owners dropped both men, citing Stengel's age of seventy and Weiss's of sixty-five. For a time, relying mainly on the talent acquired by Weiss, the Yankees continued their winning ways, capturing flags in 1961, 1962, 1963, and 1964. In 1964 the Columbia Broadcasting System purchased the franchise. Two years later, the once-mighty club sank all the way to the cellar of the ten-team league, and they failed to win another flag until the Steinbrenner era fifteen years later.

But neither Weiss nor Stengel was yet through with the game. In 1962 the New York Mets, a NL expansion team, hired Weiss as general manager, and he promptly employed Stengel as his field manager. The Mets were as inept as the Yankees had been adept, but Weiss and Stengel put together a team that excelled the Yankees in attendance, media attention, and the affection of its fans. They became, in Stengel's words, "The Amazin' Mets," good enough to capture the World Series in 1969 but under the field-generalship of Gil Hodges rather than Stengel. In 1965, Stengel finally retired.

⊡   ⊡   ⊡

Unlike the Yankees, the Brooklyn Dodgers did not have a long heritage of winning pennants. Larry MacPhail, who came to Brooklyn in 1938 after having served as general manager at Cincinnati, initiated a new era of Dodger baseball. By making clever trades, freely spending money the penurious Dodgers did not have, and employing Leo Durocher as his field manager, he brought Brooklyn a pennant in 1941, their first since 1920. When MacPhail left to join the army in 1942, Branch Rickey moved from St. Louis to Brooklyn to become the Dodgers' president and general manager. During the war, Rickey got a jump on his more lethargic and slow-witted colleagues by embarking on a nationwide campaign to sign up a bevy of promising high school prospects and by tapping the large, untouched reservoir of black talent. With the arrival of Jackie Robinson in 1947, Brooklyn began its Golden Decade, one in which it won six pennants and twice finished a close second.

By far the most distinguishing feature of the Dodgers in the Golden Decade was their use of African-American players. Although the Dodgers rarely had more than three blacks in their lineup in any given game, most other teams during the 1940s and 1950s had none or at the most a token of only one. Blacks Jackie Robinson and Roy Campanella, who together received four Most Valuable Player awards, joined such white fence-busters as Gil Hodges and Duke Snider to give the Dodgers the most consistently potent offense in baseball. No team overpowered its league more than the 1953 Dodgers, which outscored opponents more than one run per game and hit nineteen points and slugged sixty-three points above the league average. Towering pitcher Don Newcombe, another recruit from the black leagues, made direct contributions to Dodger pennants in 1949, 1955, and 1956; Newcombe compiled a stunning cumulative 64-20 won-lost mark for these three seasons.

Whereas the Dodgers of the Golden Decade were mostly the products of Branch Rickey's handiwork, the Dodgers of the 1960s represented the fruits of new Brooklyn management. Walter O'Malley drove out Rickey in 1950. O'Malley directed the business and promotional side of the franchise, and he hired Emil J. "Buzzie" Bavasi to serve as general manager, although his official title was vice president. Bavasi, who had apprenticed in the Dodgers farm system, hired Walter Alston in 1954 as field manager; for the next twenty-three seasons Alston managed the club on one-year contracts. Like Weiss with the Yankees, Bavasi used the Dodgers' farm surplus to trade for players with proven big league capabilities. Acquisitions from other clubs that made important contributions to Dodger pennants included outfielders Wally Moon and Frank Howard and pitchers Ron Perranowski and Claude Osteen.

Under Bavasi's direction, the Dodgers eventually became a different kind of team. Although Jackie Robinson's baserunning had for a time terrorized NL opponents, and pitchers Elwin "Preacher" Roe and Don Newcombe were among the league's best, the hallmark of the Dodgers of the 1940s and 1950s had been slugging. After the Dodgers moved into the Los Angeles Coliseum, with its distant right-field wall, in 1958 and then into spacious Dodger Stadium in 1962, the club became better known for its super pitching and lightning speed on the base paths. During the first year that the team occupied Dodger Stadium, shortstop Maury Wills became the first major-leaguer in the twentieth century to steal 100 bases in a season; the Dodger total for stolen bases that season doubled that of any rival. "I'm convinced it's easier to find a man who can run and field, and who has above-average speed, than it is to scout a man who has home-run power potential," Bavasi observed in 1966.

An enlarged strike zone introduced in 1963 aided the already powerful Los Angeles pitching staff. Until Sandy Koufax prematurely retired after the 1966 season with an arthritic arm, he teamed with Don Drysdale to overwhelm Dodger rivals. For the 1963 through 1966 seasons, Koufax recorded ninety-seven wins and twenty-seven losses and had seasonal earned run averages of 1.88, 1.74, 2.04, and 1.73. He pitched a no-hitter in each of these seasons. Never before in the game's history had a pitcher put together such an impressive string of performances.

⊟ ⊟ ⊟

For a brief interlude, the six seasons of 1963 through 1968, pitchers regained an ascendancy over the hitters that they had not enjoyed since the first two decades of the twentieth century. Although batting averages (but not home runs) had been slipping downward prior to 1963 (thirty points between the mid-1930s and the early 1960s), in the 1963 season major league run totals fell by 1,681, home runs by 297, batting averages by twelve points, and bases on balls by 1,345. Pitchers recorded 1,206 more strikeouts than in 1962. The 1963 totals became the standard for the next five years. Carl Yastrzemski won the American League batting crown in 1968 with an average of .301, the lowest in big league history.

In part, the precipitous decline in hitting simply reflected a long-term trend. Statistics demonstrated conclusively that night games reduced batting averages, and by the mid-1960s more than half the games were played at night. Efforts of more players to hit home runs rather than singles, the popularity of the slider in the 1950s and afterward, bigger and better fielding gloves, and the increased use of relief specialists also adversely affected batting averages. Finally, the eleven new ballparks built between 1954 and 1969 all favored the pitchers; in particular, foul ball territory had been enlarged, and friendly fences in such facilities as Sportsman's Park in St. Louis, cozy Ebbets Field, and the Polo Grounds were all gone. However, none of these factors explains the sudden drop in 1963. Apparently in an effort to speed up games (the charge had been made that baseball's pace was too slow for modern spectators) and to clarify the size of the strike zone, the Baseball Rules Committee instructed the umpires in 1963 to begin calling pitches at the bottom of the knees to the top of the shoulders strikes. The larger strike zone was mainly responsible for the hitting depression of the 1963–68 era.

Initially, the big leagues did nothing to counter the hitting drought, and baseball fans were treated to dozens of low-scoring pitching contests. "The power pitchers were in complete command of the game," concluded Bill James. "Sequential offense—four singles in an inning—[was] almost impossible." Thus, teams had to build their offenses around the home run.

Finally, for the 1969 season, the first of the two-divisional era, the majors lowered the pitching mound from fifteen to ten inches (thereby reducing the effectiveness of the curve and slider) and apparently ordered the umpires to reduce the size of the strike zone. Officially, the strike zone extended from the knees to the armpits, but to be certain of obtaining a called strike, pitchers now had to throw the ball between the knees and the belt. Five teams moved their fences closer to home plate. And in 1973 the AL replaced pitchers in the batting order with designated hitters, an innovation eventually copied by the minor leagues, the colleges, Little League, and one of the two Japanese major leagues. Only the NL remained a holdout. During the 1970s and 1980s the cumulative changes introduced between 1969 and 1973 increased offensive output, but not to the pre-1963 levels.

⊞　⊞　⊞

Until the 1960s, when Sandy Koufax began to work his magic, the way the game was played had changed little from earlier decades. True, the offenses had become more one-dimensional, but the trend away from "station-to-station," or one-base-at-a-time, baseball had been under way since the hitting revolution had commenced in the 1920s. Furthermore, until the 1960s, the game continued to be played on grass in ballparks built mostly in the early years of the century. Only the proliferation of night games and the conspicuous presence of black players made the game of the 1950s visibly different from what it had been earlier. Yet there were unmistakable signs that the old game was passing into a new and more troubled era.

13

Baseball
in Trouble

No sign of change in the game was more revealing than Walter O'Malley's decision in 1958 to move his team from Brooklyn to Los Angeles. No matter that a century earlier Brooklyn had been described as the "City of Base Ball Clubs," that it had once hosted the famed Excelsiors and the equally successful Atlantics, that a major league team had resided there since the 1880s, that Brooklyn was in effect the fourth largest city in the nation, that the Dodgers had more than any other institution given the borough its distinctive identity, or that the Dodgers had been for the past decade one of baseball's most successful money-making enterprises. The future prospects for baseball in Brooklyn were not bright. Even though the Dodgers had consistently fielded a pennant contender for more than a decade, Brooklynites had given the team only lukewarm support. Since 1952 attendance had averaged 14,081 fans per game, less than half the capacity of Ebbets Field. Without better fan support, queried O'Malley, how were the Dodgers to compete with the Braves, who had moved west in 1953 and were pulling in twice as many fans in Milwaukee?

The answer seemed simple enough. The Dodgers needed a new stadium that had plenty of parking and was easily accessible by car. Ebbets Field, the home of the Dodgers, was difficult to reach by car, had only 700 parking spaces, and was located in a decaying neighborhood. Unfortunately, obtaining a stadium site of several hundred acres, which was necessary for a ballpark in the automobile age, was not easy to do in New York City. If the Dodgers had purchased it from small landholders, the price would have been far beyond the club's financial means. Only a gift of municipally owned land, such as parks, or the use of the city's power of eminent domain to obtain private property could make such a project feasible.

The city of New York refused to do either. Even though the Dodgers promised to bear all the construction costs of a new stadium, Robert Moses, the powerful head of the city's public parks department, blocked O'Malley's efforts to acquire an ideal site at the Atlantic Avenue Railroad terminal. Moses argued that the acquisition would erase $110 million from the city's tax rolls. Fortunately for Los Angeles, it already owned Chavez Ravine, a choice hilltop area overlooking the downtown area that the city had purchased for a public housing project. Seizing on a growing hostility in southern California toward public housing and anxious to attract the Dodgers, city officials quickly decided that transferring the land to O'Malley for nominal considerations constituted a proper use of the land. Radio appeals by cowboy singer Gene Autry and telethon pleas by actors Groucho Marx, George Burns, and Ronald Reagan helped persuade Los Angeles voters to support the transaction; it passed by a narrow vote in a public referendum.

Despite an agonized cry of betrayal by Brooklyn fans, O'Malley found the proposal irresistible. In addition to giving him an ideal site for a stadium with access to the area's marvelous freeway system, Los Angeles offered O'Malley an uncontested media market in the nation's third-largest metropolitan area. In the meantime, O'Malley had already convinced Horace Stoneham of the Giants that the two teams should move to the West Coast in tandem so they could continue their longstanding rivalry and reduce the travel costs for the other NL clubs.

O'Malley's decision to transfer the Dodgers from the East to the West Coast vividly exemplified both baseball's growing troubles and the additional opportunities that had become available to the game in the postwar era. By the 1950s and 1960s, baseball could no longer ignore the shifting character of leisure in American cities, the rapid growth of new metropolises, or the new technological marvel of television. In response, the big leagues moved to exploit the new population centers, embarked on a new stadium-building boom, and sought to control the dangers and capitalize on the opportunities presented by television.

⊞   ⊞   ⊞

Well before O'Malley made his daring move, the men who ran organized baseball recognized that the industry was in serious trouble. As early as 1946, the players began demanding more (see chapter 14); a lawsuit brought by Danny Gardella even threatened the sanctity of the reserve clause before the case was settled out of court. Political pressures mounted in Washington. One or both houses of Congress held hearings on some aspect of baseball in 1951, 1953, 1954, 1957, 1958, 1959, and 1960. Labeling organized baseball "the horsehide cartel," Republican congressman Patrick Hillings of Los Angeles pressed for big league expansion to the West Coast or for recognition of the Pacific Coast League as a third major league, while House Judiciary Committee chairman Emanuel Cellar called for Congress to strip organized baseball of its antitrust exemption.

More frightening than potential congressional action was declining attendance (see table 9). During the war years of the early 1940s, major league attendance rebounded from the Great Depression with vigor, and in the immediate postwar era it took another sharp leap upward, more than doubling the per game average of the wartime years. But attendance fell again in the 1950s. In terms of the population of the metropolitan areas served by major league baseball, attendance never caught up with the late 1940s; indeed, per game averages did not recover the earlier figures until 1978.

The minor leagues fared even worse. After increasing from 18.5 million to 42 million between 1939 and 1949, attendance fell precipitously, reaching 15.5 million by 1957. Although the figures for them are not easily documented, town and sandlot baseball may have been hit even harder. Hundreds of such teams appear to have folded in the 1950s. Only the most sanguine observer could disagree with Bill Veeck, the former owner of the Cleveland Indians, the Chicago White Sox, and the St. Louis Browns, who concluded in 1958 that baseball was no longer "America's only game in town."

Table 9. Average Major League Per-Game Attendance, 1920–69

	1920–29	1930–39	1940–45	1946–49	1950–59	1960–69
Attendance	7,531	6,578	7,438	16,027	13,366	14,047

Baseball's soaring popularity in the wake of the Great Depression and World War II rested on the return of economic prosperity. After a decade and a half of deprivations, infusions of vast quantities of new disposable income in the postwar era triggered a general explosion of consumer spending. Expenditures on all forms of recreation shot upward at a dizzying pace. Major league baseball may have also contributed to its own recovery. For one thing, the increased number of night games made it easier for fans to attend games. In addition, several close pennant races in the late 1940s excited unusual fan interest. Both the regular NL season of 1946 and the AL season of 1948 ended in ties, and a single game in both leagues separated the first- and second-place teams in 1949.

The decline in attendance in the 1950s and the agonizingly slow recovery thereafter is less easily explained. Historically, attendance had been tied closely to general economic performance, but the baseball slump of the fifties and sixties came amid a period of steady, even spectacular economic gains. Baseball's attendance problems lay elsewhere, mainly in a fundamental shift in urban leisure patterns.

In the post–World War II era, decaying inner cities and fast-growing suburbs drastically affected all metropolitan spare-time activities. The suburbs pulled both jobs and the more prosperous families away from the inner city. The exodus to the suburbs left the inner city with large numbers of lower-income residents who could not afford tickets to big league games. To put it another way, the nonwhite proportion of the population of the central cities grew from 39 percent in 1950 to 51 percent in 1960. In 1958, Bill Furlong, a *Chicago Tribune* reporter secretly listening through a hotel air vent, heard Clark Griffith, president of the Washington Senators, explain why he wanted to move his team to Minneapolis. "The trend in Washington is getting to be all colored," Griffith bluntly told his fellow AL owners.

Outside the inner city, suburbanites chose to spend more of their spare time in activities other than watching ball games. The automobile itself became a supreme instrument of pleasure. Families used their cars to get away to the countryside on the weekends, to take extended vacations, and to visit relatives across the nation or simply on the other side of town. The home became a self-sufficient recreation center, or a "family playpen," to use anthropologist Margaret Mead's apt metaphor. According to the popular media of the postwar era, the enjoyment of children and "family togetherness" became virtually a moral obligation. Do-it-yourself projects, home repairs, and conquering the "crabgrass frontier" consumed more of the suburbanite's time. "Why should a guy with a boat in the driveway, golf clubs in the car, bowling ball and tennis racket in the closet, a trunkful of camping equipment, two boys in Little League and a body full of energy left over from shorter working hours pay to sit and do nothing but watch a mediocre game?" asked W. Travis Walton of Abilene, Texas, in a letter to *Sports Illustrated* in 1958.

Television likewise contributed to the relocation of leisure from public places to the privacy of the home. "And so the monumental change began in our lives and those of millions of other Americans," recalled one man about the effects of his family's purchase of their first television set in 1950. "More than a year passed before we again visited a movie theater. Money which previously would have been spent for books was saved for TV payments. Social evenings with friends became fewer and fewer still." By 1956 three of four families owned television sets; those families watched television an average of thirty-five hours each week. Novelty alone did not account for the new medium's magnetism; Americans persisted long afterward in spending a staggering amount of their free time watching television. Instead of making their way to the local ballpark, more and more Americans spent their leisure time watching for free *Gunsmoke, Milton Berle, I Love Lucy,* or the New York Yankees on television.

Ironically, the spectacular growth of a particular suburban institution, Little League baseball, seriously reduced attendance at all other forms of baseball. Carl Stotz, a twenty-nine-year old clerical employee of a Williamsport, Pennsylvania, sandpaper factory, founded Little League in 1939. Its survival remained in doubt until after World War II. In 1947, when the United States Rubber Company became the sponsor and financial angel of Little League, it had only sixty teams and some 1,000 players. Little League then suddenly took root, especially flourishing in the fast-growing suburbs. Within a decade, nearly a million boys played on 19,500 teams in forty-seven states and in twenty-two nations abroad. Soon no other youth organization in the world had so many members.

Unlike earlier adult-directed youth programs managed by recreational professionals, Little League was the product of untrained adult volunteers. Stotz explained that he had dreamed up the league for nine- to twelve-year-old boys in response to his own frustrations as a youth with unsupervised, chaotic play. The colorful team uniforms, use of a regular baseball, outfield fences, dugouts, and even a player draft system all provided a way for the adult volunteers to play out vicariously the unfulfilled fantasies of their own youth. The showpiece of Little League became its World Series, played annually at Williamsport and first televised in 1953. By the 1950s, in nearly every suburb in the nation, millions of adults gathered on dozens of afternoons each summer to watch their preadolescent boys play a facsimile of big league baseball. Paradoxically, at the same time, popular forms of unorganized ball playing by youngsters on empty lots and schoolgrounds declined.

The fans who did venture downtown to ballparks in the 1950s, at least to the big league parks, confronted a series of possible adversities. Multilane, limited-access thoroughfares had not yet been cut into the heart of the cities; thus, these fans needed a Job-like patience to fight creeping traffic. Upon arrival at the park, there was frequently a problem with parking. All the stadiums had been built long before the automobile became ascendant. Fans who were fortunate enough to find a parking place within easy walking distance of the ballpark might then encounter street urchins—or worse—who threatened their cars, their persons, or both.

Finally, there was the ballpark itself. All but three of the parks had been built prior to 1923. In 1957 Robert Creamer called the Polo Grounds (built in 1911) an "antiquated museum"; a year earlier James Murray described Pittsburgh's Forbes Field, once the most elegant ball field in the nation, as a "museum decorated with pigeon droppings." In many parks, support posts obstructed a clear view of the field, the parks were frequently dirty, and all were without lounges. Instead of evoking a pastoral retreat, many of the rickety stadiums reminded fans of the inner city's general squalor. By contrast, Murray noted that the recently built horse-racing tracks featured escalators, courteous personnel, restaurants, cocktail lounges, and cushioned seats. Acutely conscious of the bottom line and resting confidently on the belief that Americans would remain loyal to the national game regardless of personal discomforts, baseball franchise holders were slow to renovate their facilities.

Besides being victims of the new leisure patterns that adversely affected all levels of baseball, minor league baseball suffered from other difficulties. The minors had overexpanded in the wake of World War II. Anxious to take advantage of the postwar boom, small businessmen invested in minor league clubs in record numbers, and, eager to emulate the success of the Cardinals and the Yankees, every club in the big leagues set out to build a large farm system. At the same time, however, the major clubs faced rising costs from competing with one another to sign untried "bonus babies," and to counteract the dominance of such clubs as the Yankees, Cardinals, and Dodgers, the majors adopted rules making it impossible to control hundreds of farm players, shuffling them back and forth and stock-piling them for use at a later date. As early as 1947, the Cincinnati Reds announced that they intended to reduce the size of their farm operations and concentrate on signing only top prospects. Before long, other clubs were cutting costs by streamlining their farm systems. The number of minor league clubs owned by the majors dropped from 207 in 1951 to a mere 38 six years later. Finally, television broadcasts of big league games, particularly night and weekend contests, in minor league territories also damaged the minor leagues.

◫   ◫   ◫

No one could be certain whether television should be viewed as a cause or a possible solution to big league baseball's troubles. The growing popularity of home-centered leisure confounded all attempts to isolate the precise impact of television on big league attendance. Nonetheless, several owners believed that the television history of the Boston and Milwaukee Braves illustrated the ill effects of the medium. In 1948, when the Braves won the NL pennant, they drew nearly 1.5 million fans to their home games. They then sold the rights to telecast all Braves games locally for the 1951 and 1952 seasons (for the paltry sum of $40,000); seasonal attendance dropped sharply from 944,341 in 1950 to 487,477 in 1951 and then to an abysmal 281,278 in 1952, the season before the Braves departed for Milwaukee.

Although big league owners repeatedly cited the Boston experience when justifying restrictive television policies, the evidence that television was the main culprit behind the Braves' woes is far from conclusive. Apart from pennant contenders, nearly all the teams, regardless of their television policies, saw their attendance drop sharply during these same years, and the Braves were not pennant contenders. In 1952 the team tumbled from fourth to seventh place. Furthermore, in 1952 ownership of a television set, even in a metropolitan area like Boston, was still something of a rarity. Nevertheless, on his arrival in Milwaukee, team owner Lou Perini banned all telecasts of Braves games. Other team owners tried to guess the precise point at which the revenues accrued from televising additional games were offset by decreases in attendance.

Until 1961, when the Sports Broadcasting Act legalized league-wide "package" contracts, the national networks had agreements only with individual clubs. Because of their market size, the franchises in larger cities obtained such contracts easily, whereas several clubs in smaller cities never had their games broadcast on national television. Moreover, fans in the smaller cities might be confronted with a choice of going out to watch their local team or watching a telecast of a game or games between big league teams from the larger cities.

By 1958, on each weekend, fans had a bonanza of network baseball telecasts available at their fingertips. The CBS network, with Dizzy Dean and Buddy Blattner doing the play-by-play, carried games on both Saturday and Sunday. For fans, many of whom had never before seen big league baseball, Dean, the ex-Cardinals pitching star, became something of a national celebrity. Dean himself frequently took the center stage, letting the game provide the background for the spell of his personality. He enthralled viewers with his country drawl, unusual verb conjugations, and anecdotes. (When Dean heard that the St. Louis school teachers had complained about his syntax, he shot back, "Sin Tax. Are them jokers in Washington puttin' a tax on that too?") NBC countered with a weekly game featuring Lindsey Nelson and Leo Durocher. Local stations also joined the parade. Perhaps the saturation point was reached in 1958 when television stations WFIL of Philadelphia, WOR of New York, WLW of Cincinnati, WLWD of Dayton, and the CBS network all carried the same game from Philadelphia. Altogether, *TV Guide* estimated that 800 major league games appeared on television in 1958.

Yet except for the World Series and the All-Star contests, baseball games were not especially popular television fare. Used initially by the networks and local stations to fill the yawning gaps in summer weekend programming, the games captured only 7 or 8 percent of the potential television audience. (By the 1960s regular season professional football drew more than twice as many television viewers.) Unlike football, baseball had to compete with myriad other activities during warm summer days, and the essence of baseball translated poorly onto a television screen. The ball was too small to follow easily, and an appreciation of baseball required an acute awareness of the entire playing area. Although fans enjoyed isolated instances of action—the pitch, hit, catch, or throw—they also wanted to see the runners leading off base, the coaches, the position of fielders, the relationship of the hit ball to the field, and the responses of the players to the hit ball. Only the fan in the stands, not the television viewer, could command all these perspectives. Unlike football fans, few baseball followers claimed that watching a televised game was superior to watching one live.

The networks' payments for television rights to baseball, though substantial, soon lagged far behind those extended to pro football. After the passage of the Sports Broadcasting Act of 1961, the major leagues negotiated contracts with the television networks in which all clubs shared equally in revenues. The size of the network contracts slowly drifted upward, paralleling the rate of inflation until 1983. In that year, an era when the networks were slugging it out for television rights for the major sports, baseball saw its payments suddenly increase to $4 million annually per club, more than four times what each franchise had received a year earlier. The 1990–93 package contracts with CBS and ESPN yielded an even more startling increase. Each team received $14.4 million annually from these agreements, a figure comparable to that of the National Football League clubs.

In contrast to pro football teams, franchises in baseball retained control of local media rights. By 1987 each club averaged nearly $6 million annually from local television and radio rights. The franchises in the larger market areas such as New York, where the Yankees received $41 million for the 1990 season, garnered far more from the media than those in smaller cities such as Milwaukee, where the Brewers earned a mere $3 million from their local contract. These differences in club broadcast earnings resulted in much larger disparities in gross income among baseball franchises than among those of pro football.

◨ ◨ ◨

Franchise relocations, league expansion, and a new stadia were baseball's main response to troubled times. Prior to the National Agreement of 1903, when the AL became a major circuit, the big league clubs had frequently shifted sites, and in the minor leagues, both leagues and teams continued in the twentieth century to come and go with startling frequency. But after 1903 the big league map had remained frozen for a half century; not a single team changed cities. The immutability of the structure cast in 1903 rested partly on painful memories of the sport's more chaotic days and partly on the weight of tradition. The big league owners had always taken pride in baseball's resistance to change. To guard against acting capriciously, the major leagues had a rule (repealed in 1952) that required the unanimous consent of the owners in both leagues before a franchise could be moved.

Initially, the leagues permitted only the poorest-drawing clubs in the two-franchise cities to abandon their longtime homes. No franchise was worse off than the dismal Browns, who had to share the small city of St. Louis with the far more popular Cardinals. As early as 1941 there had been talk of moving the Browns to Los Angeles. After having used a panoply of gimmicks to promote attendance without much success, maverick Bill Veeck in 1952 tried to move his club to Milwaukee or to Los Angeles, only to meet the adamant resistance of his fellow AL owners. Angry with Veeck for his proposal of an unrestricted minor league draft and for his unorthodox promotional stunts, including his use of Eddie Gaedel, a midget pinch hitter, they sought to drive him out of baseball.

A year later, the club owners approved the transfer of Lou Perini's Boston Braves to Milwaukee. Faring poorly in his competition with the more popular Red Sox, Perini welcomed the opportunity to relocate his Braves to a city that offered him use of a new $6.6-million stadium and an uncontested local media market. Perini's ownership of the Milwaukee minor league franchise also eased the process of relocation. The next year, after Veeck had sold the club and after witnessing the success of the Braves in Milwaukee, the AL permitted the Browns to depart for Baltimore, a city that had a strong minor league tradition and a new stadium but was geographically hemmed in by the nearby big league cities of Washington and Philadelphia. A year after that, the miserable Philadelphia Athletics departed for Kansas City. The migrations between 1953 and 1955 left only New York and Chicago with multiple franchises.

The relocation of the Braves, Browns, and Athletics by no means solved big league attendance problems. In the first year in their new homes all the teams did well as fans poured out to experience the novelty of big league baseball, but only the Milwaukee Braves, who were one of the most consistently winning teams in the 1950s, sustained their initial success. Baltimore and Kansas City, who regularly resided deep in the AL's second division, suffered a more than 20 percent drop in attendance. The Athletics did little better off the field; between 1955 and 1960 the Yankees repeatedly bested them in a series of sixteen player deals, one of which included the Yankees' acquisition of slugger Roger Maris (who was to break Babe Ruth's single-season record of sixty home runs in 1961), which did nothing to aid the cause of baseball in Kansas City.

The next relocations, the Dodgers' and Giants' to the West Coast in 1958, entailed far more than responses to declining fan support, although both teams had seen their attendance fall in the 1950s. Both clubs hungered after the favors offered by fast-growing California; Los Angeles was already pushing its way up into the number-three spot among American cities, and the San Francisco–Oakland metropolitan area occupied eleventh place among the nation's population centers. As early as 1946 professional football leagues had planted franchises in both cities, and the Pacific Coast League had petitioned unsuccessfully for major league status. By 1958 improvements in air travel had made regular trips to the West Coast more economical and practicable than in the past.

San Francisco offered Giants owner Horace Stoneham a new stadium built by the city, but O'Malley was unable to gain a similar concession from the city of Los Angeles. O'Malley built his own park, Dodger Stadium, on a municipally furnished site with access to the city's freeway system; the stadium cost $18 million when completed in 1962. A magnificent facility, Dodger Stadium seated 56,000 fans, had parking spaces for 24,000 cars, and featured a giant electric scoreboard that could flash up in an instant Maury Wills's lifetime stolen base totals or the closing Wall Street averages. O'Malley spent more than a million dollars on landscaping; he had olive and palm trees planted in the parking lots and installed a Japanese garden in center field, all ensuring what John Merwin has described as a "Disneylike atmosphere for the paying fans." The Dodgers broke all attendance records; by the 1980s they regularly drew more than 3 million fans per season. The Giants were not so fortunate. Candlestick Park was poorly located for cars and was buffeted regularly by high bay winds.

The transfer of the Giants and Dodgers to the West Coast left a yawning gap in the nation's most populous metropolis, New York City. The Yankees were for a time Gotham's sole occupants, but not for long; William Shea and Branch Rickey rushed to fill the vacuum. They planned to plant one of the franchises in their newly proposed Continental League in a new stadium to be built in Queens. Disturbed by nightmares of the Federal League War, big leagues dreaded the very thought of a third major league. At the same time, congressional hearings revealed the profound sense of loss that Brooklyn fans experienced when the Dodgers departed and raised questions about why the major leagues refused to expand.

Frightened by the congressional hearings and the prospects of competing with the Continental League, the majors worked out a deal calling for the expansion of each big league from eight to ten teams and the dissolution of the Continental League. For permitting the NL to place a new club in New York, which was to become known as the Metropolitans or the Mets, O'Malley had to agree to allow the AL to place a new franchise (the Angels) in his Los Angeles territory. In exchange for freeing Calvin Griffith to move his Senators to Minnesota's Twin Cities, the AL agreed to put a

new club in Washington, D.C. Finally, the NL added a franchise in fast-
growing Houston, Texas. The new ten-team AL began play in 1961, and
the NL followed suit with its ten-team circuit a year later.

Expansion had mixed results. It took place at the expense of the already
hard-pressed minor leagues, which had to surrender their best markets to
the majors. Nor were the established big league clubs generous to the new-
comers. Each new entry had to pay an initiation fee of $1.8 million plus
$75,000 for each player purchased from a pool of second-rate perform-
ers set aside for them by the existing clubs. Prior to the 1969 season, none
of the expansion teams except the Angels managed to finish higher than
seventh place in the league standings. Unfortunately for the Angels, they
had to play at first in a ramshackle minor league park and then as tenants
in O'Malley's Dodger Stadium. Although Washington provided its expansion team with a new stadium, its team performed poorly and drew mea-
ger crowds. The NL neophytes fared better. Houston, which initially played
in humid, mosquito-infested Colt Stadium, prospered when it moved into
its new domed park, and even though the Mets broke twentieth-century
records for losing games, they endeared themselves to New Yorkers by their
sheer ineptitude. In the late 1960s, when they moved to Shea Stadium, the
Mets even outdrew the fading Yankees.

Although extremely modest gains in attendance in the 1960s hardly
justified an enthusiasm for expansion, petitions from other cities seeking
franchises, congressional pressures, and power struggles between the two
leagues triggered another round of franchise additions in 1969. The departure of the Braves from Milwaukee in 1966 for a low-rent stadium and
a better local media contract in Atlanta and that of the Athletics from
Kansas City in 1967 to Oakland for similar reasons provoked a flurry of
lawsuits and protests on the floor of Congress. Did such carpetbagging
portend a new era of complete promiscuity and disloyalty to host cities,
queried baseball observers? No one could say, but the AL planted new
franchises in Kansas City and Seattle, while the NL agreed to the creation
of new teams in San Diego and Montreal.

With twelve teams in each league beginning play in 1969, the leagues
adopted a completely new format. Copying the enormously successful
example of the National Football League, both leagues formed eastern and
western divisions of six teams each, with the winners of the divisions to
meet in a playoff to decide the league championship. The creation of divisions helped solve the problem of having too many teams with abysmal
season records and helped sustain interest throughout the season. The

divisional playoffs also attracted lucrative television rights payments. On the other hand, the divisions, additional teams, and the NL's geographic illogic of having Cincinnati and Atlanta in its western division made the mental management of big league franchises far more difficult than in the past. As in 1961, the established clubs exacted a heavy price on the new-comers; the new AL clubs paid a $5.25-million entry fee, and the NL charged its new entrants $10 million each. In addition, the new franchises had to pay $175,000 each for the second-rate players they drafted from a pool set aside for them by the existing clubs.

The 1969 franchises did not remain in place for long. The Seattle club went bankrupt in its first season, so the AL took over the franchise and shifted it to Milwaukee. The faltering franchises in both Washington and Cleveland coveted the Dallas–Fort Worth metropolitan area. Risking the wrath of Congress, the protests of Washington fans, and the heated resis-tance of commissioner Bowie Kuhn, the AL permitted Washington to move there. In 1976, the AL unilaterally added franchises in Seattle and Toron-to, stealing a step on the NL and ending the third wave of expansion.

Major League Baseball Franchises, 1977–92

American League

Eastern Division	Western Division
Baltimore Orioles	California Angels
Boston Red Sox	Chicago White Sox
Cleveland Indians	Kansas City Royals
Detroit Tigers	Minnesota Twins
Milwaukee Brewers	Oakland Athletics
New York Yankees	Seattle Mariners
Toronto Blue Jays	Texas Rangers

National League

Eastern Division	Western Division
Chicago Cubs	Atlanta Braves
Montreal Expos	Cincinnati Reds
New York Mets	Houston Astros
Philadelphia Phillies	Los Angeles Dodgers
Pittsburgh Pirates	San Diego Padres
St. Louis Cardinals	San Francisco Giants

Nothing abetted relocation and expansion more than cities offering franchises subsidized playing areas. In the park-building movement of the postwar era, Dodger Stadium was the only one to be erected with private funds. Just as the cathedral represented the spirit of the Middle Ages and the great railway terminals that of nineteenth-century America, supporters of publicly financed stadiums saw them as the quintessential symbols of the modern city. Not only could the edifices serve as great cultural monuments, enthusiasts argued, but they could stimulate downtown revitalization and lure tourist and investment dollars to the cities.

Several team owners seized the advantage that such thinking made possible. They presented cities with ultimatums: Either the cities built new stadiums (or granted other specified subsidies) or the franchises would move elsewhere. In the early 1960s the price tag on a modest stadium ran to some $30 million, but Houston's Astrodome, the first stadium with a roof for all-season play, cost $45 million to complete in 1965. However, the cost of the Astrodome paled compared to that of the Louisiana Superdome, which reached $300 million before it was finished in 1975. The operating deficit alone cost Louisiana taxpayers $8 million annually, and New Orleans did not even have a big league baseball franchise.

Publicly built facilities had their critics. They protested that cities should use the funds to solve more pressing problems, that building stadiums or arenas in the suburbs encouraged the further decay of the inner city (or conversely, that building downtown wiped out large areas of cheap housing), that the financial benefits attributed to big league franchises were grossly exaggerated by supporters, and that, in effect, stadium building with public funds meant that all residents subsidized the entertainment of the "advantaged." Yet in the long run, opponents rarely blocked stadium-building projects. In the 1980s nearly two dozen of the largest sixty-five metropolitan areas built new facilities, several of which were domed. Enthusiasm ran so high for stadiums and arenas that several cities even built them before receiving assurance of a major league sport franchise.

The new stadiums differed significantly from their predecessors. Though still built of steel and concrete, they had more seating capacity (nearly all in the 40,000 to 50,000 range) and sometimes featured a roof for all-weather play; nearly all of them were multipurpose facilities (sharing their field with a professional football team), nearly half of them had artificial playing surfaces, and about 20 percent of them were located in suburban satellite cities well away from the metropolitan core. Each of the new stadiums featured huge electronic score and message boards; the message boards even told fans when to cheer or jeer. Each came equipped with a large "instant replay" screen so that fans would not feel cheated by watching the game at the park rather than at home on television. Each had plush, glass-enclosed, air-conditioned boxes, sometimes with cooking facilities and beds, for corporations and wealthy patrons who were willing to pay an annual fee of $15,000 or more.

Earlier stadiums had been built to conform to strictures of the sites, whereas the newer ones transformed the site to the requirements of the stadium. Consequently, bulldozers leveled acre after acre of inner city or suburban land to provide ample space for parking and access roads. Once built, the new stadiums stood alone, separated from all other structures by vast, open spaces of concrete parking lots or garages and access roads. Without site constraints, the new stadiums were nearly all symmetrical; the distance to the foul pole in left and right field was usually the same. They were all nearly identical to one another in other respects; a fan could wake up in the middle of a stadium in Cincinnati, Pittsburgh, St. Louis, or Philadelphia and not know where he or she was.

◻ ◻ ◻

The greater number of franchises and the new multilane super highways around and through metropolitan areas increased the ease with which more people could see big league games. In 1950 the sixteen big league teams played a 154-game schedule in ten cities; forty years later there were twenty-six teams playing a 162-game schedule in twenty-four cities (including the Canadian cities of Montreal and Toronto), a 70 percent increase in the number of regular season games. Gross attendance increased, but per game attendance continued to lag proportionately to the population areas served by big league clubs. Minor league, sandlot, and semipro baseball never recovered the popularity that they had lost in the 1950s, nor was that baseball's only problem. Beginning in the 1960s major league baseball faced yet another trouble: a new uprising by the players.

14

The Empowerment of the Players

Baseball's spring training camps in 1966 had an unusual visitor. He was Marvin J. Miller, the recently appointed executive director of the Major League Baseball Players Association (MLBPA). Although he had been a long-time employee of the United Steelworkers Union as an economist and negotiator, Miller did not look like the archetype of a union boss. Indeed, he was a wiry little man whom a hostile reporter once described as an "insipid-looking" individual with a "waxed mustache and racetrack clothes." Miller spoke quietly and earnestly. Rather than outlining a program of what he intended to do, he sought to know from the ball players what they wanted him to do. In a referendum requested by Miller at the end of his spring training trip, the players endorsed his selection by a vote of 489 to 136.

Miller's appointment was a turning point in the history of baseball's player-management relationship. Before Miller, the player association had been moribund, an organization routinely used and manipulated by the owners for their own ends. After Miller, the MLBPA became a powerful counterweight to management, the reserve clause fell into shambles, and the players eventually obtained astronomical salary increases. Miller was "the Moses who led Baseball's Children of Israel out of the land of bondage," wrote labor arbitrator Peter Seitz in the *New York Times*. But player empowerment was not due solely to Miller, although it is difficult to overstate his importance. Legislation friendly to organized labor that came out of the New Deal era, favorable court rulings, and disunity within the ranks of the owners also contributed in important ways to the enhancement of player power.

◘   ◘   ◘

The story of player empowerment has its indirect origins in the immediate post–World War II era. In selecting a new commissioner of baseball in 1945, the owners were certain of only one thing: They did not want another Landis. Their choice, U.S. Senator A. B. "Happy" Chandler from Kentucky, seemed at first glance to be quite unlike his predecessor. A professional politician, Chandler was a big man, amiable and always smiling. The owners assumed that he would be easy to work with and would acquiesce to their sense of what was good for the game. They were mistaken. Chandler, like most Americans, blithely accepted the myth that the baseball commissioner stood above the interests of the individual team owners. "You don't own the game . . . ," he once brazenly lectured the owners, "the game belongs to the American people."

Such independent thinking soon got Chandler into trouble with his employers. Many disliked his acquiescence to Branch Rickey's assault on baseball's racial segregation, as well as his year's suspension of popular Dodgers manager Leo Durocher for consorting with gamblers. Chandler may have angered even more owners by his handling of the players who succumbed to the fabulous offers of the Mexican League in 1946. Although Stan Musial of the St. Louis Cardinals resisted the blandishments of Mexico, stars Mickey Owen of the Dodgers and Vern Stephens of the St. Louis Browns, along with eleven other players, jumped their contracts. Following the precedents established by Landis, Chandler banished the players from organized baseball for life. Most of the exiles soon became disillusioned with the Mexican League, but they were not permitted to return to organized baseball until 1949, when the owners were threatened by two antitrust suits brought by disgruntled players.

During the same year that Chandler banned the Mexican League defectors, Robert Murphy, an idealistic young labor lawyer with the Congress of Industrial Organizations, tried to form a new players' union, which he called the American Baseball Guild. "Ask Babe Ruth and Jimmie Foxx what they think of the one-sidedness of the baseball setup," Murphy suggested in a letter to all big-leaguers. Perhaps unduly frightened, the owners acted quickly to counter Murphy. Led by Larry MacPhail, the new joint-owner of the New York Yankees, they formed a committee that scheduled a series of meetings over the summer with the players but without Murphy. "A healthier relationship between club and player," the MacPhail committee reported, "will be effective in resisting attempts at unionization by outsiders." The owners extended tangible benefits as well. They agreed to provide a spring training allowance of $25 a week (called "Murphy money" by the players then and since), a $5,000 minimum salary, a modest player pension plan, and formal representation of the players on a council of the owners and league presidents. The results apparently pleased both sides. The owners savored the collapse of Murphy's union, and the players now had a pension fund.

Only the pension fund remained a potentially serious source of conflict. When the fund was unable to meet its obligations in 1949, Chandler forestalled contention with the players by assigning it $1 million annually from the broadcast rights to the World Series and the All Star Games. Two years later the owners dismissed Chandler, in part because they disliked his allocation of media receipts to the pension fund. The new commissioner, Ford Frick, a former sportswriter and president of the NL since 1934, was far more reliable than Chandler in representing the interests of the owners. In 1953 Frick refused to provide the players with a full accounting of the pension fund, and the owners rejected a player proposal to raise the minimum salary to $8,000. The players responded by hiring an attorney, J. Norman Lewis, to represent them. "All we want from Lewis is legal advice," player representative Ralph Kiner assured the owners. If Lewis were to so much as hint that he was interested in a union, "out he goes," added Kiner.

Although initially amiable toward Lewis, the owners suddenly and unexpectedly barred him from their December talks with the player representatives. The players then broke off further discussions and in 1954 founded the Major League Baseball Players Association. After reconsidering their hasty action, the owners reversed themselves, permitting Lewis to attend the joint meetings, and in April 1954 the parties reached an agreement on a new pension plan. As a part-time employee of the MLBPA, Lewis continued to press for a larger players' share of the media revenues for the pension fund, but apparently seeking to mollify the angry owners, the players fired him early in 1959.

The association's new legal adviser, Judge Robert Cannon of Milwaukee, managed the players' affairs in the interests of harmony and the owners' pocketbooks. He publicly endorsed the reserve clause, praised the pension fund as the "finest in existence," and told a congressional committee in 1964 that the "thinking of the average major league ballplayer" was that "we have it so good we don't know what to ask for next." In January 1966 the players offered Cannon the full-time post as "administrator" of the MLBPA at a salary of $50,000. Delighted with the players' choice, the owners promptly set aside 35 percent of the profits from the All-Star Game to pay for Cannon's salary and office expenses. To the surprise of the owners and players alike, Cannon declined the offer. Perhaps he was miffed that the owners passed him over for the position of commissioner of baseball, selecting instead ex–Air Force general William Eckert to replace Ford Frick, who retired in 1965. According to Robin Roberts, star pitcher with the Philadelphia Phillies and a leader of the effort to rejuvenate the association, while Cannon was reconsidering his decision, he "pissed off a number of player reps [representatives] by demanding additional conditions." The players then withdrew their offer to Cannon.

The determination to make the association's chief officer a full-time position reflected a vague but growing discontent among the players. Although personally conservative, mostly satisfied with the reserve clause, and emphatically opposed to forming a regular labor union, the players were not completely immune to the social strife swirling about them. In the late 1960s nearly every social group seemed to be clamoring for or against something. The ball players also observed the rapid escalation of professional football salaries, the expansion of baseball franchises, and the increasing amount of money pouring into sports by television, all of which suggested that the players might not be getting an equitable share of the sport's earnings. Finally, the success of a highly publicized holdout by Sandy Koufax and Don Drysdale in the spring of 1966 was not lost on the players. The star Dodgers pitchers had hired a Hollywood lawyer to represent them and banded together to stage the first successful collective holdout for higher salaries in baseball history.

◻ ◻ ◻

Neither the players nor the owners knew for sure what to expect from the new executive director of the MLBPA, Marvin Miller. Miller started his tenure cautiously. "I am very anxious to get the views of the players and find out what they would like this association to become," he said during his tour of the training camps in 1966. He discovered that the players did not want the association to represent them in negotiating their individual salaries; in this crucial sense the MLBPA never resembled a typical trade union. On the other hand, Miller found deep, smoldering resentments among great numbers of players on the issues of minimum salary and the pension fund. In the past, any changes in the pension fund or in minimum salaries had come only at the discretion of the owners. By initially focusing on these issues, Miller pitched the association's appeal to the ordinary rather than the star players.

At the same time, the owners abetted Miller; they were "my biggest allies," he later recalled. "When some of them tried to talk their players out of hiring me in 1966, the men simply concluded: Anybody the owners hate that much can't be all bad!" Another owner ploy backfired as well. In an effort to drive a wedge between Miller and the players, the owners reneged on their earlier promise to fund the Player Association's office. The owners squeezed out of their commitment by raising their payment to the pension fund and eliminating entirely the players' contribution. The players were then given the option of pocketing the money that they had formerly paid into the pension fund or setting it aside to cover the costs of Miller's salary and his office. The players opted for the latter. The compromise not only increased the owners' contribution to the pension fund but also made it less painful financially for the players to belong to the association.

By the end of 1966 the owners had learned more about Miller's intentions. They now knew that he planned nothing less than a fundamental reordering of the relationship between management and the players. No longer would the owners be able to decide unilaterally on minimum salaries, working conditions, or the size of their contribution to the pension fund. In the future, such issues would be decided at the bargaining table. To the utter amazement of the owners, the players stood firmly behind their new leader.

As talks dragged on through 1967 and into 1968, the owners recognized in Miller a formidable adversary, one who was familiar with labor law, experienced in negotiations, and adept at using the media. They appointed a special Player Relations Committee (PRC), composed of the league presidents and three owners from each league, and employed a professional negotiator, John J. Gaherin, to represent them in dealing with Miller. When Miller threatened to call in federal mediators in January 1968, the owners reluctantly signed a "Basic Agreement." The two-year contract, the first ever negotiated in any sport, called for an increase of the minimum salary from $7,000 to $10,000, granted to the players the right to be represented in their contract negotiations by agents, and established a formal grievance procedure.

If the threat of federal law worked on behalf of the players in 1968, the threat of NBC television withholding its payments for big league games helped bring a settlement in 1969. When the owners resisted linking pension fund contributions to growing television revenues, the union asked its members to refuse to sign their contracts. Veteran players boycotted spring training; at least 391 players were missing from the camps. With the regular season endangered, an NBC executive warned the owners that his network would not pay "major league prices for minor league games." In the meantime, the owners had fired Eckert, who because of his low profile had acquired the ignoble nickname "The Unknown Soldier." With the commissionership vacant, the PRC called in one of the NL lawyers, Bowie Kuhn, a big, strapping man, to try to work out an agreement. Kuhn successfully soothed the hard feelings of the owners. The players won an increase in their pension fund, and the owners resisted tying the fund to television income.

In retrospect (but not recognized at the time), the players won a far more important concession in 1970. Henceforth, disputes between players and owners, unless they involved the "integrity of the game," would be resolved by an independent arbitrator rather than the commissioner of baseball. Before the 1970s ended, the independent arbitration procedure served, in the apt words of Leonard Koppett, "as the lever that brought down the whole reserve structure." In the meantime, in 1969, the owners appointed Bowie Kuhn as baseball's new commissioner. During his tenure as commissioner (1969–84), Kuhn usually played a negligible role in labor relations.

In 1972 baseball experienced its first real strike, one that delayed the start of the season by three weeks and that *The Sporting News* described as the "darkest day in sports history." Ostensibly, the strike revolved around issues of how the players' pension fund would be financed, but in the background hovered the general agreement that would be negotiated in 1973 and the status of the reserve clause that was being argued before the Supreme Court. Even though the owners had just negotiated a new television contract with NBC for $70 million, they initially rejected any increase in the share going to the player pension fund. A powerful minority of the owners wanted to seize the opportunity to break the union. "We're not going to give another god-damn cent," exclaimed August Busch, owner of the St. Louis Cardinals. "And if they want to strike, let them strike."

Despite public appearances to the contrary, the owner-player confrontation in the spring of 1972 was, in the words of James Miller, "a classic mismatch." The owners tried to disguise their fundamental disunity behind tough talk. In reality, most of them were part-time baseball men, relished the prestige of owning a big league club, enjoyed their association with youthful heroes, and thus did not want to completely alienate their players. On the other hand, by obtaining incremental concessions over a period of years and keeping the players well-informed on the issues, Marvin Miller had created a cohesive union. The players held firm, voting 663-10 to strike, while owner unity vanished. Miller not only obtained his demands in 1972 but also forced the owners to make major concessions in the 1973 negotiations.

Of utmost importance in the 1973 agreement was the acceptance by the owners of "final-offer salary arbitration," a procedure by which players who had two years of experience in the majors could have their salaries decided by an "impartial" arbitrator. After having heard testimony by both sides about the player's performance and the salaries of other players whose performance was roughly equivalent, the arbitrator then chose one of two figures, one proposed by the player or one proposed by the owner, as the player's future salary. An average of about 100 players a year filed for arbitration. Each side won about half of the cases, but the mere threat of arbitration encouraged clubs to pay higher salaries. An arbitration hearing "can have a devastating effect on a player because he has to be present at the hearing and he has to listen to his employer say things the player doesn't want to hear," explained Henry Peters of the Baltimore Orioles. To avoid player ill-will and repeated salary controversies, the owners began negotiating multiyear pacts.

⊡   ⊡   ⊡

Rather than using contract negotiations, the players escaped bondage to the reserve clause by an indirect path. An initial frontal assault through the courts failed. In 1969 Curt Flood, a St. Louis Cardinals outfielder, refused to be traded to the Philadelphia Phillies. Given the reserve clause, Flood's only choice was to negotiate a contract with the Phillies or retire from baseball. Flood convinced Miller of his determination to become a free agent, even if it meant taking the issue all the way to the Supreme Court and ending his playing career. With the financial and moral support of the MLBPA and with former Supreme Court justice Arthur Goldberg representing him as legal counsel, Flood filed a suit in federal court charging that the reserve clause was an owner conspiracy in violation of antitrust law. In 1972 the Supreme Court, citing the 1922 precedent of baseball's exemption from antitrust law, ruled five to three against Flood. Lurking in the background of the decision was the judges' uncertainty about the consequences of striking down the reserve clause; perhaps it would even mean the collapse of major league baseball. At any rate, the adverse decision hardened the determination of the players to alter the reserve clause through contract negotiations.

A harbinger of the revolutionary new era of free agency came two years later when star pitcher Jim "Catfish" Hunter took Oakland owner Charley Finley to arbitration for a contract violation. Arbitrator Peter Seitz ruled that, since Finley had failed to fulfill all the terms of Hunter's contract, the pitcher was a free agent. Initially, the owners tried to hold firm and force Hunter to sign with Oakland. But the owner conspiracy collapsed within two weeks when owner George Steinbrenner, who was bent on rebuilding the New York Yankees, offered Hunter a five-year, $3.75-million contract. Other owners, the media, and the players gasped in utter astonishment at the munificent terms of the agreement. "Baseball's establishment will live to regret the Catfish Hunter case," *The Sporting News* predicted, "and baseball players will live to profit from it."

The owners were soon to hear even more bad news from Peter Seitz. Pitchers Andy Messersmith and Dave McNally refused to sign contracts for the 1975 season; invoking the reserve clause, their teams forced them to report anyway. Both players played, but without a new contract. Miller tried to obtain from the owners a revision of the reserve clause, but they refused to make any concessions. Already paying out higher salaries as a result of arbitration, they saw the reserve clause as the only dike holding back an explosion in player salaries.

As provided by the agreement between the owners and the players, Messersmith's case (McNally had in the meantime retired) went to a three-man arbitration panel consisting of Miller of the MLBPA, Gaherin of the own-

ers, and the independent Seitz as the chair. Seitz warned the owners that
the weight of the case was with the players and that they should try to
negotiate a modification in the reserve clause, but they again refused. On
23 December 1975 Seitz ruled that Messersmith was a free agent. He noted that there was no specific provision for baseball's reserve system in player
contracts and that the reserve clause bound a player for only one year after the expiration of his prior contract. The owners promptly appealed the
Seitz decision to a federal district court and the U.S. Court of Appeals. In
both instances the courts ruled in favor of Messersmith. Perhaps appropriately for the nation's bicentennial year and the NL's centennial year, the
decision meant that every player in baseball (except those with multiyear
contracts) could become a free agent simply by playing out the 1976 season without a contract.

Even Marvin Miller worried about this possible scenario. Complete free
agency for every player at the end of each season might cause a massive
defection of fans from the game and actually lower overall player salaries.
Therefore, Miller sought to use the newly won right as a bargaining chip
in the association's 1976 negotiations. In the meantime, hoping for a court
reversal of the Seitz decision, the owners took a hard stand against any
modification in the reserve clause; they even locked the players out of the
spring training camps. But on March 9 the federal courts upheld Seitz's
decision. With this adverse ruling, with the owners divided among themselves on strategy, and with the start of the 1976 season in peril, Kuhn
ordered the camps reopened. In July the two parties finally reached a settlement calling for a modified reservation system: a player became eligible for free agency after six years of play, and teams that lost free agents
would receive no compensation except raw rookies from the annual amateur draft.

When put together, the impartial arbitration procedure adopted in 1970,
the right of salary arbitration won in 1973, the Seitz decision in 1975, and
the Basic Agreement of 1976 represented revolutionary gains in player
power. Never again would the players be at the mercy of one-sided negotiations that favored the owners. Beginning in 1977, the owners had to bid
annually for the services of veterans with six years of big league experience; sometimes they even paid surprisingly high salaries to aging stars and
journeymen.

Free agency and salary arbitration furnished openings for individual
players to hire agents to represent them in their negotiations. Player agents
soon became so important as power brokers that they even worried Mar-

vin Miller. Ironically, the commission received by an agent for negotiating the contract of a single star frequently exceeded the entire budget of the MLBPA. In the new milieu, player salaries shot up at a spectacular rate, from an average of $52,300 in 1976, the first year of free agency, to an average of $146,000 by 1980 (see table 10).

Table 10. Average Major League Player Salaries in Selected Years, 1970–2000

	1970	1975	1980	1985	1990	1995	2000
Salary	$29,000	$46,000	$146,000	$369,000	$589,000	$1,094,000	$1,984,000

In the meantime, another set of baseball employees, the umpires, sought their own empowerment. In 1970, after a one-game strike of the championship playoffs, the owners recognized the newly formed Major League Umpires Association as the arbiters' bargaining agency and awarded them a minimum salary of $22,000. The 1979 season opened with "scabs," while the regular umpires picketed outside the parks for a higher minimum salary and better working conditions. The strike continued until May 18, when, amid many complaints about the quality of umpiring, the league presidents finally agreed to a new contract. Newly appointed commissioner of baseball Peter Ueberroth resolved a strike during the 1984 playoffs by awarding the umpires a sizable increase in payments for working the playoffs; the following year they won another increase (this time from arbitrator Richard M. Nixon) for working in the expanded best-of-seven divisional playoff series. Although the players and managers frequently complained that the newly empowered umpires were far more confrontational and "short-fused" than their predecessors, the officials no longer had to meekly endure abuse to retain their jobs.

⊞ ⊞ ⊞

In the 1980s the free-spending owners sought to achieve pacts with the players' union that would place a cap on the size of arbitration awards and curb their own impulses to bid up salaries by signing free agents. One way of dampening owner enthusiasm for bidding would be to force a team that signed a free agent to give up a player or players of equal value to the team that had lost a player. A majority of the owners girded themselves for an all-out campaign to accomplish such an aim in the 1980 contract negotiations. "I've never seen the owners more unified and prepared for a strike," declared George Steinbrenner. "Unless he handles this right, it could be Waterloo for Marvin Miller." The owners set aside 2 percent of their home gate receipts for a strike fund, took out special strike insurance, hired as their chief negotiator Raymond Grebey (a hard-nosed veteran of negotiations with industrial unions), imposed a gag rule on themselves that called for a $500,000 fine on any owner who discussed labor issues publicly, and launched a media blitz to convince the public that free agency was driving baseball into bankruptcy. The last owner strategy ran counter to the fact that the price of buying a big league franchise was escalating as fast as player salaries.

The players had no intention of giving up something in collective bargaining that they had gained from the Seitz decision and the Basic Agreement of 1976. They, too, began to accumulate a strike fund. Complicated maneuvering, which resulted in a decision to put off negotiations on compensation for free agents until 1981, prevented a strike in 1980, but on 19 February 1981 the owners announced the unilateral implementation of their own compensation plan. On June 12 the players went on strike (see table 11). "I can't imagine [any player] coming back and saying to the owners he didn't want to strike anymore," Kansas City star George Brett told an Associated Press reporter. "Anybody who does that is going to spend the rest of his career in the dirt, ducking pitches thrown at his head." The rival sides rejected compromises offered by both federal mediator Kenneth Moffett and secretary of labor Raymond Donovan. Grebey, in particular, seemed to believe that a firm stand would break the players' union. The fans, by and large, sided with the owners.

Finally, seven weeks into the Great Strike, owner unity wavered. Even though the owners had collected a reported $44 million in strike insurance,

Table 11. Baseball's Work Stoppages, 1972–95

Year	Work Stoppage	Games Missed	Length (days)	Major Issue
1972	Strike	86	13	Pensions
1973	Lockout	0	17	Salary arbitration
1976	Lockout	0	17	Free agency
1980	Strike	0	8	Free-agent compensation
1981	First Great Strike	712	50	Free-agent compensation
1985	Strike	0	2	Salary arbitration
1990	Lockout	0	32	Salary arbitration and salary cap
1994–95	Second Great Strike	920	232	Salary cap and revenue sharing

the cancellation of 713 games had cost them a reported $72 million in ticket sales and broadcast revenues. (The players had lost about $30 million in salaries.) The owners' strike insurance was also due to expire within a week. Only a speedy resumption of play could salvage any more revenue from the 1981 season. In the meantime, AL president Lee MacPhail had skillfully isolated Grebey and taken negotiations into his own hands. In a classic understatement, MacPhail recalled that "there was feeling between Miller and Grebey [that] . . . was impeding our ability to get things done."

Settlement of the Great Strike of 1981 entailed retreats on both sides but an especially drastic one by the owners. The players agreed to a new compensation plan by which each team could protect twenty-six of its forty-man playing roster. The remaining fourteen players entered a pool from which a team that lost a player by free agency could compensate itself. Because the players in the pool were of marginal quality—aging veterans, substitutes, untried minor leaguers, and the like—their value was not equivalent to the athlete lost through free agency. Consequently, the new compensation system did little to curtail owner bidding for the services of free agents.

An uneasy peace followed the 1981 strike. The retirement of Marvin Miller and his replacement by the more conciliatory Kenneth Moffett, the federal mediator in the Great Strike, and the replacement of Raymond Grebey by the more amiable Lee MacPhail contributed to a more pacific relationship between management and labor. Nonetheless, arbitration's leverage on salaries remained a continuing source of owner discontent. The two sides also tangled over player drug use. Charges of alcohol abuse in baseball had a long history, extending back to the origins of the game. In the 1970s and 1980s, the drinking binges and barroom brawls of Billy Martin, the highly charged manager of several big league clubs, repeatedly made headlines. In the late 1970s news reports about widespread player use of amphetamines and cocaine began to surface. Whitey Herzog, manager of the St. Louis Cardinals, in a not atypical disclosure, later estimated that "about eleven" members of his 1980 team were "heavy users" of cocaine. In the spring of 1985 more than twenty players admitted cocaine usage in testimony before a grand jury in Pittsburgh. "Why should I be sorry?" Pittsburgh star Dave Parker reportedly said. "It was a fad. . . . I never missed a game."

Without first consulting or working with the MLBPA, Commissioner Kuhn tried unilaterally to set up a drug assistance program, only to meet the widespread indifference of most of the owners and the stout resistance of most of the players. When Moffett revealed an apparent willingness to cooperate with Kuhn in developing a drug program, the players fired him and recalled Miller on an interim basis. In 1983, Donald Fehr, the players' attorney and Miller's protégé, became the new MLBPA's executive director. In 1984 the players and owners finally reached a truce on drugs. Henceforth, the teams would pay the costs of player treatment but not require testing for drug use.

While hoping to avoid another disastrous strike and simultaneously curtail upward salary pressures, the owners in 1985 proposed a cap on the total amount of money spent on salaries, arbitration limited to veterans of three years or more of big league service, and a limit on arbitration awards to 100 percent of the player's current salary. To strengthen their case for a salary ceiling, the clubs provided the MLBPA with financial data purporting to show that eighteen teams had lost money in 1984 and that the teams expected a deficit of $155 million by 1988. Fehr scoffed at the figures, claiming they were examples of "voodoo economics." (Tax breaks, in particular, made calculations of actual franchise profits difficult.) A two-day strike in August 1985 ended when Peter Ueberroth, who had replaced Kuhn as commissioner in 1984, intervened. Neither side won a clearcut victory. The players agreed to an increase in the amount of time before a player was eligible for salary arbitration from two to three years, and the owners agreed to restore the amateur draft system of compensation for free agents.

Unable to negotiate an agreement that would limit salary escalation and persistently harangued by Ueberroth, the owners discontinued bidding for free agents in 1985. "We must stop daydreaming that one free agent signing will bring a pennant," MacPhail told the owners. For the first time in recent baseball history the ascent of salaries suddenly leveled off. "[It's] not a conspiracy," explained Peter Ueberroth, "it's common sense. The pot is dry." The prize among the 1985 free agents, slugger Kirk Gibson, who had taken Detroit to the 1984 World Championship while hitting twenty-nine home runs, knocking in ninety-seven runs, and batting .287, did not receive a single outside offer. He had to re-sign with the Tigers. By refusing to sign free agents, the owners had, in effect, reinstituted the reserve clause.

But in 1987 the players won a major victory when arbitrator Thomas Roberts found the owners to have violated their contract with the players by a "concerted conduct" to limit the market for free agents. He ordered compensation awards to players who had become free agents during the time that the owners had colluded. Another arbitration judgment in 1988 reaffirmed Roberts's 1987 decision, resulting in a whopping $280-million damage award by the owners to the players affected by the collusion. Nor did the new Basic Agreement of 1990 do anything to stem the upward salary momentum. In fact, free agency and salary arbitration, when combined with the spectacular infusions of new money into baseball from television in the 1990s, set off yet another upward spiral in salaries. Arbitration awards jumped 102 percent in 1991 alone and for the first time averaged more than $1 million for a season. When the 1991 season opened, nearly a third of the 624 major-leaguers earned at least $1 million annually.

The salary explosion, the growing importance of player agents, long-term contracts, free agency, unions, and strikes had significant implications for the public's perception of the players. Earlier, management usually imposed an iron curtain of silence on salary figures, but after free agency and arbitration both the players and the owners often turned to the press to assist them in their negotiations. Salaries rather than home runs or strikeouts often became the bottom line for defining a player's identity and status. Little wonder, then, that the players became more concerned with salaries. As players heard that a teammate or a player elsewhere of similar caliber enjoyed a more lucrative contract, envy and imagined grievances mounted. Resentful players often demanded that their salaries be renegotiated. Salary disputes led fans to suspect that a preoccupation with money reduced the players' enthusiasm for the game and loyalty to their team.

▣   ▣   ▣

A revised system of baseball governance accompanied the empowerment of the players. In a move reflecting baseball's growing legal entanglements, the owners in 1969 had hired Bowie Kuhn, a Wall Street lawyer, as commissioner. Kuhn did not limit himself to legal matters. Concerned with the diminishing popularity of big league baseball, during the first two years of his tenure he signed a contract for the telecast of Monday night games, scheduled games three, four, and five of the World Series at night, and delayed the start of the series until the second Saturday in October so television could beam two weekends of games. Acting more boldly in respect to the owners than even Landis had, Kuhn suspended the Yankees' George Steinbrenner for two years and the Braves' Ted Turner for one, and in 1976 he blocked efforts by Oakland's Charley Finley to sell three of his stars for $3.5 million. He aroused an equal furor by forcing Willie Mays and Mickey

Mantle to sever their relationships with organized baseball because they had become employees of gambling casinos.

Kuhn eventually became the casualty of accumulated owner grievances and his own lack of diplomatic skills. The owners who had been the victims of his punishment never forgave him; he narrowly averted an effort to unseat him as early as 1975. When Kuhn proposed to redistribute some of the local media revenues among all clubs, he encountered the opposition of the franchises that held lucrative local contracts. (The individual franchises had always retained local media receipts, which had resulted in huge disparities between such clubs as the Yankees and the Kansas City Royals.) In 1983 a minority consisting of eight of the twenty-six owners finally obtained Kuhn's dismissal; he continued to serve on an interim basis until a new commissioner took office in 1984.

The new commissioner, Peter Ueberroth, who was hired after his spectacular success in managing the 1984 Olympic Games in Los Angeles, brought to the job unusual skills in public relations, promotion, and management. Before taking charge, Ueberroth insisted that the owners relinquish extensive powers to the commissioner's office. By becoming the major league's chief executive officer, a position roughly parallel to that of a corporate executive, Ueberroth not only obtained the authority to interpret and enforce the cartel's rules but also assumed a far larger role than past commissioners in the decisions that affected the economic welfare of each individual franchise.

Ueberroth soon made his mark. His $1.08-billion, four-year (1990–93) television contract with CBS and additional money from ESPN brought in an average of $14.4 million in national media receipts annually for each franchise. Ueberroth also obtained a sixteenfold increase in licensing income from merchandise marketed by major league baseball. During his reign (1984–89), baseball lost only one game because of labor relations, headline-producing drug cases declined, and player salaries leveled off. But, like Ronald Reagan, the nation's president during the 1980s, Ueberroth achieved part of his success by mortgaging the future. His legacy included the $280 million that the owners had to pay to the players in the 1990s for their collusion against signing free agents in the 1980s.

Ueberroth bequeathed another unfortunate legacy to his successors. That was the case of Pete Rose, nicknamed "Charlie Hustle" for his extraordinary grit and determination on the playing field. No player in baseball was more popular with the ordinary fans than Rose. In 1984 he was appointed player-manager of the Cincinnati Reds, and in the next season he broke

Ty Cobb's longstanding record for the most career hits. In 1989 charges surfaced that Rose had regularly bet on sporting events, including baseball games. Rather than immediately suspending Rose, Ueberroth left the resolution of the issue to A. Bartlett Giamatti, the former president of Yale University and the game's new commissioner. With memories of the Black Sox scandal still lurking in the background, Giamatti ordered a full-scale investigation. Although the 258-page report failed to prove in a strict legal sense that Rose wagered on baseball games—a charge that Rose repeatedly denied—Giamatti banished him from baseball.

Only days after the decision, Giamatti died from a massive heart attack, but the Rose case did not go away. Tenaciously refusing to acknowledge any wrongdoing, Rose apparently believed that his continuing popularity with the fans would one day lead to his reinstatement. Partly because of a huge public relations blitz launched by Rose himself and partly because of public sympathy for Rose that resulted from a hostile interview of Rose by Jim Gray on nationwide television during the 1999 World Series, public support for Rose's admission into the Hall of Fame (from which he was barred by his lifetime ban from the game) rose from 56 percent in 1989 to 74 percent in 1999. However, baseball authorities continued to insist that Rose make some kind of acknowledgment of his guilt before his reinstatement could be considered. Rose refused.

In 1989, the owners also appointed Giamatti's assistant, Fay Vincent, as the new commissioner. A lawyer who had formerly been the chief executive officer of Columbia Pictures, Vincent not only saw himself as guardian of the fan's interest but (like Ueberroth) he thought that the commissioner should be in charge of baseball's overall business operations. In effect, Vincent believed the club owners should serve, in the words of Leonard Koppett, as the commissioner's "department heads." Such a mind set promptly brought him into conflict with his employers. When Vincent discovered in 1990 that George Steinbrenner had been paying money to an informer to avoid negative publicity regarding matters not directly relevant to baseball, he banished the Yankee owner from baseball for life (although in fact the suspension lasted only two years). The owners also resented Vincent's intervention in the labor negotiations of 1990, his refusal to exempt himself from labor negotiations in 1992, and his attempt to unilaterally implement new divisional realignments. Upon receiving a no-confidence vote from the owners in 1992, Vincent tendered his resignation.

The governance of baseball then passed on to an executive council of the owners, headed by Allan H. "Bud" Selig, the owner of the Milwaukee Brewers. In effect, the owners resumed complete command of major league baseball's operations; Selig could take no actions of consequence without the owners' approval. In 1999 the owners named Selig permanent commissioner, and in 2000 they drew up a new national agreement that in principle enormously expanded Selig's authority.

⊞ ⊞ ⊞

The implications of player empowerment reached beyond salaries, strikes, agents, pensions, and a new commissioner system. Neither the owners nor commissioners now ruled baseball with unrestricted authority. The owners argued that player power would dampen public enthusiasm for the sport, that the fans might find it difficult to identify with such well-paid, mobile players. And polls did consistently reveal that the fans resented player strikes and believed that the players were overpaid. Yet the fans did not punish them by staying away from the ballparks. Indeed, in the seasons following each strike, attendance rose. Nor did dire predictions by the owners that free agency would result in the richest teams cornering the best talent prove accurate. On the contrary, though not due to free agency alone, the two-divisional era of baseball history (1969–93) witnessed the demise of team dynasties.

15

The Demise of Dynasties

In the 1970s and 1980s, the glory that had once been baseball in New York City passed away. Nearly a century and a half had elapsed since the Knickerbockers had first taken the field, and few if any recalled the fabulous Atlantics or the renowned Excelsiors. With each passing decade, memories of John J. McGraw's Giants and Jackie Robinson's Brooklyn Dodgers also faded. The Yankees remained in town, and, for a time in the late 1970s and early 1980s, it seemed as though they might regain their former eminence. With shipbuilding magnate George Steinbrenner spending freely, they captured three consecutive divisional titles (1976–78) and two more in 1980 and 1981 but then sank again into obscurity. For nearly a decade, the newcomers to the Big Apple, the Mets, excited interest with their displays of sheer ineptitude. Eventually the Mets began to win, but their scattered divisional titles in 1969, 1973, 1986, and 1988 bore only the faintest resemblance to the supernal consistency that had belonged to the Dodgers, the Giants, and the Yankees of old.

The decline in the performance of New York teams was part of a larger pattern. Teams in the two-divisional era (from 1969 through 1993 each league had two divisions) had far greater difficulty than in the past in sustaining season after season of high play. The age of dynasties, of winning pennants or being a runner-up for decades on end, was over. No teams replaced the Giants, Cardinals, Yankees, or Dodgers of old as the long-term rulers of their respective leagues. The expansion in the number of big league franchises, the adoption of an amateur player draft in 1965, and even free agency introduced a new era of competitive balance.

⊞　⊟　⊞

All comparisons between performances in the two-divisional era and earlier baseball history point toward greater parity in team competition (see tables 7, 8, 12, and 13). Whereas the Yankees in the 1946–68 era captured twelve more pennants than they would have had each AL team captured an equal number of flags, in the 1969–93 era Oakland exceeded hypothetical equality by only three pennants, Baltimore by two, and New York by one. Whereas in the 1946–68 era the Dodgers won seven more flags than they would have had all teams in the NL been of equal strength, in the 1969–93 era the Cincinnati Reds, and the Dodgers exceeded hypothetical equality by 2.5 pennants and the New York Mets and St. Louis Cardinals by only one flag. Those with a statistical bent will also be interested in learning that the standard deviation in win percentages for both leagues for the 1969–93 era was the lowest in big league history. Furthermore, economist Gerald W. Scully found in 1989 that the "margin by which pennants are won is narrower today than in the past, and the margin separating the nonpennant clubs is narrowing." During the 1980s, only three of the twenty-six clubs failed to capture at least one divisional flag (see tables 12 and 13). In 1991, for the first time in major league history, teams that had finished in the cellar of their respective divisions in the previous season (Atlanta and Minnesota) won league championships. Two seasons later, Philadelphia accomplished the same feat.

Simply expanding the number of big league franchises increased the odds against a particular team winning the pennant. Instead of eight teams competing for a single title, beginning in 1969 each league had twelve (the AL had fourteen beginning in 1977), thereby reducing the likelihood of a particular team winning the title by 33 percent if the selection were random. But of course, not everything was random. All the expansion teams

Table 12. National League Pennant Winners in the Two-Divisional Era, 1969–93

Cincinnati	Los Angeles	New York	St. Louis	Philadelphia	Pittsburgh	Atlanta	San Francisco	San Diego
1990	1988	1986	1987	1993	1979	1992	1989	1984
1976	1981	1973	1985	1983	1971	1991		
1975	1978	1969	1982	1980				
1972	1977							
1970	1974							

Table 13. American League Pennant Winners in the Two-Divisional Era, 1969–93

Oakland	Baltimore	New York	Boston	Kansas City	Minnesota	Toronto	Detroit	Milwaukee
1990	1983	1981	1986	1985	1991	1993	1984	1982
1989	1979	1978	1975	1980	1987	1992		
1988	1971	1977						
1974	1970	1976						
1973	1969							
1972								

had to build from nothing, and some teams had special advantages such as larger market areas, more lucrative media contracts, richer, freer-spending owners, and more astute management. The home city's size was no longer as important in determining team success as it had once been. In the two-divisional era, the smaller cities of St. Louis and Cincinnati in the NL won as many flags as the giant metropolises of New York, Los Angeles, and Chicago put together, and Oakland and Baltimore won seven more championships than the AL's New York, Chicago, and California franchises combined, which indicated that the traditional relationship between city size and on-field success no longer held true.

New modes of player acquisition encouraged team equality, in particular the amateur free-agent draft implemented in 1965. With the growing popularity of farm systems in the 1930s and 1940s, the major rather than the minor league clubs had become the primary agencies for procuring new talent. The majors then found themselves in direct competition with one another for new players. Even in the depressed 1930s a few raw recruits obtained large bonuses. In 1936 the Yankees stunned the baseball world by offering Tommy Henrich $25,000 to sign, but four years later the Detroit

Tigers paid out a $52,000 bonus to obtain the contract of Dick Wakefield, who was fresh off the campus of the University of Michigan. After World War II the bidding prices for "bonus babies" escalated even higher. By 1961, the *New York Times* estimated that bonuses had cost major league franchises a total of $12 million.

Over the adamant opposition of the Yankees, Dodgers, Cardinals, and Mets—the franchises that could more easily afford to pay large bonuses— the owners adopted an amateur draft to take effect in 1965. The new rule permitted clubs to draft (in reverse order of their standings in the previous season) the rights to negotiate with any unsigned amateur player. Once drafted, the player could sign with the team that drafted him or wait six months to have his name placed in the draft pool again. "I've been pushing for this thing for 20 years," exclaimed a delighted Gabe Paul, vice president of the Cleveland Indians. The amateur free-agent draft decidedly reduced the advantages that the richer franchises had long enjoyed in the procurement of promising high school and college players.

After the draft, bonuses to amateurs and scouting costs also fell sharply. Whereas Rick Reichardt had signed for $200,000 in 1964, Rick Monday, an even more promising prospect, received only about half that much to sign in 1965. With the draft, clubs no longer needed to employ thirty to forty full-time scouts to locate and convince youths to sign with their team. The draft "made everything automatic and meaningless," grumbled scout Jack Brown of the Philadelphia Phillies. Scouting pools such as the Major League Scouting Bureau, founded in 1968 by former Chicago Cubs executive Vedie Himsl, now identified prospects, who could then be further evaluated by a team's own skeletal scouting staffs. By 1981 most big league clubs employed fewer than twenty full-time scouts.

Stockpiling superior players became more difficult than in the past. In the first place, the forty-player roster limit imposed on each big league club made it impossible for a team to keep under contract large numbers of surplus big league–caliber players. In the second place, as Leonard Koppett has observed, the new era witnessed "an equalization of the power of money." Although some owners had greater fortunes than others, nearly all the owners in the two-divisional era commanded vast financial resources that they had gained from their other businesses. Only the O'Malleys of Los Angeles and the Griffiths of the Minnesota Twins depended any longer on baseball as their sole or main source of income. The owners no longer had to sell superior talent simply to make ends meet. Moreover, an edict by commissioner Bowie Kuhn in 1976 made it virtually impossible for a club to profit from player sales. In that season, citing "the best interests of baseball," Kuhn blocked the sales by Charley Finley, owner of the Oakland Athletics, of three of his stars for $3.5 million and imposed a $400,000 limit thereafter on all player-cash transactions between clubs. In an era in which few players were worth less than $400,000, the Kuhn edict in effect ended cash-for-player transactions.

Despite historical evidence to the contrary, defenders of the reserve clause had always argued that it was essential in maintaining competitive parity. Without the reserve clause, they insisted, the richer franchises would corner the best talent. And indeed, after the collapse of the reserve system in 1975, evidence initially seemed to support their contention. George Steinbrenner, the free-spending owner of the New York Yankees, was particularly effective in wooing established star players to his team. Aided by veteran free agents, the Yankees won five divisional titles between 1976 and 1981, but then their success turned sour; until 1994, they did not win another divisional crown. Several of Steinbrenner's high-priced stars failed to perform well and, in the 1985–87 era, the Yankee owner joined the other owners in refusing to sign free agents. In fact, as Dean Chadwin has argued, the owner collusion against free agency in the late 1980s may have in its own right contributed to the demise of team dynasties.

Regardless, assessing the aggregate effects of free agency on team parity in the two-divisional era is difficult. In the 1970s, free agency ignited the dispersal of both Cincinnati's Big Red Machine and the mighty Oakland A's. Neither Finley of the A's nor Robert Howsam of the Reds was willing to pay out huge sums to hold onto their high-priced stars. Other owners frequently tried to preempt roster raids via free agency simply by signing their better players to multiyear contracts; therefore, many of those potentially eligible for free agency never filed for it. The players who did switch clubs seemed to have had, on the whole, a negligible impact on the performance of the teams that they joined.

Data collected by Bill James on the relationship between aging and performance in the 1980s may help to explain why. James found that players achieved their peak value at the age of twenty-seven; after twenty-seven, performance began to fade rapidly. Because a player could not become a free agent until he had been in the big leagues for six years, most free agents had reached or passed their prime by the time they signed with a new team. Because a club losing a free agent received compensation in the form of younger players from the amateur draft, or (from 1981 to 1990) from a pool of marginal players, such a club might in the long run even benefit from having lost an aging star. On the other hand, in the three-divisional era beginning in 1994, a renewed bidding war for free agents contributed to the coming of a new age of team dynasties (see chapter 16).

▣ ▣ ▣

Although no teams in the two-divisional era established dynasties that even approached the dominance of the Giants, Yankees, Cardinals, or Dodgers of earlier times, in the 1969–93 era six teams performed consistently better than the others. When combined, Cincinnati and Los Angeles collected thirty-one of the forty-nine first or runner-up spots in the NL West, and Pittsburgh won fourteen such places in the NL East. Kansas City and Oakland combined for twenty-eight of the top two spots in the AL West, and Baltimore took fourteen in the AL East. In other words, fans could expect to see these six teams finishing in first or second place in their respective divisional races more than half of the time. Table 14 also reveals a cyclical pattern of divisional dominance.

Kansas City, Baltimore, Pittsburgh, Cincinnati, and Los Angeles shared some striking similarities. A disposition to delegate responsibility and an unusual stability in front office personnel and field managers characterized these clubs. The Los Angeles Dodgers were a classic instance. Both Walter O'Malley, the club's president until 1970, and his son, Peter, who followed,

Table 14. Cycles of Superiority by Divisional Titles, 1969–93

National League				
Cincinnati	Pittsburgh	Philadelphia	Los Angeles	Atlanta
1976	1975	1980	1985	1993
1975	1974	1978	1983	1992
1973	1972	1977	1981	1991
1972	1971	1976		
1970	1970			

American League					
Oakland	Oakland	New York	Baltimore	Kansas City	Toronto
1975	1992	1981	1974	1980	1993
1974	1990	1980	1973	1978	1992
1973	1989	1978	1971	1977	1991
1972	1988	1977	1970	1976	1989
1971		1976	1969		

Note: As reflected in divisional titles interrupted by only one or no seasonal flags.

delegated the nonbusiness side of their franchise to subordinates. Of the some 225 executives and staff in the Dodgers' front office, a study by John Merwin in 1982 found that most of them had been with the team for more than two decades and a few for forty years. Walter Alston managed the Dodgers for twenty-three seasons before retiring voluntarily in 1976; he was replaced by Tommy Lasorda, who was with the organization for forty-seven years. Baltimore had an almost equal stability; Earl Weaver served as their field manager for eighteen seasons.

Even the successful franchises that changed managers more frequently— Pittsburgh six times, Cincinnati seven, Kansas City eight, and Oakland twelve—can be contrasted with George Steinbrenner's Yankees, who had twenty-one managers, including Billy Martin five times, Bob Lemon twice, Gene Michael twice, and Lou Piniella twice. (Major league franchises in the two-divisional era averaged a new manager every two years.) In addition, the Yankees had twenty-nine pitching coaches, twelve club presidents, fifteen general managers, and eleven public relations directors during the 1970s and 1980s. On the other hand, Kansas City, an expansion team that enjoyed a better overall record than the Yankees, had front office men John Schuerholz and Herk Robinson, who were with the Royals from the beginning and served in several capacities while working their way up the organizational ladder.

Personnel permanency may not, of course, have been a cause of team success; it may simply have been a result of success. Despite almost constant turmoil in the front office and on the field, with the exception of the 1979 season the Yankees dominated the AL-East between 1976 and 1981. Yet personnel stability may have also reflected a consistency in strategy and a determination to achieve long- rather than short-term goals. Furthermore, economist Gerald Scully, using a sophisticated statistical model known as the frontier production function, has found that field managers in the 1961–80 era did not reach their "maximum efficiency" until their twelfth or thirteenth year of experience. In descending order, Earl Weaver of Baltimore, Sparky Anderson (mostly with Cincinnati), and Walter Alston of Los Angeles had the best performance measures, whereas, among the veteran managers, Gene Mauch, Dave Bristol, and Leo Durocher had the worst. Another way of stating Scully's findings is to say that Weaver was worth seven to eight more wins per season than the mercurial Billy Martin. Martin ranked tenth in Scully's measure of managerial efficiency.

In addition to possessing seasoned front office personnel and managers, nearly all the successful teams seemed to enjoy a special esprit de corps.

Even the individualistic Oakland Athletics of the early 1970s held in common their shaggy hair, mustaches, flashy uniforms, and a hatred of their owner, Charley Finley. Although the two-divisional era was racked with heated disputes between players and management, some franchises went to great lengths to cultivate team loyalty and tradition. The Dodgers, for example, invited all their minor league prospects to Dodgertown, a specially constructed village in Vero Beach, Florida, in the spring to train and to meet and socialize with such Dodgers legends as Roy Campanella and Sandy Koufax. To encourage team loyalty, the Dodgers also pursued a policy of trying to sign their own veterans to long-term contracts rather than regularly entering the free-agent market.

In addition, a few individual players seemed to have special capacities to inspire their mates. For more than a decade, the Pittsburgh Pirates looked to slugger Willie Stargell for leadership. In the latter part of his career, when he was known as "Pops," Stargell generated a special affection among his younger teammates. Perhaps even more impressive was Don Baylor, who, regardless of his direct contribution on the field, seemed to arouse his teammates to superior performances wherever he played. Baylor, known for his enthusiasm and positive thinking, played on AL championship teams for three different franchises.

In procuring new player talent, which was the single most important variable in determining team performance, all the successful teams except the Yankees pursued a roughly similar strategy. All of them tried to develop a core group of players from within their own organizations rather than through trades or free agency. Acquiring the core began with the amateur draft. Even for the most astute judges of talent, the draft was something like a giant crapshoot. Only about one in thirty-five picks actually made it to the big leagues. Even in the first round of the draft, a club had only a one in two chance of picking a starter, and pitchers were an even bigger risk. "Pitchers who were drafted very high (one through ten spots) in the years 1965–83 proved on the whole to be terrible investments," Bill James has found. Reliance on the draft for new talent also took an uncommon patience. Typically, a drafted player did not reach his peak value until six to eight years later. Nonetheless, astute drafting helped build such mini-dynasties as the Oakland and Los Angeles teams in the early 1970s and Atlanta in the 1990s.

The successful management of a farm system demanded an equal persistence. With the Branch Rickey system and its imitators, the assumption was that out of the sheer quantity of players would arise a few quality athletes. "It was a Darwinian thing," explained Philadelphia Phillies general manager Lee Thomas in 1990. "But each major league team had twenty farm clubs then, and the players were forced to claw their way upward. Now we have only five to seven minor league teams apiece, and the emphasis is on teaching." With the big league club paying in full the salaries of players on their minor league affiliates and having far fewer players under their control than in the past, each club tried to maximize the likelihood of each of its minor league prospects reaching the majors.

A marked impatience for quick results characterized the history of the less successful franchises. Only six franchises had the same ownership for the entire two-divisional era, and fourteen new owners arrived in the 1980s alone. All the new owners obtained their wealth from outside baseball. Such owners tended to view their teams as hobbies and as agencies for them to gain public attention. "No one pays attention to a shipbuilder," George Steinbrenner once candidly confessed. For the hobby to furnish immediate gratification or public recognition to the franchise owner, club officials had to build winners quickly. They were thus tempted to spend freely in the free-agent market and to trade younger, unproven men for veteran players. After 1975, Steinbrenner, who loved to be called "The Boss," signed a record-shattering forty-eight free agents, and Yankees star second baseman Willie Randolph had thirty-one different double-play partners in thirteen seasons. If free agents and trades failed to bring instant pennants, which they usually did, the owners often fired their general managers and field managers. With a large part of their own egos invested in their clubs, two of the owners, Steinbrenner and Ray Kroc of San Diego, even criticized the performance of their players publicly.

◫ ◫ ◫

Although offensive and defensive statistics per game remained essentially unchanged in the two-divisional era, the fans witnessed a different kind of game. It featured raw power, dazzling speed, and specialized pitching. Like athletes in most other sports, the ball players reflected the general increase in the size of Americans, the huge pool of new talent added by those of African and Latin descent, and doubtless in several instances the use of steroids or growth hormones. In the 1950s, only a dozen or so players in all of big league baseball weighed 200 pounds or more, but teams such as the Oakland Athletics of 1990 fielded a lineup that had a half dozen 200-pounders; in 1908, the average player stood at just under five feet ten inches, but in 1990 he stood at just under six feet three inches, a full five inches taller than his predecessors. The big men were just as agile as their smaller counterparts of earlier eras, probably on the average more so. For example, Baltimore shortstop Cal Ripken Jr., who stood at more than six feet, four inches tall and weighed about 220 pounds, led the AL in assists five times and double plays three times; in 1990 Ripken became the first shortstop in big league history to make only three errors in a complete season of play. The players were also better conditioned than their predecessors; many of them carefully monitored their diets and lifted weights in both the regular season and the off-seasons.

Even the smaller men had the power to hit twenty or so home runs per season. No player exhibited multiple talents more emphatically than Cincinnati's Joe Morgan, who stood only five feet, seven inches tall and weighed a mere 160 pounds. In 1976, the muscular Morgan had one of the best single season performances in big league history. In the final NL figures, he was second in runs scored (113), fourth in home runs (27), second in runs batted in (111), second in bases on balls (114), fifth in batting average (.320), first in on-base percentage (.453), first in slugging average (.576), second in stolen bases (60), and, for the third straight season, first in Thomas Boswell's measurement of total offensive production. With more than sufficient reason, the baseball writers named Morgan as the NL's Most Valuable Player for 1976, the second year in a row that he captured the honor.

Sheer speed, both in the field and on the base paths, also sharply separated the two-divisional era from earlier baseball. Defensive players had to be able to react more quickly and cover more area to stop the ground balls that rocketed through the infield off the artificial surfaces. Quickness and strong arms permitted shortstops and second basemen to play several feet deeper than in the past; weak-armed shortstops, such as Phil Rizzutto and Lou Boudreau, who played only a step or two behind the baseline in the 1940s, could never have held down such a vital position in the two-divisional era. "I couldn't have played the short leftfield that guys do today," admitted Rizzutto in 1990. Furthermore, with the spacious new parks, few teams could afford to play even one plodding outfielder. With their added quickness, range, and use of larger, form-fitted gloves, the modern players, especially the infielders, transformed what would earlier have been considered spectacular plays into routine outs.

The return of the stolen base was also indicative of baseball's growing speed. With the hitting revolution that commenced in the 1920s, stolen base totals began to fall rapidly, until the stratagem all but disappeared in the

1940s and 1950s; entire teams during these decades averaged fewer than 50 stolen bases per season. But even then, a tiny contingent of Caribbean basin and black players hinted at what lay ahead. In 1959 Luis Aparicio stole 56 bases and proceeded to top 40 thefts in four of the next five seasons. In 1962, Maury Wills, the Los Angeles shortstop, was successful in 104 attempts, breaking Ty Cobb's record of 96, which had stood since 1915. The Dodgers as a team stole 198, the most for a club since 1918. Wills's role in the Dodgers' NL championships in 1963, 1965, and 1966 and Lou Brock's similar one for the Cardinals in 1964, 1967, and 1968 encouraged managers to look more favorably on base stealing and the recruitment of players with superior speed.

In the two-divisional era the base thieves broke all earlier records. NL teams, the beneficiaries of more artificial surfaces and a tougher enforcement of the balk rule than the AL, averaged more than 150 thefts per season, three times the figures for the 1940s and 1950s, while the AL teams lagged about 50 behind the senior circuit. Black and Latino players led the way; of the ninety two league titles between 1947, when Jackie Robinson broke into the big leagues, and 1993, a black or Latino player won eighty-five times. Of the top twenty all-time base stealers in 1993, twelve of them played most of their careers since 1960. Although a few successful managers eschewed base stealing as a critical weapon (notably Earl Weaver of the Baltimore Orioles), the Cincinnati Reds of the early 1970s, the Philadelphia Phillies of the late 1970s, and the Oakland Athletics of both the early 1970s and late 1980s exhibited a remarkable combination of both speed on the base paths and home run prowess. In 1988 sportswriters hailed Jose Canseco as a superman when he became the first player in baseball history to hit forty home runs and steal forty bases in the same season.

No innovation of the two-divisional era was more important than the use of relief pitchers. Reflecting the game's fundamental conservatism and, more specifically, its attachment to the complete game mystique, managers were amazingly obtuse (in retrospect) in their reluctance to use more relief pitching. No example in the game's history suffices more adequately than Bucky Harris's failure to relieve the legendary Walter Johnson in game 7 of the 1925 World Series. Harris left Johnson, who had already pitched two complete games in the series, in for the entire nine innings while Washington wasted leads of 4-0, 5-3, and 7-6 before finally losing to Pittsburgh 9-7. Pittsburgh used four pitchers who allowed seven hits, while Harris let the thirty-eight-year-old Johnson take a fifteen-hit pounding. In the bullpen, Harris had the best reliever in baseball, Fred "Firpo" Marberry, who had appeared in fifty-five regular season games, recorded fifteen saves, and had eight wins, all in relief. Asked afterward by AL president Ban Johnson why he stuck with his starter so long, Harris replied, "I went down with my best."

Even the hitting revolution of the 1920s failed to spawn much experimentation with relief pitching. Completed game percentages remained essentially unchanged from the 1920s until the late 1940s. Nearly all the relievers were veteran starters whose stamina was suspect or who were experiencing other difficulties, youngsters from the farm clubs who were looking for a chance to show off their abilities, or starters working overtime. Finally, in the late 1940s and in the 1950s managers began to turn to their bullpens more frequently, especially during World Series time. Even then, relievers were usually employed only when the starter was manifestly struggling or when he had to be removed for a pinch hitter.

Managers slowly but in the end decisively altered the use of pitchers (see table 15). For the two-divisional era as a whole, the percentage of complete games pitched plummeted; on the average, pitchers finished less than one in ten games for the 1989–93 seasons. (At the beginning of the century, starters completed more than two-thirds of all games.) Sparky Anderson led the way while serving as manager of the Cincinnati Reds from 1970 through 1978. Earning the sobriquet "Captain Hook," Anderson allowed the starting pitchers on his divisional championship teams of 1970, 1972, 1973, 1975, and 1976 to complete only 32, 25, 39, 22, and 33 games, respectively. Although no Reds relievers stood among the league leaders in any category (except for Clay Carroll in 1972), in 1974 Mike Marshall of the Dodgers became the first relief pitcher to win the Cy Young Award for the best pitcher in the NL. Three years later, another reliever, the Yan-

Table 15. Percentage of Completed Games and Saves in the Two-Divisional Era, 1969–93

Seasons	National League		American League	
	Complete Games	Saves	Complete Games	Saves
1969–74	25.4	—	27.1	—
1975–79	20.1	20.4	23.4	17.5
1980–84	14.1	23.9	20.6	21.2
1985–88	12.3	24.6	15.4	23.1
1989–91	9.8	25.4	10.4	27.1
1992–93	8.0	25.8	9.9	26.7

Note: A new "save" rule, adopted in 1974, makes the 1969–74 seasons not comparable to the 1975–93 seasons.

kees' Sparky Lyle, garnered the AL's Cy Young Award; in 1981, Rollie
Fingers of Milwaukee won both the Cy Young Award and the AL's Most
Valuable Player Award; and in 1992 Dennis Eckersley became the first
pitcher to record forty saves in four different seasons.

By the 1980s the term *saver* replaced *reliever* as the more significant way
of describing substitute pitchers. Managers no longer planned or necessarily even hoped that their starters would complete an entire game. Rather
than coasting through the early innings, they urged their starters to pitch
their best and hardest from the outset. If the starter revealed any signs of
fatigue or ineffectiveness, the manager rushed in his middle or long reliever;
he was followed by the setup pitcher. Then, in the eighth or ninth inning,
regardless of how well the starter, middle reliever, or setup pitcher was
doing, many of the managers brought in a closer. The (usually) big, power-
pitching closers became the bullpen kings. Instead of building their mound
corps from the starters, many clubs began to erect their pitching staffs from
the closers backward.

Despite all this, the relief pitchers did not occupy all the limelight in the
two-divisional era. Especially early in the era there were some remarkable
starters as well. Bob Gibson and Juan Marichal finished their careers in 1975
with 251 and 243 victories, respectively. Steve Carlton, Don Sutton, Gaylord Perry, Tom Seaver, and Nolan Ryan stood among the all-time top twenty
pitchers for career wins. These pitchers also held down the first five places
in all-time career strikeouts. Ryan, who did not retire until the age of forty-
six in 1993, stood far ahead of all other hurlers in career strikeouts. He was
the only pitcher to throw no-hitters for three different teams (and in three
different decades as well), the only pitcher since Cy Young in 1901 to win
his 300th game in a year in which he gave up the fewest hits per game in his
league, the only pitcher to win 194 games by allowing no more than one
run, and the only pitcher to win 115 games in which he allowed no more
than three hits. Ryan seemed ageless; after reaching the age of forty, he proceeded to lead his league in strikeouts for four consecutive years.

Specialized pitchers, along with the development of the slider, the split-
finger fastball or fork ball (the "new" pitch of the 1980s apparently invented by San Francisco's Roger Craig), and better fielding, helped offset
the smaller strike zone and the growing strength of the hitters. "It usually
takes a hitter two or three at bats to gauge a pitcher," complained slugger
Mike Schmidt. "Now you probably get no more than two looks at a starter.
The next at bat you get another guy, usually with one outstanding pitch.
And for the final at bat, you get the closer with one *great* pitch."

Home runs per game crept up only slightly during the divisional era, and only two players scaled the fifty-home-runs-in-a-season plateau. Apart from Frank Robinson, Harmon Killebrew, Willie McCovey, and Hank Aaron, who completed their careers in the 1970s, only Reggie Jackson (with 563) and Mike Schmidt (with 548) broke into the top ten career home run ranks. At the end of the two-divisional era in 1993, only two active players had accumulated 400 home runs, and, even with the additional eight games per season, more often than not the league leader totaled fewer than forty home runs for the season. With the exception of Aaron's brief tenure in the divisional era, none of the strong men hit for consistently high batting averages. The hitters achieved an even more dubious distinction; twenty-two of the top forty career strikeout leaders played during the 1980s.

❑ ❑ ❑

To the question of whether baseball continued to hold a vital place in American life during the two-divisional era, the answer was uncertain. Public opinion polls from the mid-1960s on revealed that when Americans were asked to name their favorite spectator sport, they usually chose football. Nearly everyone agreed that football was better suited than baseball to television, and some speculated that Americans themselves had changed, that they now wanted in their games more violence, continuous action, and the kind of team coordination needed for success in the nation's bureaucracies where most of them worked. Moreover, baseball's once vast and thriving middle ground—the baseball of the sandlot, town teams, semi-pro teams, and American Legion squads—had all but disappeared. Besides the big leagues, only adult-directed Little League baseball, its imitators, and to some extent intercollegiate and minor league baseball remained successful enterprises.

Yet there were grounds for optimism. Spurred on by improved economic conditions and greater parity on the playing field, big league attendance jumped from 45 to 55 million between 1982 and 1990. Subsidized by television profits and the receipts that accrued from playing so many games, the owners were able to keep ticket prices below those for most forms of competing commercial entertainment. They were particularly successful in selling large blocs of season tickets to corporations.

As in the past, audiences varied in their composition. The White Sox, located on Chicago's South Side, for example, continued to rely mainly on white ethnics, whereas the Kansas City Royals pulled in a large regional following. Reflecting in part the distribution of income along racial lines and in part the perception of baseball as the most "white" of American team sports, no franchise succeeded in capturing a percentage of African-American fans that was anywhere near proportionate to their numbers in the general population of the host cities. "It is clear that black fans, after a romance with baseball that began at the turn of the century and flourished through the early 1950s," asserted Brent Staples, an editor at the *New York Times* in 1990, "have abandoned the national pastime." Baseball lost more than just black fan support. Whereas the percentage of black or racially mixed players in other team sports increased in the 1980s, the figures declined for baseball.

Although never regaining the position that they occupied for much of the first half of the twentieth century, the minor leagues experienced a rapid growth in the 1980s and 1990s (see table 16). Attendance during the 1980s rose more than 50 percent; in 1989 the Buffalo Bisons of the International League outdrew the Chicago White Sox and the Atlanta Braves. In the 1990s, teams located in the suburbs of cities with major league franchises led the minor league renaissance; in the 2000 season the greater Chicago area alone hosted three minor league clubs. "It all comes down to price, proximity and price," explained Steve Arch, a club official with the Crestwood Cheetahs in suburban Chicago. The revival of minor league baseball also benefitted from promotional gimmicks and big league subsidies. Although the major league clubs rarely continued to own minor league franchises, by the end of the 1980s each big league franchise was spending $5 to $7 million apiece (mostly in salaries) supporting their minor league affiliates.

Intercollegiate and international baseball prospered as well. Though not approaching the interest manifested in or the money generated by intercollegiate football, by the mid-1980s some 10 million fans attended col-

Table 16. Minor League Baseball Activity in Selected Years, 1949–99

Season	Leagues	Clubs	Attendance (millions)	Club Average
1949	59	n.a.	41.8	n.a.
1952	43	324	24.0	74,149
1961	22	147	9.8	66,438
1968	21	152	9.9	65,048
1979	18	154	15.2	98,731
1989	19	190	23.1	121,597
1999	16	182	35.2	193,294

lege baseball games annually. The season climaxed with a televised College World Series scheduled at Omaha, Nebraska. Playing nearly 100 games in a season, the major college programs in the sunbelt region featured a quality of ball equal to that of the lower minor leagues. With more than 70 percent of the big league rosters containing ex-collegians, the colleges also became an integral part of big league player development plans. Finally, the sport appeared to be spreading internationally. There already was a long tradition of flourishing baseball in the Caribbean basin countries and Japan, but in addition, the International Baseball Association reported a doubling of its membership (to sixty-eight countries) in the 1980s.

The most startling evidence of baseball's continuing perseverance arose from unexpected quarters, from the ranks of the button-down, white-collar professional classes. As part of a widespread quest for ties beyond the self, these men (and some women) created and supported a flourishing auxiliary baseball culture of memorabilia, magazines, books, movies, games, and organizations. The popular movies *Eight Men Out* (1988), *Field of Dreams* (1989), and *A League of Their Own* (1992) evoked images of an earlier, presumably simpler and more heroic age of baseball.

Perhaps reacting to feelings of impotency and sometimes disgust with current big league baseball, a contingent of fans sought to take charge of their own baseball experiences. Some attended fantasy camps where they were provided with big league uniforms and could play alongside former big league stars. Fans published more than fifty baseball newsletters, ranging from *The San Diego Baseball Update,* a newsletter featuring the personal observations of a fan on the Padres, to *Basewomen,* a newsletter devoted to women in baseball. Each February and March found a flood of annual baseball publications at newsstands and supermarkets. Dozens of Rotisserie Leagues allowed fans themselves to own and direct imaginary big league teams. The Society for American Baseball Research, which by the 1990s had a membership of nearly 6,000 and an annual budget of more than a quarter of a million dollars, attracted fans interested in even the most arcane aspects of the game's past.

◘　◘　◘

The two-divisional era, which spanned the 1969–93 major league seasons, was a momentous one for baseball history. As revealed in chapter 14, it witnessed the empowerment of the players; never again would the owners be able to exercise unbridled authority over the actors in baseball's drama. The two-divisional era also saw the end of the great team dynasties of the past; no single team or small groups of teams completely dominated league play for season after season. In the two-divisional era, fans watched a different kind of game; as never before, size, strength, speed, and specialized pitching characterized the game between the foul lines. What no one foresaw in 1993 was the revolutionary changes that lay ahead.

16

A New Era

During the 1990s nothing more dramatically heralded the arrival of a new era in baseball history than a momentous home run duel between Mark McGwire of the St. Louis Cardinals and Sammy Sosa of the Chicago Cubs. Seeking to stake his claim as baseball's new Babe Ruth, on September 8, 1998, McGwire first broke Roger Maris's thirty-seven-year record of sixty-one homers. As McGwire exuberantly trotted around the bases, each of the Cubs' infielders congratulated him, and, upon reaching home plate, he was hugged by the Cardinals batboy, who happened to be his son, Matt. After briefly basking in the adulation of his fellow players and the sellout crowd, McGwire climbed into the stands to share the occasion with members of Maris's family who were at Busch Stadium in St. Louis to witness the epochal event. True to the form that he had displayed all season, McGwire responded humbly by saying, "I can't believe I did it."

McGwire's sixty-second home run was only one episode, albeit the most exciting one, in what turned out to be the mightiest home run derby in major league history. Adding the stunning total of twenty homers in June to the thirteen he had hit earlier, the ever-smiling and self-deprecating Sammy Sosa unexpectedly challenged McGwire. "The two made for a wonderful Only-in-America pairing: McGwire the blue-eyed Paul Bunyan, and Sosa the dark-skinned Dominican from a Caribbean island overflowing with baseball players," explained Steve McKee of the *Wall Street Journal*. On the final weekend of the season, Sosa hit number sixty-six, his last one for that summer, to take the lead—but only for 45 minutes. McGwire then smashed five homers in his last eleven at bats, to end the season with an incredible total of seventy home runs.

As had not been the case for nearly a half century, or perhaps even longer, the home run derby riveted the nation's attention to baseball. America's game seemed to be alive and well after all. Fans addressed one another with a hypothetical question: "If you got your hands on one of those home run record balls, would you keep it, sell it, or give it back?" And fans judged one another by their responses. (Upon recovering McGwire's seventieth home-run ball, Philip Ozersky, a research scientist at Washington University's Human Genome Laboratory in St. Louis, auctioned it off for $3 million.) The historic assault on the single-season home run benchmark came at a propitious time in the game's history. Along with Cal Ripken's breaking of Lou Gehrig's consecutive game streak in 1995 and the performance of a couple of dozen other future Hall of Famers in the 1990s, it "saved baseball's ass," announced baseball's chief bard, Roger Angell of the *New Yorker*.

The direct origins of this new era in baseball's history go back earlier, perhaps four or five years earlier. In 1993 the NL expanded to twelve teams (the same as the AL) and a new offensive barrage, one that even surpassed that of the 1920s, got under way. In 1994 each league split into three divisions and the major leagues set up a new wild-card playoff system similar to professional football. Also in 1994 a strike—the Second Great Strike—cut short the season, canceled the World Series, and delayed the start of the 1995 season. In 1994 the Public Broadcasting System released Ken Burns's *Baseball: An American Epic,* the most monumental historical television documentary ever made. Other epochal developments in the new era were not so directly tied to 1993 and 1994. These included a new age of ballpark building, new mini-dynasties in Atlanta, Cleveland, and New York (the Yankees again), the "invasion" of an army of new playing talent from Latin America, and the advent of the Internet as a tool by which fans could relate to America's game in new ways, both real and imaginary.

▣   ▣   ▣

Expanding the number of big league franchises ushered in the new era. In 1993, the NL added franchises in Denver (called the Colorado Rockies) and Miami (called the Florida Marlins), which, by giving each league fourteen teams, ended an imbalance in the number of franchises between the two leagues that had prevailed since 1977. Playing in cavernous Mile High Stadium, which hitherto had been almost exclusively a football field, the Colorado Rockies in their first season broke all big league attendance records. Continuing the big league march toward the rapidly expanding population centers in the Sunbelt, in 1998 the AL added a franchise in Tampa Bay and the NL one in Phoenix (called the Arizona Diamondbacks). That same year, Milwaukee switched from the AL to the NL.

The owners broke with other time-honored traditions. Reasoning that they could spur greater fan interest by having more teams in contention for the pennant through the regular season and permitting more teams to participate in the playoffs, in 1994 they created three divisions in each league and established a new four-team playoff format that included divisional winners plus a wild-card team (the divisional second-place finisher with the best season record). Hoping to bring back to the parks fans who were angry about the 1994–95 strike, the majors inaugurated an experiment with limited interleague play in 1997. This step, plus the creation of a single major league umpiring staff and the abolition of the league presidencies in 2000, all but wiped out baseball's venerable tradition of distinctively National and American leagues.

Baseball's new stadium-building era began with the construction of Toronto's Skydome in 1989. Though conforming in general to the 1960s design of multipurpose ovals, the Skydome boasted a retractable roof, a Hard Rock Cafe, and a hotel behind the outfield wall. So popular was Toronto's new technologically sophisticated park that for the next three seasons the Blue Jays broke all big league attendance records. Then, in 1992, came the first of the "retroparks," a popular name for the new parks that was something of an oxymoron. Built near the harbor and within two blocks of Babe Ruth's birthplace, Camden Yards in Baltimore combined the fan intimacy of parks built early in the twentieth century with the latest high-tech razzmatazz. Camden Yards not only featured an asymmetrical playing field and natural grass but a view of downtown Baltimore, escalators, elevators, climate-controlled lounges, Disneyesque play areas for children, and luxury suites that could be leased for a minimum of $75,000 annual-

ly. "This is a fan's park," enthused Roger Angell. "They've done it at last."
The popularity of Camden Yards soon inspired more than a dozen imitators.

In nearly all instances, the park-building drama played out according to
a common script. It began with a team owner throwing up his or her hands
in despair. The old ballpark would no longer do, the owner said. Without
a new park that generated millions of dollars more in revenues, the local
team could not possibly compete with other franchises in securing the best
playing talent. Unless city, county, state, or some combination of these
governments built a new facility, one that included an ample quantity of
luxury boxes, suites, and shopping malls, the owner threatened to take the
team and leave town. To preserve the older ballparks or to halt the use of
their tax dollars to build new "playpens for the rich," ordinary fans and
taxpayers often resisted club owner pleas. But the politicians often found
ingenious ways to provide public funds for construction that bypassed voter
approval, and, in the end, the parks usually got built anyway. This fact, plus
the naming of stadia after corporate sponsors who were willing to pay more
than $50 million for the privilege, reflected, in baseball's business opera-
tions, a loss of local autonomy and the growing clout of global capital.

Although the question of whether the new parks fulfilled the promises
of downtown revitalization remained problematic, other propositions were
far less debatable. With the construction of each new park, attendance
increased and each of the teams experienced huge transfusions of fresh
funds from luxury seats, concessions, mountains of licensed merchandise,
and the rental of retail spaces. But with each park opening, fans also found
fewer seats at affordable prices. According to a Vanderbilt University study
published in 1998, when a team moved into a new park, ticket prices rose
on average by 35 percent. Teams sold most of the seats in the new parks
to season ticket holders, the majority of whom were corporations. Despite
a decade of exceptionally modest inflation, the average ticket price for big
league games shot up from $8.64 in 1991 to $14.91 in 1999. The price
for concessions jumped an equal amount or perhaps even more; the advent of the five-dollar hotdog in 1996 was emblematic of a general shift
in the socioeconomic characteristics of baseball fans. In increasing numbers, baseball's patrons, like the fans of other professional team sports,
came from the ranks of the well-to-do. Put another way, baseball's patrons
increasingly represented the upper end of the late twentieth-century's fast-
growing inequalities in income and wealth.

By 2000, the experience of attending a big league game had changed radically in another respect. In the spirit of the National Hockey League and the National Basketball Association and operating on the premise that the game itself was no longer enough to hold the fans' attention, baseball decided to fill every moment of the fans' time with, in the words of Jeff MacGregor in *Sports Illustrated*, "a deafening infusion of prerecorded enthusiasm." Fans found themselves bombarded by musical cues, big-screen replays, and big-screen commercials. "Forget about turning to your kids and remarking on that dandy 6-4-3 double play," remarked MacGregor, "they can't hear you because its dance time!" Almost nothing in the experience of the game went unmediated. In vital respects, attending a game became more and more like watching television, except that the ads and the music were much louder.

▣ ▣ ▣

In the meantime, baseball's Second Great Strike in 1994–95 threatened to undo much of the fan enthusiasm that had been generated by the new stadia and the new playoff system. During the 1990s, the owners continued to find galling the recently won player rights of salary arbitration and free agency. But rather than directly assaulting these player gains—strategies that had misfired in the past—the owners rallied behind a new ploy. By calling for a salary cap and a redistribution of money from large- to small-market teams, the owners sought to halt or turn back the escalation of player salaries while simultaneously addressing the financial woes of small-market teams. Neither proposal received a warm welcome from Donald Fehr, the executive director of the Major League Baseball Players Association (MLBPA). Fehr reasoned that a salary cap would reduce the total revenues available for player salaries, and a redistribution of team revenues would reduce owner enthusiasm for signing free agents.

According to labor law, if both parties bargained in good faith and no agreement had been reached by the end of the 1994 season, the owners could then declare a bargaining impasse and impose a salary cap unilaterally. Given this likely scenario, the players concluded that they had no choice but to call a peremptory strike. The players decided to halt play on 12 August 1994, before postseason play was to begin, and thereby inflict the heaviest damage on the owners' pocketbooks. On September 14, acting commissioner Bud Selig announced that for the first time since 1904, there would be no World Series. The season-ending strike, the first in the history of professional sports, cost the owners an estimated $442 million in revenue, and the players sacrificed some $236 million in salaries. The players continued to stand firm; they vowed to never accept a salary cap "even if we have to stay out 92 years," said San Francisco Giant pitcher Rich Monteleone.

Likewise, the owners refused to budge. The small-market owners rallied around Selig's insistence on tying a new labor agreement to a "share the wealth" plan. Several new owners, having paid big price tags for their franchises and hoping that they could curtail escalating costs in player payrolls, were equally enthusiastic about holding firm. And so were several of the big-market owners, who saw the conflict as an opportunity to crush the players' union. Reflecting the owners' intractability was their decision to adopt a new rule requiring the approval of three-fourths (rather than a majority) of their numbers for any agreement reached with the players. "If such a requirement . . . applied to all elections," exclaimed Marvin Miller, the legendary director of the MLBPA from 1966 to 1983, "we would never elect a president." With neither side willing to make more than minor concessions, the owners threatened to employ replacement players for the 1995 season. In March, spring training camps opened for all clubs (except Baltimore) using "scabs"—minor-leaguers, semipros, and a few recently retired big-leaguers—rather than bona fide big league players.

Finally, after 232 days and 20 minutes before the first pitch of the 1995 season had been scheduled, the strike ended—but not because of the signing of a new labor pact. Instead, a district court judge found that by failing to bargain in good faith, the owners had violated federal law. In the wake of the court's decision, both the players and owners agreed to play a foreshortened 1995 season of 144 games under the terms of the old labor agreement. Average game attendance in 1995 plummeted 17 percent. Bud Selig claimed that, for the 1995 season, twenty-three of the twenty-eight big league teams lost money.

In November 1996 the players and the owners finally reached a new agreement. With the decision by Chicago White Sox owner Jerry Reinsdorf, previously an influential spokesperson for fiscal restraint by owners, to sign free agent slugger Albert Belle for $55 million over five years (a figure well above that any previous player had received), opposition by the owners to a settlement dissolved. The new pact kept salary arbitration and free agency in place. However, the players did agree to a team payroll tax; teams whose payrolls exceeded $51 million in 1997 would pay 35 percent on the dollars above that figure to the clubs with smaller payrolls. However, by 2000 the payroll tax was to be phased out. Although the payroll tax was at least a symbolic concession to the owners, the new agreement accomplished little in curbing the upward trend in salaries or improving the capacity of small-market franchises to field more competitive teams.

Nor did the payroll tax, expansion in the number of franchises, the creation of a new divisional system, new stadia, interleague play, and efforts to speed up the pace of the games solve all of baseball's attendance problems. Aided by the addition of franchises in Denver and Miami in 1993 and the opening of new retroparks in Baltimore (1992) and Cleveland in (1994), average game attendance for regular season games reached all-time highs in 1993 and 1994. But afterwards average game attendance never fully recovered, in part because of the Second Great Strike of 1994–95. Even the great hitting barrage of the late 1990s and the addition of new franchises in Phoenix and Tampa Bay failed to raise per game attendance enough to reach the marks achieved in the 1993–94 seasons.

▣   ▣   ▣

In the final years of the 1990s, wide disparities in team performances reappeared. In the previous decade, divisional and league titles had been spread out among the teams in a roughly equal fashion. But in the three-divisional era that began in 1994, three teams—the Atlanta Braves, the Cleveland Indians, and the New York Yankees—won five consecutive divisional titles (1995–99). (Because of the Second Great Strike, there were no official divisional winners in 1994.) In the same era, one of these three teams won eight of the ten league championships and four of five World Series. Because there were more teams than ever before and teams had to claw their way through two rounds of playoffs to win league pennants— two more minefields per season than the dynasties of old—these feats were all the more remarkable.

In the new era, no statistic predicted team success or failure more accurately than the size of a club's payroll. Of the teams with the four highest average seasonal payrolls for the 1995–99 era, only Baltimore failed to appear in every single playoff (see table 17). In 2000, the World Series featured the number one payroll team (the Yankees) against the number three payroll team (the New York Mets). The converse was also true. Teams with the lowest average seasonal payrolls rarely or never made it to the playoffs, and when they did they failed to win a single postseason game in the 1995–99 era.

During the 1990s, the payroll disparities between the haves and the have-

Table 17. Seasons in the Playoffs for the Teams with the Seven Highest Average Annual Payrolls, 1995–99

New York (AL)	Baltimore	Atlanta	Cleveland	Texas	Boston	Los Angeles
1999	1997	1999	1999	1999	1999	1996
1998	1996	1998	1998	1998	1998	1995
1997		1997	1997	1996	1995	
1996		1996	1996			
1995		1995	1995			

Note: In descending order of average seasonal payrolls for 1995–99. Of the remaining twenty-three teams, seventeen never appeared in the playoffs.

nots widened. The seven largest payrolls were 2.6 times the seven lowest in 1995, and the ratio swelled to 3.9 to 1 by 1999. In 1999, the Yankees alone doled out $88 million, a figure that exceeded the payrolls of the Florida, Kansas City, Minnesota, and Montreal franchises combined. Furthermore, in 1999 these "bottom feeders" won only 40.1 percent of their games. "You look at the bottom tier of teams, and those guys aren't making any more money than they did four or five years ago," complained Houston Astros owner Drayton McLane Jr. in 1999. "It comes down to the elite. . . . A few people got all the money." Small-market teams with losing records struggled to stay afloat. In 1999, the Montreal Expos, for example, averaged a mere 6,254 fans for a three-game home series against the Colorado Rockies.

The widening disparities in team revenues arose from several sources. One was the new retroparks. Revenues from sold-out stadia, luxury boxes, and concessions aided both Baltimore and Cleveland in generating the funds necessary to maintain their high team payrolls. Another was rich, free-spending owners with lucrative local media markets; these large revenue streams allowed both the Atlanta Braves and the New York Yankees to spend more on players than their poorer counterparts. In 1999, for example, the Yankees got $55 million from local media, whereas the Kansas City Royals received a measly $5 million. And then there were the new corporate owners who had their own motives for doling out larger payrolls. In particular, the media giants (in the 1990s Disney obtained ownership of the Angels, Time Warner the Braves, Tribune Company the Cubs, and Fox the Dodgers) saw in successful baseball teams a valuable source of programming.

Disparities in team revenues changed the process of player acquisition and retention. In the first place, the prices of free agents escalated in the nineties beyond the wildest imaginations of anyone who contemplated the future of baseball salaries at the beginning of the decade. The signing in 1996 of Albert Belle by the Chicago White Sox triggered a general runup in the costs of obtaining and retaining free agents. In 2000, Ken Griffey Jr., arguably the most valuable player in the game and seemingly destined to break Henry Aaron's career home run record, signed a nine-year deal with the Cincinnati Reds calling for $116.5 million. The signing of Griffey was a gamble for the small-market Reds. "It's up to the fans to determine what [the financial impact] is [on the franchise]," said John Allen, the Reds chief operating officer. If the fans failed to come out in record numbers to see Griffey play, the signing of the superstar could wreak havoc with the team's finances. Furthermore, Griffey's salary could absorb so much of the team's financial resources that the Reds would be unable to recruit and retain other superior players.

Nothing illustrated the brute power of money in the new free-agency market more than the experience of the Florida Marlins. In 1996, Wayne Huizenga, who had garnered a fortune from Blockbuster video stores and owned the Miami Dolphins in the National Football League, decided to transform his losing expansion team into a winner. Within twenty-one days, Huizenga startled the baseball world by spending a record-shattering $89 million on free agents, a figure four times as high as the entire payroll of the Pittsburgh Pirates. Big spending paid equally big dividends; the Marlins, who had won less than half their games in the previous season, swept to the NL championship and defeated the Cleveland Indians in the 1997 World Series. Despite increased attendance, Huizenga claimed that his team had lost $34 million. To reduce the team's payroll, Florida promptly traded its high-priced stars for untried minor-leaguers. In 1998 the team sank to the cellar of the NL's Eastern Division.

In the second place, the growing inequalities in franchise revenues brought about the virtual collapse of baseball's amateur draft system. Since its inception in 1965, the draft had led to an equalization of talent. But aware that the wealthier franchises were willing to pay large signing bonuses and salaries, in the 1990s outstanding prospects began to ask for more. If the team that had drafted them was unable to meet their demands, the draftees insisted on having their signing rights traded to another club that would pay them what they asked. If this tactic failed, they would sit out a year so that they could reenter the next amateur draft. In addition, the sudden appearance in the late 1990s of Cuban refugees (reportedly more than thirty players), who (not being American citizens) were ineligible for the draft, distorted player acquisition in favor of teams that could afford to pay larger bonuses and salaries.

In the third place, the larger pool of salary funds in the hands of the richer franchises sharply increased salary-arbitration awards. According to the owner-player labor agreement, once a player had been in the league for three years, he was eligible for salary arbitration. If a player enjoyed some success on the field, the small-market teams often found that they could not afford to pay the subsequent arbitration award. They were then forced to trade such a player to a large-market team. In 1998, in something of an understatement, John Schuerholz, the general manager of the Atlanta Braves, summed up the situation: "We fairly well have separated ourselves from that era, when a team could be competitive without being in a major market."

True enough. Yet the successes of all three of the 1990s dynasties entailed something more than the sheer capacity to generate revenues. As in the past, front office personnel permanency and commitment to a long-term strategy enhanced a team's prospects for winning. Take the instance of Atlanta. Even before the arrival of John Schuerholz in Atlanta in 1990 from Kansas City, the Braves front office, led by Bobby Cox, who was then the team's general manager, had built a strong minor league system and astutely drafted a bevy of future stars. In 1992, Schuerholz entered the free-agent market and added Greg Maddux, who was destined to become the decade's most successful pitcher. Aided by the expansive pocketbooks of Ted Turner and the Time-Warner media consortium (which obtained control of the Braves in 1996), Schuerholz concentrated his abundant resources on keeping in place an outstanding pitching corps.

The story of Cleveland's rebirth was more complex. Upon purchasing the team in 1987, Richard Jacobs, a local shopping mall developer, invested heavily in the club's farm system. In 1991, he named fast-talking John Hart as the franchise's general manager. Identifying promising prospects early in their careers, Hart defied conventional baseball wisdom by signing them to long-term contracts. Such a strategy paid off. Not only did Hart lock in such stars as Albert Belle, Carlos Baerga, Jim Thome, Sandy Alomar Jr., and Charles Nagy, but he saved money on arbitration awards and enhanced the value of such players for trading purposes. With growing success on the playing field and the opening of a new park—Jacobs Field in 1994—Cleveland experienced a sharp rise in revenues. These additional funds permitted Hart to enter the expensive free-agent market from which he repeatedly filled key gaps in Cleveland's lineup with veteran players.

Perhaps nothing surprised baseball fans in the 1990s more than the return to supremacy of the New York Yankees. The Yankees had gone without a pennant from 1964 to 1976 and again from 1981 to 1996. But then in the second half of the 1990s the Yankees rebounded in a spectacular fashion. In 1999 the Yankee juggernaut capped off the team's domination of twentieth-century baseball by capturing the franchise's twenty-fifth World Series and its third AL championship in four seasons. It was plausible to argue that the 1990s team outperformed earlier Yankee dynasties. In 1999 the team posted the first set of consecutive series sweeps since the Yankees in 1938–39 and capped off its domination of twentieth-century baseball by completing an incredible run of eighteen victories in nineteen postseason games. Although their streak of consecutive game wins in the Fall Classic ended in 2000, that season the Yankees won their third straight World Series.

Even lifelong Yankee haters had difficulty sustaining their hostility toward the new dynasty. Unlike earlier Yankee behemoths, the 1990s Yankees had no sluggers the equivalent of Ruth, Gehrig, DiMaggio, or Mantle. (Though often overlooked, the team did have a superstar pitching staff). Instead, the team featured unspectacular but superior players all the way up and down the lineup. In their 22-3 run through the 1998 and 1999 postseasons, ten different Yankees drove in the run that put them ahead to stay. "Only someone who regards baseball intelligence as an oxymoron could fail to marvel at a team that excels in the little things—working the count, going with the pitch, hitting-and-running, knowing which pitch to use in every situation," wrote essayist Roger Rosenblatt.

The Yankees seemed to thrive on adversity. In 1999 alone, their manager, the stolid Joe Torre, fought to overcome prostate cancer, and during the season three of his players saw their fathers pass away. The 1999 team also evoked a special nostalgia. The players wore number 5 patches on their uniform sleeves to honor Joe DiMaggio, who died in March, and then added black armbands in honor of Jim "Catfish" Hunter, who passed away in September. As a baseball museum, Yankee Stadium continued to rival Cooperstown. Before pitching each game, Roger Clemens went out to touch Babe Ruth's monument, located beyond the left field wall. Around the stadium were other reminders of the team's glorious past: pictures of such heroes as Ruth and Yogi Berra, of Lou Gehrig's farewell speech, and of DiMaggio, who had said, "I thank the good Lord for making me a Yankee."

Why the Yankee revival? "The Boss," George Steinbrenner, had changed his behavior—at least a little bit. Though still a "crass blowhard" in the words of sportswriter Adrian Wojnarowski, Steinbrenner reluctantly learned to share some of his power and decision making with his subordinates. Along with Steinbrenner himself, three general managers put together the "team of the nineties": Gene Michael (who served from 1990 to 1995), Bob Watson (1995–98), and Brian Cashman (1998–). More than in the past, Steinbrenner listened to the entreaties of his general managers before impulsively entering the free-agent market. With financial resources larger than those of any other team in baseball, the Yankee management seized on the opportunities offered by the new player market. They used the draft judiciously, they paid large bonuses to sign Cuban and Japanese stars, they preyed on less well-to-do teams to obtain players who had received expensive salary arbitration awards, they signed key free agents, and, to retain the services of the team's veteran stars, the Yankees doled out generous salaries.

In the meantime, at the beginning of the new century a movement to reverse the growing income disparities between franchises gained momentum. In 2000 a Blue Ribbon Panel on Baseball Economics recommended increasing revenue sharing up to as much as 50 percent of local earnings and sharply increasing the "luxury" tax on payrolls. To deter poorer owners from simply putting the new money in their bank accounts, the panel recommended that the small-market franchises pay out a minimum of $40 million in salaries. That same year major league baseball rewrote its agreement, or "constitution." The owners handed over to Allan H. "Bud" Selig, the newly appointed commissioner (in 1999), enormous powers, which, in theory, exceeded even those obtained by Landis in 1921. Selig could "take such action as he deem[ed] appropriate to ensure an appropriate level of long-term competitive balance" between the teams. The early press reports presumed that Selig might take away millions of dollars in television revenues from teams such as the Yankees and Braves and redistribute them to such have-not clubs as the Montreal Expos and the Minnesota Twins.

Such a prospect was highly unlikely. Unlike those of Landis, any action taken by Selig was subject to approval by the players' union. Assuming that transferring money from the haves to the have-nots might have a dampening effect on salaries, the players looked upon Selig's new powers with well-founded suspicion. Furthermore, a move to arbitrarily reassign large amounts of revenue to the poorer teams would surely encounter resistance from the richer franchises. During the 1990s, some of the small-market team owners had pocketed the luxury tax received from the richer clubs rather than using it to improve their teams, which had galled big-market owners such as George Steinbrenner. "What's Steinbrenner's incentive to give money to his 29 friends?" rhetorically queried University of Chicago economist Allen Sanderson.

◫ ◫ ◫

In the three-divisional era of the 1990s the game's long hitting drought finally ended. During the two-divisional era (1969–93), the overall offensive output of the big leagues had never fully recovered from its nadir of the 1960s. True, lowering the pitching mound in 1969, decreasing the size of the strike zone in the same season, and the American League's adoption of the designated hitter in 1973 did lead to slight improvements in hitting. But both runs and home runs per game remained well below the marks achieved in the 1921–60 era. Indeed, during the two-divisional era's twenty-five seasons, nearly half the time league leaders failed to scale the modest plateau of forty home runs, and only two players (George Foster with fifty-two in 1977 and Cecil Fielder with fifty-one in 1990) managed to hit more than fifty homers in a single season.

Then, with a suddenness reminiscent of 1920 and 1921, the 1993 and 1994 seasons signaled the arrival of a new hitting barrage (see table 18). An omen of the great reversal in hitting arrived with the 1987 season; during that exceptionally hot summer the sluggers banged out more than two homers per game, an all-time big league record. But the upturn in hitting was only temporary; in the next season scoring and home runs plummeted again and remained in a trough through 1992. In 1993, the offensive explosion began anew. Batting averages jumped nine points, runs per game rose from 8.6 to 9.2, and for the first time since 1969 five men hit forty or more home runs in a season. The 1993 season proved a modest harbinger of what lay ahead. While playing in only 112 games, in 1996

Table 18. The Great Offensive Barrage

Seasons	Batting Averages	Runs/Game	Home Runs/Game
1969–93 (avg.)[a]	.257	8.1	1.5
1992	.256	8.6	1.5
1993	.265	9.2	1.8
1994	.270	9.8	2.1
1994–99 (avg.)[b]	.281	9.8	2.1

a. For two-divisional era.
b. For three-divisional era.

Mark McGwire clobbered a stunning forty-seven home runs. In 1999, in the twentieth century's final season, runs per game shot up to a record-shattering 10.7, an average of 2.6 more than in the two-divisional era. Likewise, beleaguered pitchers saw their earned run averages soar to startling new heights.

Home runs were at the center of the new hitting barrage. In Ruth's heyday homers were something of a rarity; they came at a rate of only one for each ninety-one at bats. But in 1999, the sluggers averaged one homer for each thirty at bats. In other words, when visiting a ballpark in 1999 fans were three times more likely to see a home run hit than had they been present at a game in the 1920s. Moreover, when Mark McGwire's and Sammy Sosa's feats were taken together for the 1998 and 1999 seasons, they completely wiped out the game's historic frame of reference for home run productivity. Ruth's seasonal record of sixty home runs had stood for thirty years, and Roger Maris's sixty-one home runs had remained unblemished for thirty-seven years. But McGwire's and Sosa's success in scaling the sixty-home-run barrier in 1998 stood for only a single season. In the very next summer, McGwire (with sixty-five) and Sosa (with sixty-three) again hit more than sixty homers. Their repeat performance in 1999 overshadowed not only the feats of Ruth and Maris but also some of the mystique growing from McGwire's and Sosa's own accomplishments in 1998. "If there is going to be an assault on 60 every year, why should anyone get excited about it?" exclaimed broadcaster Bob Costas. "When you have too much of a good thing, the wonder of it fades."

Like the offensive breakthrough of the 1920s, the great hitting barrage of the 1990s included the minor leagues. But although the sharp upturn in hitting in the majors began with the 1993 season, it did not reach the AAA minor leagues until the 1996 season. For the last four seasons of the twentieth century, home run and run productivity in these leagues shot up nearly 60 percent over the previous four seasons.

As with the great hitting breakthrough in the 1920s, several hypotheses have been offered to explain the new hitting revolution. These include a more resilient or "juiced-up" ball; a dilution of pitching talent occasioned by the expansion in the number of teams in 1993 and 1998; more hitter-friendly parks; lighter bats; umpires decreasing the size of the strike zone, leading to a new style of hitting; and hitters muscling up through weight training and the use of dietary supplements.

Despite a plethora of anecdotal evidence (especially from pitchers) and the claims of such baseball sages as Leonard Koppett, the most questionable of these explanations is the juiced-up ball hypothesis. (A variant of the more resilient ball hypothesis included the idea that the protrusion of the ball's seams had been reduced.) According to a popular version of this idea, the owners reasoned that the fans wanted to see more offense, particularly home runs, so they conspired with Rawlings, the manufacturer of the baseballs, to make the balls more resilient. However, simple experiments testing the coefficient of resolution (COR)—how far the ball rebounds after having struck a hard surface—of the ball in the 1980s and 1990s performed by Richard Larsen and Ofer Rind at the Brookhaven National Laboratory under the direction of Yale physics professor Robert Adair and similar experiments by Professor Jim Sherwood at the University of Massachusetts at Lowell offer little support for the juiced-up ball hypothesis.

Nor is there strong support for the idea that expanding the number of teams caused the hitting revolution of the 1990s. True, in the short run expansion is likely to improve the performance of superior players; in other words, both the better hitters and the better pitchers will confront more weak players than in the previous season. Therefore, in the seasons immediately after expansion, outstanding players should do even better, and so it was that Maris's (1961) and McGwire's (1998) record-setting home run seasons and Rod Carew's run at batting .400 (in 1977) all came in the first year after the expansion of their respective leagues.

But, although in theory the dilution of talent should bolster the numbers of the exceptional players, aggregate hitting and pitching statistics should remain unchanged. A comparison of seasonal statistics before and after expansion supports this conclusion. In 1961, the first season of AL expansion, the improvement in hitting in the NL (which retained eight franchises) actually exceeded that of the AL (which expanded to ten franchises), and in 1962 both the AL and the expanded NL experienced a similar slight drop in offensive production. In 1977 both the expanded NL and the nonexpanded AL witnessed similar improvements in offense, and in 1998 the AL and the expanded NL saw almost no change in hitting output.

At first glance, there seem to be two major exceptions to the theory that expansion has no significant effect on aggregate offensive or defensive output. First, when both leagues increased their number of teams from ten to twelve in 1969, hitting in both leagues improved sharply. Yet rather than expansion, changes in baseball rules and practices in 1969—namely lowering the mound from fifteen to ten inches and decreasing the size of the de facto strike zone—appear to account for the upsurge in hitting during that season. Second, in 1993 both leagues experienced a significant improvement in hitting, but the increase was larger for the NL. That season the NL increased from twelve to fourteen teams. Yet rather than expansion per se, the addition of new hitter-friendly ballparks in Miami and Denver in 1993 appear to be largely responsible for the NL's improved hitting. Denver's extraordinarily high altitude favored the hitters; at Mile High Stadium, the Colorado Rockies and their opponents scored runs at a rate 30 percent above the league average. If the data for Denver are ignored, then the NL's increased productivity in 1993 is no larger than the AL's.

As popular as expansion and the juiced-up ball explanations for the offensive revolution of the 1990s has been the cozy ballpark hypothesis. According to this argument, the owners believed that the fans wanted more offense; therefore, they shortened the distances to the fences (especially in the new retroparks) to produce more home runs. Certainly the owners often toyed with the distances to the outfield walls, but on the average, contrary to popular belief, the distance to the fences in major league ballparks remained almost unchanged in the 1990s (see table 19).

Although neither cozier parks nor juiced-up balls significantly affected hitting output, lighter bats may have contributed to the offensive revolution. "Everyone talks about the [juiced-up] balls; no one talks about the bats," said Tony Gwynn, the perennial National League batting champion, in 1996. "I think they're the biggest reason." Apparently triggered by the experience of using lighter, big-barreled aluminum bats in high school and college (the big leagues retained the requirement that bats be made of wood), beginning in about 1992, according to bat manufacturers, big-leaguers started using lighter bats en masse. According to bat manufacturers, the average major league bat weight dropped from thirty-three ounces in 1991 to thirty-one ounces by 1996. Even Seattle's Ken Griffey Jr. and Edgar Martinez, two of the strongest hitters in the game, used thirty-

Table 19. Average Distances (in Feet) to the Fences of Major League Parks

Season	Left Foul Line	Left Field Power Alley	Center Field	Right Field Power Alley	Right Foul Line	Average
1990	330	378	406	375	326	363
1998	331	376	406	374	328	363
Change	+1	−2	0	−1	+2	0

Source: Adapted from Philip J. Lowry, "Ballparks," in *Total Baseball,* ed. John Thorn et al., 6th ed. (New York: Total Sports, 1999).

one-ounce bats. With lighter bats, proponents insisted, the hitters could wait longer and still have time to whip their bats through the hitting zone. With their thinner handles, bats broke far more often than in the past.

Equally important in bringing about the new hitting barrage were changes in the size and shape of the de facto strike zone (that called by the umpires rather than that provided by the rules). Well before the 1990s hitting outburst, obtaining a strike from a high pitch (essentially pitches above the belt) was problematic. That the percentage of base on balls increased slightly more than home runs from 1987 to 1999 suggested the possibility that the umpires had decreased the size of the strike zone. Dozens of pitchers echoed the complaint of pitcher Kirk McCaskill of the Chicago White Sox in 1994. "You don't get the high strike at all anymore," McCaskill said. "[And] you don't get the inside strike." In 1988, after a series of brawls, umpires were given the authority to expel a pitcher immediately if, in the umpire's judgment, the pitcher had deliberately thrown at the hitter. The introduction and growing popularity in the 1990s of large-cushioned elbow pads to protect the arms from inside pitches also emboldened the hitters. It seems that in the 1990s both the hitters and the pitchers began to accept a new convention, namely that it was no longer permissible to repeatedly bust the inside of the plate with high fast balls.

As the 1990s wore on, hitters felt increasingly comfortable about standing closer to the plate and, when striding into the pitch, planting their front foot in a straight line with their back foot or even toward the opposite field rather than away from the plate. No longer did they have to worry as much about bailing out from a brush-back pitch or being hit in the arm by an inside pitch, or so it seemed. Indeed, most baseball aficionados believe that in the 1990s opposite field home runs proliferated, though perhaps as much from the increasing strength of the hitters as from their striding into pitches on the outside part of the plate.

The development of stronger hitters also contributed to the offensive barrage. By the 1990s, nearly every team's lineup featured one or more behemoths whose physiques resembled those of professional football linemen (as well as a half-dozen more players whose size and shapes resembled professional football linebackers) rather than such earlier sluggers as Ted Williams and Stan Musial. Multiple regression analysis of the 1990 and 1999 seasons indicates that players with higher height/weight ratios also hit more home runs than their smaller counterparts. Yet sheer size does not explain the hitting revolution of the late 1990s, for the average weight and height of players in 1990 and in 1999 was almost identical. Of course,

weight and height do not determine the actual strength of players. It is likely
that on the average the hitters were stronger in 1999 than in 1990. By 1999,
systematic weightlifting had become almost an obligation for every player. By then, each team employed a full-time strength and conditioning
coach.

To add to their size and strength, the players increasingly turned to dietary supplements. According to Tom Verducci in a *Sports Illustrated* cover
story of 23 March 1998, nearly every big league locker room included
machines that dispensed protein drinks spiked with creatine, a muscle-
building supplement. According to locker room scuttlebutt, anywhere
between 15 and 30 percent of the players regularly used illegal steroids.
In August 1998, Mark McGwire admitted that he had been taking androstenedione, a steroid, although he said he had discontinued its use four
months earlier. (In 1999, the year after McGwire's confession, the nationwide sales of the testosterone booster shot up 1,000 percent according to
industry figures). Though legal in baseball, androstenedione was banned
by the Olympics, in college sports, and in pro football and basketball.
Muscle-bulking apparently helped hitters more than pitchers. "As a pitcher,
what can you do?" queried Yankee star David Cone in 1998. "Lifting
weights is not going to translate into having better stuff, not the way getting stronger can make someone a better hitter."

⬚ ⬚ ⬚

In the meantime, the "Latino invasion" resulted in a quieter revolution than
the hitting barrage. Although players of Hispanic origin had been prominent in the big leagues as early as the 1960s, it was no exaggeration to say
that during the 1990s America's game took on a distinctively Latin flavor.
The percentage of Latinos (including those born within and outside the
United States) in the big leagues suddenly doubled, from 12 percent to 24
percent. Consider the 1995 Cleveland Indians; its roster included four
Dominicans, two Puerto Ricans, two Venezuelans, and one Nicaraguan.
"Some days it's easy to forget what country you're in with all the Spanish
being spoken and the salsa music," said Mike Hargrove, the team's manager. Whereas DiMaggio's Yankees played in World Series involving nine
foreign-born players, Derek Jeter's Yankees of the 1990s played with or
against forty-six foreign-born athletes. In the minor leagues, the Latino
presence was even more striking; by 1998, 36 percent of all minor league
players had been born in the Caribbean basin.

Latinos outperformed non-Latinos in nearly every phase of the game. Not only did Sammy Sosa of the Dominican Republic slam more than sixty home runs in both 1998 and 1999, but Latinos captured more than half of the top five spots in home runs for both the NL and the AL during these two seasons. And in 1999, Cuban exile Pedro Martinez established a strong claim for having pitched the finest single season in baseball history. Although the Red Sox ace's numbers (23-4 won-lost, 2.08 earned run average, 312 strikeouts, and only thirty-seven walks) were not clearly superior to Sandy Koufax's in 1965 or Ron Guidry's in 1978, his earned run average was nearly three runs below the league average, a far better mark than had been achieved by any prior hurler in the game's history.

In retrospect, the precipitants of the great influx of Latinos into American baseball are clear. In the first place, the Latinos helped to fill a vacuum created by the failure of the United States to produce domestically as many superior players as it had in the past. The decline of baseball at the sandlot level, a trend evident as early as the 1950s, picked up momentum in the 1980s and 1990s. At the end of the twentieth century, boys whose fathers and grandfathers had once played stickball in the concrete canyons of New York City, "flies and grounders" on the empty suburban lots of Chicago, or "work up" on Missouri cow pastures now played basketball or football or engaged in virtual workouts in the comfort of their bedrooms while stationed in front of cable TV, a VCR, a video game, or a computer. In 1998, former New York Yankees general manager Bob Watson, an African American who grew up in Los Angeles, explained it this way: "What's happening is that kids in Latin America are playing baseball the way I did when I was growing up. We'd play eight, nine games a day. . . . [Today] the stud athletes [in the United States] are playing football and basketball."

In the second place, in the 1980s and 1990s the major leagues began to take full advantage of the opportunities that the Caribbean basin offered for securing new talent. Unlike in the United States, no amateur draft restricted the recruitment of players south of the border. Not only did big league franchises begin to devote additional resources to scouring the Caribbean for potential players who might step directly into the lineups of their minor league affiliates or perhaps "the show" itself, but thirty major league clubs set up special "academies" in the Dominican Republic. (The Dominican Republic became an astonishing incubator of baseball talent; with a population of less than 8 million, the tiny island republic produced more big league players per capita—89 total in 1998—than even California, the leading domestic producer of talent.) For thirty days, promising youngsters between ages fourteen and seventeen lived in special compounds where they received hour after hour of professional instruction. "Believe me, these kids have balls," explained Luis Mayoral, the Texas Ranger's Latin American liaison man, "because for them, growing up was so much harder than for the typical U.S. kid." Initially the major leagues could sign the hungry Latino recruits cheaply, but toward the end of the century the more promising of them began to employ agents and obtain substantial signing bonuses.

Unlike the Latinos, African Americans in baseball became less prominent than in the past. Not only did the percentage of black fans continue to lag far behind their percentage of the urban populations with big league franchises, but the proportion of African-American players in the majors dropped from one in four in the late 1960s to one in six in the 1990s. Apparently the big leagues reached the optimum number of black field managers with five in the 1993; only one black, Bob Watson (with Houston from 1994 to 1996 and the Yankees from 1996 to 1997) served as a club's general manager. In a not-very-successful effort to entice black youth back to the diamond, the major leagues embraced John Young's RBI (Reviving Baseball in the Inner Cities) program. In 1997, the majors also sought to capitalize on the fiftieth anniversary of baseball's "finest moment," the debut of Jackie Robinson. They dedicated the season to Robinson's memory; players wore arm patches honoring his breaking of the color ban, President Bill Clinton addressed the nation on the significance of Robinson's act, and acting commissioner Bud Selig announced that all teams would henceforth retire Robinson's number (42) forever.

In other ways, baseball reflected the nation's growing ethnic and racial diversity. With the rapidly expanding Latino population in the sunbelt, the Los Angeles Dodgers, California Angels, San Diego Padres, Texas Rangers, and Florida Marlins pioneered in carrying Spanish-language broadcasts of their games. Clubs began printing special Spanish-language brochures, the Marlins threw *Parrandas* (block parties) for Latino fans, and in 1997 the Padres began chartering buses each Sunday to bring fans from Tijuana, Mexico, to their games.

Even though baseball had long been popular in Japan, for the first time the big league teams began to recruit substantial numbers of Japanese players. In 1997, only two years after the Los Angeles Dodgers' Hideo Nomo had begun to baffle NL hitters with his spiraling windup and dazzling forkball-fastball combination, eleven Japanese pitchers reported to major and minor league spring training camps. In the first official big league game played outside the North American continent, the Chicago Cubs and the New York Mets opened the 2000 season by playing two games in Tokyo.

◻ ◻ ◻

As baseball entered the twenty-first century, there were positive signs that it would remain America's game. "We've tried and tried to ruin this game," observed Sparky Anderson, manager of the Detroit Tigers in 1990, "and we just can't do it." Perhaps so. Historically, baseball has shown a striking resistance to internal and external threats, but all involved in the professional game should be acutely conscious and repeatedly reminded of what the late A. Bartlett Giamatti was wise enough to see, that baseball is a "strenuously nostalgic" game. No other team sport has such a remarkable capacity for evoking a plethora of sharply defined and deeply felt images from the past. The game's connectedness with America's past is both its special strength and its special vulnerability.

Bibliographical Essay

GENERAL WORKS

As befits the importance of the subject, baseball's literature is immense. For those seeking a far more complete bibliography than this one, there is *Baseball: A Comprehensive Bibliography* (Jefferson, N.C., 1986, 1998), compiled by Myron J. Smith. See also Donald E. Walker and B. Lee Cooper, eds., *Baseball and American Culture: A Thematic Bibliography of Over 4,000 Titles* (Jefferson, N.C., 1995). For baseball historiography, see Larry R. Gerlach, "Not Quite Ready for Prime Time: Baseball History, 1983–1993," *Journal of Sport History* 21.2 (Summer 1994). Other valuable references are Jonathan F. Light, *Cultural Encyclopedia of Baseball* (Jefferson, N.C., 1997); David L. Porter, ed., *The Biographical Dictionary of American Sports: Baseball* (New York, 1987); and Paul Dickson, *The Baseball Dictionary* (New York, 1987, 1999). For a comprehensive current guide to baseball's extensive historical literature, one can profitably consult *Nine: A Journal of Baseball History and Culture.* Libraries especially notable for their holdings in baseball history include the Baseball Hall of Fame and Museum Library in Cooperstown, New York, the New York Public Library, and the Sporting News Library in St. Louis.

Few historical subjects are richer in statistics than baseball is. For up-to-date statistics, there are several Web sites as well as *The Complete Baseball Record Book* (later called *The Official Major League Fact Book*), published annually by *The Sporting News* in St. Louis since 1942; *Bill James Presents Stats Major League Handbook,* published annually since 1991; and John Thorn et al., eds., *Total Baseball,* first published in 1989 and regularly updated. *Total Baseball* also includes valuable essays by authorities on subjects ranging from the history of blacks and women in baseball to the history of minor leagues and college baseball. Those intrigued by the use of statistics in baseball history should begin with the extensive writings of and statistics generated by Bill James, especially *The Bill James Historical Baseball Abstract* (New York, 1988). James invented the term *sabermetrics*. The term honors the Society for American Baseball Research (SABR), organized in 1971, and describes what is done by those who use social science methods to research baseball as it is played. Much of Robert Kemp Adair's *The Physics of Baseball,* 2d ed. (New York, 1994) is accessible to the nontutored.

Except for Albert Spalding's *America's National Game* (New York, 1911; Lincoln, Nebr., 1992), the recently republished Alfred H. Spink, *The National Game* (Carbondale, Ill., 2000), and Francis C. Richter, *Richter's History and Records of Baseball* (New York, 1914), serious general histories of baseball are rather recent. Among the more successful are Robert Smith, *Baseball* (New York, 1947, 1970); Lee Allen, *One Hundred Years of Baseball* (New York, 1950), *The National League Story* (New York, 1965), and *The American League Story* (New York, 1962); Leonard Koppett, *Koppett's Concise History of Major League Baseball* (Philadelphia, 1998); Fred Lieb, *The Baseball Story* (New York, 1950); David Voigt, *Baseball* (New York, 1987); Charles Alexander, *Our Game* (New York, 1991); John P. Rossi, *The National Game* (Chicago, 2000); and Joel Zoss and John Bowman, *Diamonds in the Rough* (New York, 1989). For an especially insightful set of essays on baseball history, see Jules Tygiel, *Past Time: Baseball as History* (New York, 2000), and for writings on baseball more generally, see Richard Peterson's *Extra Innings: Writing Baseball* (Urbana, Ill., 2001) and Tristram Potter Coffin's *The Old Ball Game* (New York, 1971), a neglected but pioneering book on baseball folklore and fiction. For a valuable anthology of scholarly articles about baseball off the playing field, see John Dreifort, ed., *Baseball History Outside the Lines: A Reader* (Lincoln, Nebr., 2001).

Baseball now has three valuable multivolume histories. Exceptionally rich in detail and understanding of the organizational side of the game's history are Harold Seymour's *Baseball: The Early Years* (New York, 1960) and *Baseball: The Golden Years* (New York, 1970), which when combined take the story of commercial baseball from its amateur beginnings in the mid-nineteenth century to about 1930. Seymour's *Baseball: The People's Game* (New York, 1990) is a large potpourri of amateur and semipro baseball. David Q. Voigt's three-volume *American Baseball* (Norman, Okla., and University Park, Pa., 1966–83) traces the history of commercial baseball from its origins to the early 1980s. Also examine Robert F. Burk's *Never Just a Game* (Chapel Hill, N.C., 1994) and *Much More Than a Game* (Chapel Hill, N.C., 2001). Despite the criticism leveled at it by careful students of the game and its uncritical perspective, no one interested in baseball history should miss Ken Burns's *Baseball,* a Public Broadcasting System documentary film released in 1994.

There are solid histories of particular facets of the game. For labor relations from the outset of professional baseball to about 1980, see Lee Lowenfish and Tony Lupien, *The Imperfect Diamond* (New York, 1980); for minor league history see Neil J. Sullivan, *The Minors* (New York, 1990), and Robert Obojski, *Bush League*

(New York, 1975); and for umpires, see Larry Gerlach, *The Men in Blue* (New York, 1980; Lincoln, Nebr., 1994), and James M. Kahn, *The Umpire Story* (New York, 1953). For the history of American Legion ball, see Kent M. Krause, "From Americanism to Athleticism: A History of the American Legion Junior Baseball Program" (Ph.D. diss., University of Nebraska, 1998).

For a history of women's participation in baseball, see Gail Berlage, *Women in Baseball* (Westport, Conn., 1994), and Barbara Gregorich, *Women at Play* (New York, 1993). Peter Levine's *Ellis Island to Ebbets Field* (New York, 1992) treats baseball in the context of the American Jewish experience.

The literature on baseball outside the United States has proliferated recently. For baseball in Latin America and Latinos in baseball in the United States, consider Peter Bjarkman, *Baseball with a Latin Beat* (Jefferson, N.C., 1994); Roberto G. Echevarria, *The Pride of Havana: A History of Cuban Baseball* (New York, 1999); Alan M. Klein, *Sugar Ball: The American Game, the Dominican Dream* (New Haven, Conn., 1993) and *Baseball South of the Border: A Tale of Two Laredos* (Princeton, N.J., 1999); Samuel L. Regalado, *Viva Baseball!: Latin Major Leaguers and Their Special Hunger* (Urbana, Ill., 1998); and Rob Ruck, *The Tropic of Baseball: Baseball in the Dominican Republic* (Lincoln, Nebr., 1999). Robert Whiting's *You Gotta Have Wa* (New York, 1989) is a marvelous introduction to Japanese baseball and culture. For Canada, see an outstanding local history, Colin D. Howell's *Northern Sandlots: A Social History of Maritime Baseball* (Toronto, 1995), and a solid general history, William Humber's *Diamonds in the North: A Concise History of Baseball in Canada* (Toronto, 1995).

African-American baseball has received a solid, pioneering treatment by Robert Peterson in *Only the Ball Was White* (Englewood Cliffs, N.J., 1970). For an especially perceptive summary of black baseball in the first half of the twentieth century, see chapter 6 of Jules Tygiel's previously cited *Past Time*. Not always trustworthy but containing interesting observations and important documents is Jerry Malloy, comp., *Sol White's History of Colored Baseball* (Lincoln, Nebr., 1995). See also Bruce Adelson, *Brushing Back Jim Crow: The Integration of Minor-League Baseball in the American South* (Charlottesville, Va., 1999); Janet Bruce, *The Kansas City Monarchs* (Lawrence, Kans., 1985); David Falkner, *Great Time Coming: The Life of Jackie Robinson from Baseball to Birmingham* (New York, 1995); John Holway, *The Life of Josh Gibson and Satchel Paige* (Westport, Conn., 1991); Mark Ribowski, *A Complete History of the Negro Leagues, 1884–1955* (New York, 1995); Donn Rogosin, *Invisible Men: Life in Baseball's Negro Leagues* (New York, 1983); Rob Ruck, *Sandlot Seasons: Sport in Black Pittsburgh* (Urbana, Ill., 1987); Jules Tygiel's classic, *Baseball's Great Experiment: Jackie Robinson and His Legacy* (New York, 1983); Arnold Rampersad's superb *Jackie Robinson* (New York, 1997); John C. Chalberg, *Rickey and Robinson* (Wheeling, Ill., 2000); and David Zang's remarkable book *Fleet Walker's Divided Heart: The Life of Baseball's First Black Major Leaguer* (Lincoln, Nebr., 1995).

THE NINETEENTH CENTURY

No book has shaped our understanding of early baseball history more deeply than Albert Spalding's *America's National Game* (New York, 1911; Lincoln, Nebr., 1992). Fortunately, the first part, that dealing with the 1845 to 1865 era, relies mainly on Henry Chadwick's writings and scrapbooks. Indeed, it may have even been written by Chadwick, who, before he died, requested that his wife turn all his materials over to Spalding. These invaluable documents are now deposited in the Spalding Collection at the New York Public Library. The second part of the book consists of Spalding's elaborate apologia for the National League and, in particular, for his role in the league's history. Neither Seymour, Voigt, Arthur Bartlett in *Baseball and Mr. Spalding* (New York, 1951), nor Peter Levine in *A. G. Spalding and the Rise of Baseball* (New York, 1985) completely escapes the spell of Spalding, although all these books add fresh perspectives. The Spalding view of early National League history can be profitably contrasted with Ted Vincent's largely neglected, somewhat idiosyncratic *Mudville's Revenge: The Rise and Fall of American Sport* (New York, 1981). Two books by Steven A. Riess, *Touching Base: Professional Baseball in the Progressive Era* (Westport, Conn., 1980; rev. ed., Urbana, Ill., 1998) and *City Games* (Urbana, Ill., 1990), present significant analysis of early professional baseball and politics, the building and location of ballparks, social reform, professional baseball as a source of social mobility, and the "invention" of a baseball ideology. Bryan D. Salvatore, *The Clever Baseballist* (New York, 1999), and David Stevens, *Baseball's Radical for All Seasons* (New York, 1999), are competent biographies of John Montgomery Ward.

Since the pioneering ventures of Seymour and Voigt, academics have given particular attention to the history of baseball before the creation of the National League in 1876. For an extensive documentation of the playing of baseball-type games long before the formation of the New York Knickerbockers, see Thomas L. Altherr, "'No Place Level Enough to Play Ball': Baseball and Baseball-Type Games in the Colonial Era, Revolutionary War, and Early American Republic," *Nine* 8 (Spring 2000). For details about the early clubs and an analysis of their membership, see especially Melvin Adelman, *A Sporting Time: New York City and the Rise of Modern Sport, 1820–1870* (Urbana, Ill., 1986); George Kirsch, *The Creation of American Team Sports: Baseball and Cricket, 1838–72* (Urbana, Ill., 1989); and the previously cited Zoss and Bowmam, *Diamonds in the Rough*. For understanding the "base ball fraternity" and the inner tensions of early baseball, consult Warren Goldstein, *Playing for Keeps* (Ithaca, N.Y., 1989). See also the provocative interpretations of Ronald Story, "The Country of the Young: The Meaning of Baseball in Early American Culture," in Alvin Hall, ed., *Cooperstown Symposium on Baseball* (Westport, Conn., 1991), and Michael S. Kimmel, "Baseball and the Reconstitution of American Masculinity, 1880–1920," *Baseball History* 3 (1990).

For contemporary sources, see Henry Chadwick's *Beadle's Dime Baseball Player,* the first guide of its sort, which began publication in 1860 and lasted until 1881, and *Spalding's Guide,* which began publication in 1877 and continued until 1941. The 1880s witnessed the beginning of three important publications: *The Reach Guide* and *Sporting Life* in 1883 and *The Sporting News* in 1886. For early era sources, see also Preston D. Orem, ed., *Baseball, From the Newspaper Accounts* (Altadena, Calif., 1961–67) and especially Dean A. Sullivan, ed., *Early Innings: A Documentary History of Baseball, 1825–1908* (Lincoln, Nebr., 1995).

1900–1950 ERA

Baseball literature for the first half of the twentieth century is immense. Apart from the general histories cited earlier, see especially G. Edward White, *Creating the National Pastime: Baseball Transforms Itself, 1903–1953* (Princeton, N.J., 1996), and Dean A. Sullivan, ed., *Middle Innings: A Documentary History of Baseball, 1900–1948* (Lincoln, Nebr., 1998). A set of team histories published by G. P. Putnam between the late 1940s and early 1950s and written by sportswriters Lee Allen, Warren Brown, Frank Graham, Harold Kaese, Franklin Lewis, Fred Lieb, and Shirley Povich remain classics of the genre. For updated franchise histories, see Peter Bjarkman, *Encyclopedia of Major League Baseball Team Histories: National League* (Westport, Conn., 1991), and *Encyclopedia of Major League Baseball Team Histories: American League* (Westport, Conn., 1991).

Biographies and reminiscences are another popular source for this era. Of the dozens of general memoirs available, Fred Lieb's *Baseball As I Have Known It* (New York, 1977) is perhaps the most revealing. Interviews with twenty-six (later thirty) players form the substance of Lawrence S. Ritter, *The Glory of Their Times* (New York, 1966), which is the best book for capturing the flavor of the early twentieth-century game. For similar books for the 1940s and 1950s, see Donald Honig, *Baseball When the Grass Was Green* (New York, 1975; Lincoln, Nebr., 1993), and *Baseball Between the Lines* (New York, 1976; Lincoln, Nebr., 1993). Of the numerous autobiographies of this era, see in particular Leo Durocher, *Nice Guys Finish Last* (New York, 1975); Hank Greenberg with Ira Berkow, *Hank Greenberg* (New York, 1989); and Ty Cobb and Al Stump, *My Life in Baseball* (Garden City, N.Y., 1961). Among the more important biographies, see Charles Alexander, *Ty Cobb* (New York, 1984) and *John McGraw* (New York, 1988); Robert W. Creamer, *Babe* (New York, 1974); Eugene Murdock, *Ban Johnson* (Westport, Conn., 1986); David Pietrusza, *Judge and Jury: The Life and Times of Kenesaw Mountain Landis* (New York, 1998); Murray Polner, *Branch Rickey* (New York, 1982); Ray Robinson, *Matty: An American Hero* (New York, 1993); J. G. Taylor Spink (apparently ghosted by Fred Lieb), *Judge Landis and Twenty-Five Years of Baseball* (New York, 1947); Al Stump, *Cobb* (Chapel Hill, N.C., 1994);

Henry W. Thomas, *Walter Johnson* (Lincoln, Nebr., 1998); and Paul J. Zingg, *Harry Hooper* (Urbana, Ill., 1993). And do not miss the award-winning documentary film *The Life and Times of Hank Greenberg*, released in 1999.

Books and articles on other aspects of baseball in the "golden age" abound. On baseball ideology, see especially Richard Crepeau, *Baseball: America's Diamond Mind, 1919–1941* (Orlando, Fla., 1980; Lincoln, Nebr., 2000); Steven A. Riess, *Touching Base* (Westport, Conn., 1980; rev. ed., Urbana, Ill., 1998); and Leverett T. Smith Jr., *The American Dream and the National Game* (Bowling Green, Ohio, 1970). See the revised edition of *Touching Base* for valuable discussions of baseball crowds, politics and baseball, ballparks and neighborhoods, Sunday baseball, and baseball as a source of social mobility. On the Black Sox scandal, see Elliot Asinof, *Eight Men Out* (New York, 1963). On the relationships between ballparks, their inhabitants, and the city in which they are located see (for Philadelphia) Bruce Kuklick, *To Every Thing a Season* (Princeton, N.J., 1991). For Detroit, see Richard Bak, *A Place for Summer* (Detroit, 1997), and Patrick J. Harrigan, *The Detroit Tigers* (Toronto, 1997). The title of William Curran's *Big Sticks: The Batting Revolution of the Twenties* (New York, 1990) is self-explanatory.

For the World War II era, see Richard Goldstein, *Spartan Season: How Baseball Survived the Second World War* (New York, 1980); Bil Gilbert, *They Also Served: Baseball and the Home Front, 1941–1945* (New York, 1992); a reissue of *Even the Browns* (Chicago, 1978), retitled *Baseball Goes to War,* by William B. Mead (Washington, D.C., 1985); and Robert Creamer, *Baseball in '41: A Celebration of the Best Baseball Season Ever—In the Year America Goes to War* (New York, 1991). Evocative of the final days of baseball in the 1950s is David Halbertstom, *Summer of '49* (New York, 1989).

Also useful are Bill Rabinowitz, "Baseball and the Great Depression," and Clark Nardinelli, "Judge Kenesaw Mountain Landis and the Art of Cartel Enforcement," in Peter Levine, ed., *Baseball History* (New York, 1989). On the origins of the Hall of Fame, see James Vlasich, *A Legend for the Legendary* (Bowling Green, Ohio, 1990). *Baseball Magazine,* an important monthly, began publication in 1908, and *You Know Me Al,* a classic baseball novel by Ring Lardner, first appeared in 1916.

1950–2000 ERA

In the second half of the twentieth century, baseball outside the foul lines has received more attention than it did in earlier eras. One may start with Dean A. Sullivan, ed., *Late Innings* (a forthcoming book). A book that contains far more on baseball in general than the title suggests is James Edward Miller, *The Baseball Business: Pennants and Profits in Baltimore* (New York, 1990). In making a case for the city ownership of the New York Yankees, Dean Chadwin in *Those Damn Yankees* (New York, 1999) throws light on the trend in the late 1990s toward a growing disparity between the small- and the large-market franchises. For valuable material on the business side of the game, see also Ralph Andreano, *No Joy in Mudville* (Cambridge, Mass., 1965); Bill Veeck, *Veeck—As in Wreck* (New York, 1962) and *The Hustler's Handbook* (New York, 1965); Harold Parrott, *The Lords of Baseball* (New York, 1976); Bowie Kuhn, *Hardball* (New York, 1987); Gerald W. Scully, *The Business of Major League Baseball* (Chicago, 1989); Kenneth Jennings, *Balls and Strikes* (New York, 1990); Mark Rosentraub, *Major League Losers* (New York, 1997); and Andrew Zimbalist, *Baseball and Billions* (New York, 1992). For a focus on baseball's labor relations, see works by Miller, Jennings, and Lowenfish (cited earlier); James B. Dworkin, *Owners Versus Players* (Boston, 1981); Daniel R. Marburger, ed. *Stee-Rike Four! What's Wrong with the Business of Baseball* (Westport, Conn., 1997); Marvin Miller, *A Whole Different Ball Game* (New York, 1991); and a forthcoming book on the Major League Baseball Players Association by Charles Korr. For broadcasting, see Red Barber, *The Broadcasters* (New York, 1970); Curt Smith, *Voices of the Game* (Chicago, 1987); and Benjamin G. Rader, *In Its Own Image: How Television Has Transformed Sports* (New York, 1984).

How the game was played, the experience of playing and watching baseball, and statistics for the post-1950 era can be found in a number of books and Web sites. Anticipating the sabermetricians was Leonard Koppett's *All about Baseball* (New York, 1974). Those interested in the analysis of statistics should consult John Thorn and Pete Palmer, *The Hidden Game of Baseball* (Garden City, N.Y., 1984); Craig R. Wright and Tom House, *The Diamond Reappraised* (New York, 1989); John Thom and John B. Holway, *The Pitcher* (New York, 1985); George F. Will, *Men at Work: The Craft of Baseball* (New York, 1990); and several books by Bill James. For baseball's most successful post-1950 manager, see Robert Creamer, *Stengel* (New York, 1984). And for perhaps the post-1950 era's most popular star, Willie Mays, see Charles Einstein, *Willie's Time* (New York, 1979). Kevin Kerrane's *Dollar Sign on the Muscle* (New York, 1984) is invaluable for the subject of scouting, and both Pat Jordan's *False Spring* (New York, 1969) and David Lamb's *Stolen Season* (New York, 1991) are indispensable for the minor league experience. Pioneers in providing inside revelations of player behavior are Jim Brosnan, *The Long Season* (New York, 1960), and the less restrained Jim Bouton, *Ball Four* (New York, 1970). Something of a classic for its look at the life of players both during and after baseball is Roger Kahn, *Boys of Summer* (New York, 1972). There are many worthwhile though sometimes pretentious books and essays treating the cultural meaning of baseball. Sample among others the writings of Roger Angell, Thomas Boswell, James T. Farrell, Peter Gammons, A. Bartlett Giamatti, Stephen Jay Gould, Allen Guttmann, David McGimpsey, Michael Novak, Richard Peterson, Jules Tygiel, and George Will.

Index

Aaron, Henry, 179, 231, 243
Adair, Robert, 249
Adams, Merle, 146
African Americans, 10–11, 28, 38, 59,
    102, 155–69 passim, 183, 228, 232,
    254
Alexander, Grover Cleveland, 137–38,
    175
Algren, Nelson, 111
Ali, Muhammad, 136
All-American Black Tourists, 157
All-American Girls Professional Baseball
    League, 173–74
Allen, John, 243
Allen, Lee, 104
Allen, Mel, 176
All-star games, 5, 153, 167
Alomar, Sandy, Jr., 244
Alston, Walter, 183, 224
Altherr, Thomas, 7
Amateur Softball Association, 173
American Association (minor league),
    131
American Association of Base Ball
    Clubs, 36, 55–60, 69–70
American Baseball Guild, 203
American Communist Party, 164
American League: origins, 80, 86–91.
    See also Major leagues

—pennant winners: 1900–1920, 101;
    1921–46, 140; 1946–68, 179; 1969–
    93, 220
American Legion baseball, 150
Amherst College, 11
Anderson, Sparky, 224, 229, 255
Angell, Roger, 236, 238
Anson, Adrian "Cap," 48, 53–54, 58,
    59, 65, 69, 74, 75, 81, 84
Anti-Semitism, 84–85, 139
Antitrust law, and baseball, 122, 208
Aparicio, Luis, 228
Arbitration, 206, 207, 209, 213, 244
Arch, Steve, 232
Arizona Diamondbacks, 237
Arlin, Harold, 151–52
Athletics (Philadelphia), 51. See also
    Kansas City Athletics; Oakland Ath-
    letics; Philadelphia Athletics
Atlanta Braves, 197, 232, 241, 242, 244
Atlantics (Brooklyn), 23–24, 27, 33, 45,
    186
Attendance, 80, 95, 142, 150, 188–89,
    192, 200, 232–33, 240, 241
Autry, Gene, 187

Baerga, Carlos, 244
Baker, Gene, 168
Baker, Newton D., 114

Baker, William, 139
Ballparks, 20–21, 38–40, 95–97, 191, 199–200, 237–38
Baltimore Orioles, 75, 76, 82, 100, 145–47, 195, 223, 224, 242
Barber, Red, 176
Barnes, Roscoe, 45–46, 48
Barnie, Billy, 70
Barnstorming teams, 37–38, 157
Barrow, Edward G., 138, 141–42, 143, 180
Baseball: early game, 5–7; origin myths, 93–95; rules of play, 8–9, 24, 72, 73, 98, 127, 185; style of play, 9, 72–77, 97–100, 124–30, 160–61, 177–79, 184–85, 226–31, 247–52. *See also* Major leagues; Minor leagues
Baseball: An American Epic (film), 236
"Baseball Fever" (song), 10
"Base ball fraternity," 2, 6–8, 13–15, 18–19, 21, 28–30, 34, 64
Baseball Hall of Fame and Museum, 94, 154
Basewomen (newsletter), 233
Bavasi, Emil J., 183
Baylor, Don, 225
Beadle's Dime Base Ball Player, 16
Bell, James "Cool Papa," 160
Belle, Albert, 240, 243, 244
Bender, Charles "Chief," 100, 102
Berra, Yogi, 180, 245
Bierbauer, Louis, 70
Black Sox Scandal, 110–11, 115–18, 120
Blattner, Buddy, 193
Bloomer Girls, 172
Blue Ribbon Panel on Baseball Economics, 246
Bostic, Joe, 165
Boston Beaneaters, 70, 75, 76, 100
Boston Braves, 192, 195
Boston Reds, 69
Boston Red Sox, 142
Boston Red Stockings, 70
Bostons, 37, 45–46, 62, 143
Boswell, Thomas, 227
Boudreau, Lou, 227
Brainard, Asa, 33
Branca, Ralph, 177
Breadon, Sam, 147

Brett, George, 211
Brewer, Chet, 164
Bridwell, Al, 103, 104
Bristol, Dave, 224
Brock, Lou, 228
Brooklyn Bridegrooms, 60, 76
Brooklyn Dodgers, 170, 177, 180, 182–84, 185–86, 195, 218, 219
Brooklyn Superbas, 86
Brotherhood of Professional Base Ball Players, 62, 66. *See also* Players League
Broun, Heywood, 175
Brown, Jack, 221
Brush, John T., 66–67, 83, 90, 92, 105, 141
Brush Purification Plan, 82
Buckeye Base Ball Club (Cincinnati), 33
Buffalo Bisons, 232
Bulkeley, Morgan G., 51
Burkett, Jesse, 74, 85
Burns, George, 187
Burns, Ken, 236
Busch, August, 207

California Angels, 197
Camden Yards (Baltimore), 237–38
Cammeyer, William H., 20–21
Campanella, Roy, 160, 167, 183, 225
Candlestick Park (San Francisco), 196
Cannon, Robert, 204
Canseco, Jose, 228
Cantor, Eddie, 103
Caray, Harry, 176
Carew, Rod, 249
Carlton, Steve, 230
Carroll, Clay, 229
Cartwright, Alexander, 7, 16
Cashman, Brian, 246
Caylor, Oliver P., 55
Cellar, Emanuel, 188
Chadwick, Henry, 15, 16, 17, 18, 21, 64, 84, 94
Chadwin, Dean, 222
Champion, Aaron B., 33
Chandler, A. B. "Happy," 165, 202–3
Chapman, Ray, 126, 128
Chase, Hal, 118
Chesbro, John, 99
Chicago American Giants, 158

Chicago Cubs, 87–88, 104–5, 132–33, 242
Chicago White Sox, 100, 110–11, 115, 231, 232
Chicago White Stockings, 33, 35, 37, 39–40, 45, 47–48, 50, 51, 53–54, 58, 83, 88
Cicotte, Eddie, 116, 118
Cincinnati Reds, 115, 152–53, 192, 222, 223, 243
Cincinnati Red Stockings, 31–32, 33–35, 42
Civil War, and baseball, 17–18
Clarke, Fred, 85
Clarkson, John, 66
Clemens, Roger, 245
Clemente, Roberto, 169
Cleveland Indians, 241, 242, 243
Cleveland Spiders, 80
Clinton, Bill, 254
Clipper (New York), 16
Cobb, Tyrus "Ty," 97, 102, 106–9, 112, 113, 118, 130, 132, 154, 228
Cochrane, Mickey, 130
Coffin, Tristram Potter, 162–63
College World Series, 233
Collins, Eddie, 115
Collins, Ripper, 138
Colorado Rockies, 237, 242, 250
Colt Stadium (Houston), 197
Combs, Earle, 142
Comiskey, Charles, 56, 58, 59, 75, 86, 87, 88, 115, 116, 117, 118, 119, 175
Comiskey Park (Chicago), 96
Cone, David, 251
Continental League, 196
Coolidge, Calvin, 134
Cooper, Gary, 154
Corbett, Joe, 76
Costas, Bob, 248
Cox, Bobby, 244
Craig, Roger, 230
Crawford, Samuel, 103, 104, 150
Creamer, Robert, 191
Creighton, James, 26–27
Croker, William, 90
Crosetti, Frankie, 138, 143
Crosley, Powel, 152
Crutchfield, Jimmie, 161–62
Cuban Giants, 38, 157

Cunningham, Bill, 130
Curran, William, 126, 130
Cushman, Charley, 73

Dark, Alvin, 177
Dauvray, Helen, 61, 80
Dauvray Cup, 80
Day, John B., 56, 83
Dean, Dizzy, 138, 148, 162, 193
Designated hitter rule, 185
Detroit Tigers, 213
Devery, William, 90
Devlin, James, 52
Devyr, Thomas B., 26
Dickey, William, 143
DiMaggio, Dom, 177
DiMaggio, Joe, 138, 139, 143, 172, 175, 245, 252
Ditmar, Al, 181
Dodger Stadium (Los Angeles), 196, 199
Dominican Republic, 253
Donovan, Raymond, 211
Doubleday, Abner, 7, 94
Doyle, Jack, 76
Draft, 91, 220–21, 225, 243
Dressen, Charlie, 177
Dreyfus, Barney, 85, 95, 118
Drinking. *See* Drugs and drinking
Dropo, Walt, 178
Drugs and drinking, 26, 64–66, 212–13, 251
Drysdale, Don, 184, 204
Duffey, Hugh, 74
Duffy, Edward, 26
Dunn, Jack, 145, 146–47
Duren, Ryan, 181
Durocher, Leo, 182, 193, 202, 224

Eastern Colored League, 158, 159
East-West All-Star Game, 159
Ebbets, Charles, 96
Ebbets Field (Brooklyn), 96–97, 186, 187
Eckersley, Dennis, 230
Eckert, William, 204, 206
Eckfords (New York), 27
Eight Men Out (film), 233
Ethiopian Clowns, 158
Etten, Nick, 171
Evans, Billy, 133
Evers, Johnny, 104

Excelsiors (Brooklyn), 14, 16–17, 22,
    23, 186
Excelsiors (Philadelphia), 10–11

Farm systems, 144–45, 147–49, 225–26
Federal League, 113–14, 120
Fehr, Donald, 213, 239
Feller, Bob, 172
Fenway Park (Boston), 96
Ferguson, Robert, 44–45, 47
Fielder, Cecil, 247
Field of Dreams (film), 233
Fingers, Rollie, 230
Finley, Charlie, 208, 214, 222, 225
Fitzgerald, F. Scott, 111
Flint, Frank, 65
Flood, Curt, 208
Florida Marlins, 237, 243, 254
Forbes Field (Pittsburgh), 95, 191
Ford, Whitey, 180
Foster, Andrew "Rube," 158, 159
Foster, George, 247
Fowler, John, 59
Foxx, Jimmie, 130
Frazee, Harry, 119, 142
Free agency, 208–9, 211, 212, 213–14,
    222–23, 242–43
Freedman, Andrew, 84–85, 86, 90
Freeman, Harry H., 38
Freeman, John, 125
Frick, Ford, 135, 167, 203
Frisch, Frankie, 154
Fullerton, Hugh, 115, 116
Fultz, David, 113

Gaedel, Eddie, 195
Gaherin, John J., 206, 209–10
Gallico, Paul, 175
Gambling, and baseball, 25–26, 47–48,
    81. *See also* Black Sox Scandal
"Game of the Day" (radio broadcasts),
    176
Gardella, Danny, 188
Gas House Gang, 138
Gehrig, Lou, 135, 138, 142, 143, 148,
    154, 172, 236, 245
German Americans, 36, 41, 55, 64
Giamatti, A. Bartlett, 216, 255
Gibson, Bob, 230
Gibson, Josh, 161
Gibson, Kirk, 213

Gillette, Gary, 128
Gillette Safety Razor Company, 176
Gilmore, James A., 113
Glasscock, John, 71
Goldberg, Arthur, 208
Goldstein, Warren, 13
Gomez, Vernon, 143
Gore, George, 65
Gould, Charles, 33
Graham, Frank, 175
Grant, Charlie, 157
Grant, Ulysses S., 31
Graves, Abner, 94
Gray, Jim, 216
Great Depression, 150–54, 159
Great Strike of 1981, 211–12
Grebey, Raymond, 211, 212
Greenberg, Hank, 139, 172
Greenlee, Gus, 159, 162
Griffey, Ken, Jr., 243, 250
Griffith, Calvin, 196
Griffith, Clark, 152, 153, 189
Grove, Robert "Lefty," 130, 146, 154
Guidry, Ron, 253
Gwynn, Tony, 250

Hamilton, William, 75
Hanlon, Ned, 76–77, 82, 86
Hargrove, Mike, 252
Harris, Bucky, 228–29
Harris, Florence, 38
Hart, James, 79, 87
Hart, John, 244
Haymakers (Troy, N.Y.), 31
Heitz, Tom, 9
Henderson, Robert W., 94
Henrich, Tommy, 220
Herrmann, August "Garry," 79, 96,
    103, 111, 112, 118, 119
Herzog, Buck, 110
Herzog, Whitey, 212
Heydler, John, 76, 119
Hicks, Robert, 47
Hillings, Patrick, 188
Himsl, Vedie, 221
Hispanics. *See* Latinos
Hitting. *See* Baseball: style of play
Hodges, Gil, 182, 183
Holmes, Howard "Ducky," 84–85, 86
Holmes, Oliver Wendell, Jr., 122
Holway, John, 167

Homestead Grays, 161
Hoover, Herbert, 133, 134, 151
Hop Bitters (Rochester, N.Y.), 37
Hornsby, Rogers, 129, 130, 137
Houston Astrodome, 199
Houston Astros, 197
Howard, Frank, 183
Howsam, Robert, 222
Huggins, Miller, 129, 134
Huizenga, Wayne, 243
Hulbert, William Ambrose, 43, 48, 51, 52, 83
Hunter, Jim "Catfish," 208, 245
Hurly, Richard, 33
Husing, Ted, 176
Huston, Tillinghast, 119, 141–42

Intercollegiate baseball, 232–33
International Association of Professional Base Ball Players, 52–53
International Baseball Association, 233
International League, 59, 130, 146–47
Irish Americans, 23–24, 41, 64, 77, 102
Irvin, Monte, 177
Italian Americans, 139

Jackson, Joe, 102, 110, 114, 115, 116, 117
Jackson, Reggie, 231
Jacobs, Richard, 244
Jacobs Field (Cleveland), 244
James, Bill, 74, 118, 126, 146, 178, 185, 222–23, 225
Japan, 172, 254–55
Jennings, Hughie, 86, 108
Jeter, Derek, 252
Jethro, Sam, 165
Jews, 36. See also Anti-Semitism
Johnson, Al, 67
Johnson, Byron Bancroft "Ban," 78, 79, 80, 86–91, 97, 100, 101, 105–6, 111–12, 114, 116, 118–20, 134, 229
Johnson, Judy, 160
Johnson, Walter, 105–6, 154, 228–29
Journalism, and baseball, 174–75
Joyce, William, 72

Kansas City Athletics, 195
Kansas City Monarchs, 152, 159, 160, 162

Kansas City Royals, 223, 224, 231–32, 242
Kauff, Benny, 122
Keeler, Willie, 75, 86
Kelley, Joe, 76
Kelly, Michael "King," 54–55, 58, 65–66, 67, 68–69, 70, 75, 86
Killebrew, Harmon, 231
Kiner, Ralph, 178, 203
Kirsch, George, 17
Kluszewski, Ted, 178
Knickerbocker Base Ball Club (New York), 7–9, 14, 17, 28–29, 218
Koenig, Mark, 142
Kontsanty, Jim, 181
Koppett, Leonard, 206, 216, 221, 248
Koufax, Sandy, 184, 185, 204, 225, 253
Kroc, Ray, 226
Kuhn, Bowie, 198, 206, 209, 212–13, 214–15
Kurys, Sophie, 174

LaGuardia, Fiorello, 164
Lajoie, Napoleon, 89, 108
Lake Front Stadium (Chicago), 39–40
Landis, Kenesaw Mountain, 111, 117, 120–22, 143, 149, 153, 164, 171, 175, 176, 202, 246
Lane, F. C., 128–29, 132
Lardner, Ring, 175
Larsen, Don, 170, 181
Larsen, Richard, 249
Lasker, Albert D., 120
Lasorda, Tommy, 224
Latinos, 102, 169, 228, 252–55
Lazzeri, Tony, 137–38, 142
Leach, Tommy, 108
League Alliance, 53
A League of Their Own (film), 233
Leggett, Joseph, 23
Lemon, Bob, 225
Lemon, Jim, 178
Leonard, Buck, 161
Lewis, J. Norman, 203–4
Lieb, Fred, 143
Little League Baseball, 190–91
A Little Pretty Pocket-Book, 7
Lockman, Whitey, 177
Long, Dale, 181
Lopat, Eddie, 181

Los Angeles Dodgers, 187, 195–96, 223–24, 225, 228, 242
Louis, Joe, 164
Louisiana Superdome (New Orleans), 199
Louisville Grays, 51
Lowry, Philip, 126
Lucas, Henry V., 57–58
Luque, Adolfo, 102
Lyle, Sparky, 230
Lynch, Tom, 85

MacGregor, Jeff, 239
Mack, Cornelius "Connie," 89, 97, 100–102, 113, 130, 139, 151, 171
MacPhail, Larry, 152–53, 182, 203
MacPhail, Lee, 212, 213
Maddux, Greg, 244
Maharg, Billy, 116
Major League Baseball Players Association, 201–7 passim, 213
Major leagues, expansion and franchise relocation in, 55–58, 90–91, 196, 198, 237. See also American League; National League
Major League Scouting Bureau, 221
Major League Umpires Association, 210
Manley, Effie, 158
Mantle, Mickey, 179, 180, 214–15, 245
Marberry, Fred, 228–29
Marichal, Juan, 169, 230
Maris, Roger, 24, 181, 195, 235, 249
Marquard, Rube, 100, 102
Marsans, Armando, 102
Marshall, Mike, 229
Martin, Billy, 212, 224
Martin, Pepper, 138
Martinez, Edgar, 250
Martinez, Pedro, 253
Marx, Groucho, 187
"Massachusetts game," 15
Mathewson, Christy, 97, 100, 105–6, 154
Mauch, Gene, 224
Mayoral, Luis, 254
Mays, Carl, 119, 128, 141
Mays, Willie, 179, 214–15
McCarthy, Joe, 143
McCarthy, Tom, 74–75
McCaskill, Kirk, 251

McCloskey, Joe, 100
McCormick, Jim, 66
McCovey, Willie, 231
McGraw, John J., 74, 82, 89, 97, 98, 101–2, 105, 121, 130, 141, 165–67, 181, 218
McGwire, Mark, 235–36, 248, 249, 251
McGwire, Matt, 235
McKee, Steve, 235
McKeever, William, 24
McLane, Drayton, Jr., 242
McMahon, John, 76
McNally, Dave, 208
McVey, Cal, 48
Mead, Margaret, 189
Medill, Joseph, 33
Merkle, Fred, 104–5
Merwin, John, 224
Messersmith, Andy, 208–9
Meusel, Emil, 130
Mexican League, 202
Meyers, John, 102
Michael, Gene, 225, 246
Mile High Stadium (Denver), 250
Miller, Marvin J., 201–2, 205, 207, 208, 209, 211, 212, 213, 240
Mills, Abraham G., 56, 94
Milwaukee Braves, 186, 192, 194, 195
Milwaukee Brewers, 194
Minnesota Twins, 196–97
Minor leagues, 52, 56, 91, 114, 119, 130–31, 145–47, 188, 191, 232, 248
Mize, Johnny, 181
Moffett, Kenneth, 211, 212
Monday, Rick, 221
Monteleone, Rich, 240
Montreal Expos, 242
Moon, Wally, 183
Moreland, Nate, 164
Morgan, Joe, 227
Moses, Robert, 187
Most Valuable Player Award, 154
Mueller, Don, 177
Mullane, Anthony, 76
Murdock, Eugene, 88
Murphy, Robert, 203
Murray, Bill, 93
Murray, James, 191
Murray, John, 100

Musial, Stan, 148, 178, 179, 202, 251
Mutual Broadcasting Company, 176
Mutuals (New York), 23–24, 26, 27, 47, 51

Nagy, Charles, 244
Nardinelli, Clark, 121–22
National Agreement: of 1892, 70, 87, 88; of 1903, 90–91, 111; of 1921, 121; of 2000, 217
National Association of Base Ball Players, 17–18, 24, 27–29
National Association of Professional Baseball Leagues, 91, 145
National Association of Professional Base Ball Players, 29, 36, 44–48
National Commission, 90–91, 111–12, 118–19
National League, 36; founding, 43–44, 48–50; reorganized in 1892, 70–71
—pennant winners: 1876–1902, 56–57; 1900–1920, 101; 1921–46, 140; 1946–68, 180; 1969–93, 220
Nationals (Washington, D.C.), 27
Native Americans, 102
Navin, Frank, 112
Negro American League, 159, 166
Negro National League, 158–59, 166
Nelson, Lindsey, 193
Newark Bears, 147
Newcombe, Don, 177, 183
New England town ball, 11
"New York game," 15–16
New York Giants, 37, 56, 61, 69, 83–85, 100–102, 104–5, 130, 144,177, 180, 195, 218
New York Highlanders, 90
New York Metropolitans, 58
New York Mets, 182, 197, 218, 219, 241
New York Yankees, 90, 119, 125, 130, 132–33, 137–38, 141–43, 149, 154, 170, 179–82, 194, 197, 218, 219, 222, 224, 241, 242, 244–45
Niagaras, 22
Nichols, Charles, 77
Night baseball, 152–53
Nixon, Richard M., 210
Nomo, Hideo, 254
Noren, Irv, 181

North Western Association of Base Ball Players, 18
Northwestern League, 56
Norworth, Jack, 93
Nugent, Gerry, 139

Oakland Athletics, 197, 219, 222, 223, 225
O'Day, Henry, 105
Okmulgee Chiefs, 131
O'Malley, Peter, 223–24
O'Malley, Walter, 183, 185–88, 196, 223–24
O'Neil, James, 74
Osteen, Claude, 183
Owen, Mickey, 202
Owens, Jesse, 164
Ozersky, Philip, 236

Pacific Coast League, 130, 188, 196
Page Fence Giants, 157
Paige, Leroy "Satchel," 160–63
Palmer, Pete, 126
Palmer, Potter, 33
Parker, Dave, 211
Paul, Gabe, 221
Payroll disparities, 141–47
Payroll tax, 240–41
Pegler, Westbrook, 175
Pennock, Herb, 142
Perini, Lou, 142, 195
Perranowski, Ron, 183
Perry, Gaylord, 230
Peters, Henry, 207
Peterson, Robert, 161
Pfeffer, Fred, 74
Philadelphia Athletics, 45, 100–102, 130, 195
Philadelphia Phillies, 56
Pidgeon, Frank, 13, 14
Piniella, Lou, 225
Pitching. See Baseball: style of play
Pittsburgh Crawfords, 159, 162
Pittsburgh Pirates, 223, 225, 228–29
Player Relations Committee, 206
Players: agents, 209–10; behavior, 13–15, 23–24, 63–65, 76–77, 102–4, 212–13; origins, 7, 10, 12–13, 76, 102, 138–39; professionalism, 64; salaries, 62–63, 67–69, 112, 113, 153,

207, 210, 213, 214; work stoppages,
206–7, 211, 213, 239–41. *See also*
Free agency; Major League Baseball
Players Association; Players League;
Reserve clause
Players Fraternity, 113
Players League, 67–69
Players' Protective Association, 88, 112
Polo Grounds (New York), 41, 191
Pond, Arlie, 76
Porter's Spirit of the Times, 16
The Pride of the Yankees (film), 154
Pulliam, Henry C., 90, 105
Pythians (Philadelphia), 10

Quinn, Bobby, 103
Quinn-Ives Act, 164

Radio, and baseball, 151–52, 175–77
Randolph, Willie, 226
Rankin, A. B., 53
Reach, Alfred J., 56, 83
Reagan, Ronald, 187
Redland Field (Cincinnati), 96
Reichardt, Rick, 221
Reinsdorf, Jerry, 240
Renfro, Othello, 162
Reserve clause, 62, 63, 66, 68–69, 87,
112, 207–9
Reynolds, Allie, 181
Rice, Grantland, 175
Rickey, Branch, 3, 138, 139, 147, 154,
155–56, 165–66, 182–83, 196, 202,
225
Riess, Steven, 97
Rind, Ofer, 249
Ripkin, Cal, Jr., 227, 236
Ritter, Lawrence, 103, 105
Rizzutto, Phil, 227
Roberts, Robin, 204
Roberts, Thomas, 213–14
Robinson, Frank, 168, 231
Robinson, Herk, 224
Robinson, Jackie, 143, 155–56, 165–67,
168, 183, 218, 228, 254
Robinson, Sharon, 167
Robison, Frank, 79, 81, 85
Roe, Elwin, 183
Roosevelt, Franklin D., 133, 151, 171
Roosevelt, Theodore, 94

Root, Charley, 133
Rose, Pete, 215–16
Rosenberg, Norman, 122
Rosenblatt, Roger, 245
Rothstein, Arnold, 121
Rotisserie leagues, 233
Rounders, 7
Rubenstein, Helena, 174
Rules. *See* Baseball: rules of play
Runyan, Damon, 175
Ruppert, Jacob, Jr., 119, 141–42, 147,
148–49, 151, 180
Rusie, Amos, 84
Ruth, George Herman "Babe," 3, 124–
29 passim, 131–36, 138, 141, 142,
143, 146, 154, 172, 175, 179, 195,
235, 245, 248
Ryan, Nolan, 230

Sain, Johnny, 181
Salaries. *See* Players: salaries
Salary cap, 239–41
Sanderson, Allen, 247
San Diego Baseball Update, 233
San Diego Padres, 254
San Francisco Giants, 195–96
Sauer, Hank, 178
Schmelling, Max, 164
Schmidt, Mike, 230, 231
Schrekengost, Ossee, 104
Schuerholz, John, 224, 244
Scientific Baseball (Pfeffer), 74
Scully, Gerald W., 168, 219, 224
Seaver, Tom, 230
Second Great Strike, 236, 239–41
Seitz, Peter, 202, 208–9
Selee, Frank, 77
Selig, Allan H. "Bud," 217, 239, 240,
246
Seymour, Harold, 52, 76, 95, 112, 113
Shantz, Bobby, 181
Shattuck, Debra, 174
Shea, William, 196
Shea Stadium (New York), 197
Sherwood, Jim, 249
Shibe, Benjamin, 95
Shibe Park (Philadelphia), 95, 96
Simmons, Al, 130
Sinclair, Harry, 113
Sisler, George, 118

Skydome (Toronto), 237
Slaughter, Enos, 181
Snider, Duke, 183
Snodgrass, Fred, 103
Society for American Baseball Research, 233
Soden, Arthur, 83
Softball, 173
Somers, Charles, 79, 80, 88
Sosa, Sammy, 235–36, 253
Soule, Asa T., 37–38
Southern League, 36
Southern Negro League, 158
Spalding, Albert, 16, 27, 36, 39, 46, 48–49, 50, 51, 53–54, 58, 62, 65–66, 68, 69, 81, 83, 90, 93–94
Spalding, J. Walter, 83
Spalding's Official Baseball Guide, 51
Spectators, 40, 82, 231–32
Spink, Alfred H., 55
The Sporting News, 171
Sports Broadcasting Act of 1961, 192, 194
Staples, Brent, 232
Stargell, Willie, 225
"The Star Spangled Banner" (national anthem), 171–72
Steinbrenner, George, 208, 211, 214, 216, 218, 222, 226, 245–46
Stengel, Charles "Casey," 181–82
Stephens, Vern, 202
Stirnweiss, George, 171
St. Louis Browns, 58, 59, 172, 195
St. Louis Brown Stockings, 35
St. Louis Cardinals, 137–38, 144, 147–48, 152, 154, 172, 176, 195, 219, 228
Stoneham, Charles A., 121, 141, 147
Stoneham, Horace, 187, 196
Stotz, Carl, 190
Stovey, George, 59–60, 61
Stovey, Harry, 70
Strikes. *See* Players: work stoppages
Subway Series, 170
Sukeforth, Clyde, 155
Sullivan, Neil J., 147
Sullivan, Tim, 90
Sunday baseball, 50, 51, 56, 81, 139, 142
Sutton, Don, 230

Taft, William Howard, 93
"Take Me Out to the Ball Game" (song), 93
Talcott, Edward, 81
Tampa Bay Bucaneers, 237
Tebeau, Oliver, 76
Television, and baseball, 190, 192–94
Temple, William C., 80
Temple Cup, 80
Tennessee Rats, 158
Terry, Ralph, 181
Texas Negro League, 158
Thomas, Lee, 226
Thome, Jim, 244
Thomson, Bobby, 177
Thorn, John, 126
Thorpe, Jim, 102
Time-Warner media consortium, 244
Toney, Fred, 112
Topping, Dan, 180
Torre, Joe, 245
Truijillo, Rafael, 162
Turley, Bob, 181
Turner, Ted, 214, 244
Twain, Mark, 94
Tweed, William Marcy "Boss," 26
Tygiel, Jules, 159, 166

Ueberroth, Peter, 210, 213, 215–16
Umpires, 8–9, 47, 76, 210
Union Association, 57–58
Uniques (Brooklyn), 11

Vanderbilt University, 236
Vassar College, 38
Vaughn, James, 100
Veeck, Bill, Jr., 3, 163, 164–65, 188, 195
Veeck, Bill, Sr., 151
Verducci, Tom, 251
Victorians, and baseball, 14–15, 26, 35, 47, 50
Vincent, Fay, 216
Vincent, Ted, 35–36
Von der Ahe, Christopher, 55–56, 60, 71
Von der Hoorst, Harry, 85–86
Von Tilzer, Albert, 93

Waddell, Rube, 104
Wagner, John "Honus," 85, 97, 106–7, 154

Wakefield, Dick, 221
Walker, Moses, 59
Walker, Welday, 59
Walsh, Christy, 135
Walsh, Ed, 99
Wansley, William, 26
Ward, Arch, 153, 175
Ward, John Montgomery, 61–62, 66, 67, 69, 72, 74–75, 81
Warner, John, 76
Washington Senators, 196, 228–29
Watson, Bob, 246, 253, 254
Weaver, Earl, 224, 228
Webb, Dell, 180
Weiss, George, 149, 180–81
Wertz, Vic, 178
Western Association, 131
Western League, 80, 87
White, Jim, 46, 48
White, Judge J. W. F., 50
White, Sol, 156
Whitman, Walt, 1
Wicker, Tom, 175
Williams, Marvin, 165
Williams, Ted, 172, 178–79, 251
Williams College, 11

Wills, Maury, 184, 228
Wojnarowski, Adrian, 246
Women, and baseball, 24–25, 38, 41–42, 172–74
Woodling, Gene, 181
Woolf, Virginia, 2
World Championship Series, 58–59
World Series, 91, 92–93, 110, 175–76, 239; predecessors, 58–59
World War I, 113–14
World War II, 171–74
Wright, George, 33, 45
Wright, Harry, 33–35, 44, 45–46, 69, 143
Wrigley, Philip K., 173–74
Wrigley, William, 147

Yankee Stadium (New York), 141
Yastrzemski, Carl, 184
Yawkey, Thomas, 139–40
Young, Denton "Cy," 85, 100, 230
Young, John, 254
Young, Nicholas, 83, 105

Zernial, Gus, 178
Zulu Cannibals, 158

BENJAMIN G. RADER is James L. Sellers Professor of History at the University of Nebraska at Lincoln. He is the author of *American Sports: From the Age of Folk Games to the Age of Television* and *American Ways: A Brief History of American Culture.*

ILLINOIS HISTORY OF SPORTS

The Olympics: A History of the Modern Games (2d ed.)   *Allen Guttmann*
Baseball: A History of America's Game (2d ed.)   *Benjamin G. Rader*
The World's Game: A History of Soccer   *Bill Murray*

The University of Illinois Press
is a founding member of the
Association of American University Presses.

Composed in 10/13 Sabon
with Aachen Bold display
by Celia Shapland
for the University of Illinois Press
Designed by Dennis Roberts
Manufactured by Thomson-Shore, Inc.

University of Illinois Press
1325 South Oak Street
Champaign, IL 61820-6903
www.press.uillinois.edu